COUNTING DOWN
SOUTHERN ROCK

Counting Down

Counting Down is a unique series of titles designed to select the best songs or musical works from major performance artists and composers in an age of design-your-own playlists. Contributors offer readers the reasons why some works stand out from others. It is the ideal companion for music lovers.

Titles in the Series

COUNTING DOWN SOUTHERN ROCK

The 100 Best Songs

C. Eric Banister

ROWMAN & LITTLEFIELD
Lanham • Boulder • New York • London

Published by Rowman & Littlefield
A wholly owned subsidiary of The Rowman & Littlefield Publishing Group, Inc.
4501 Forbes Boulevard, Suite 200, Lanham, Maryland 20706
www.rowman.com

Unit A, Whitacre Mews, 26-34 Stannary Street, London SE11 4AB

British Library Cataloguing in Publication Information Available

Library of Congress Cataloging-in-Publication Data

Names: Banister, C. Eric.
Title: Counting down southern rock : the 100 best songs / C. Eric Banister.
Description: Lanham, Maryland : Rowman & Littlefield, 2016. | Series: Counting down | Includes
   bibliographical references and index.
Identifiers: LCCN 2015040973 (print) | LCCN 2015041150 (ebook) | ISBN 9781442245396 (cloth :
   alk. paper) | ISBN 9781442245402 (electronic)
Subjects: LCSH: Rock music—Southern States—History and criticism.
Classification: LCC ML3534.3 .B3155 2016 (print) | LCC ML3534.3 (ebook) | DDC
   782.421660975—dc23 LC record available at http://lccn.loc.gov/2015040973

Printed in the United States of America

For Brittany, Porter, and Claire

CONTENTS

ACKNOWLEDGMENTS

A work such as this is always built on the foundation of those who have come before. The list of writers who have touched on Southern Rock would fill another book, so I would like to narrow it down to just a few.

First, I would point anyone interested in the history of Southern Rock to look up the work of Scott B. Bomar, who has one of the most recent works on the subject. Likewise, Alan Paul, who has done much with the history of the Allman Brothers Band, is another who has recently added to the study of Southern Rock.

By my estimation, no one has done more to further the legacy of Southern Rock than the "Ambassador of Southern Rock," Michael Buffalo Smith. Buffalo took a fan's love of the music and created a library of work that is unparalleled. From his freelance work at various publications to his own magazine, the sadly defunct *GRITZ*, to his books on the subject, no one has covered the genre the way Buffalo has and continues to do.

I would also like to thank editor Bennett Graff for giving me the opportunity to write on a subject that I have loved since childhood.

The biggest thank-you goes out to my family: my beautiful wife Brittany, my wonderful son Porter, and my fantastic daughter Claire. You all make every day better than the one before it.

INTRODUCTION

I didn't grow up in the South, and I was only a year or so old by the time the music was getting off the ground, but once I discovered it in late elementary school, I was hooked. (I've recounted much of that discovery in my book *All I Can Do Is Write about It: One Boy's Journey through Music with Lynyrd Skynyrd*.) The songs of Southern Rock provided much of the sound track of my most formative years, and I have continued to revisit them as the years progress. So when the opportunity to tackle this project came up, I jumped at the chance to dive headlong into the history of the music.

For this book, I've decided to impose a few rules on my selection process in an effort to narrow down the field. First, I looked at geography. Following the lead of Scott B. Bomar, I decided to keep to bands and artists within the states that fell under the Confederate states, with the addition of Kentucky, Oklahoma, and Texas. This means that some bands often lumped into Southern Rock, such as the Ozark Mountain Daredevils and RamJam, were excluded.

The second thing to do was set a range of time. For that, I chose 1969 through 1990. The year 1969 is an obvious one, as that is when the Allman Brothers Band released their debut album. The year 1990 may not be as obvious, but it marks the release of the Allman Brothers Band album *Seven Turns*, which marked the next phase of their career and encouraged a resurgence of interest in Southern Rock. Albums by a version of Lynyrd Skynyrd followed, as did new albums from the Black Crowes and Georgia Satellites front man Dan Baird.

When it comes to the entries contained within, in most instances I am writing about a specific recording of a song, which will be noted in the title of each entry. Sometimes I note the definitive recording but also discuss other interesting versions of the song that may lend some insight into the song's staying power.

It should go without saying, but I will say it anyway, that the list written here is my list. It is subject to my tastes and opinions. Not everyone will agree with the songs chosen or the order of those that were picked. But I hope that it will spark discussion and that even if you don't agree with some of them, you will discover or rediscover great Southern Rock from the past.

THE COUNTDOWN

100. "Are You Sure Hank Done It This Way," Hank Williams Jr. (from *Rowdy*, 1981)

Ask anyone who has ever played country music—heck, even some rockers—about influences, and the name Hank Williams is sure to come up. His songwriting and charisma caught fire with audiences, and his star was one of the brightest in the music galaxy. Another part of that influence, for good or bad, was the lifestyle that became associated with him. His drinking, while often exaggerated, became legendary. His rebellious attitude and way of doing things became a template for musicians to come. His star was extinguished much too early when he died January 1, 1953, at age twenty-nine.

His son, Randall Hank Williams, forever known as Hank Jr., was just shy of four years old when Hank died. His mother, Hank's estranged wife Audrey, worked through her grief by grooming the young son to take his father's place on the stage. At age eight, Hank Williams Jr. debuted as a performing artist on a stage in Georgia to sing the songs of his father. He was part of a package tour, a popular touring configuration of the day putting several artists together to draw a larger crowd. For the better part of the next ten years, Hank Jr. continued to tour in those package shows, sharing stages and buses with the likes of Johnny Cash and Waylon Jennings, two men who were great fans of Hank Sr. and who would become lifelong friends and mentors to Bocephus, as his father used to call him.

Those shows were filled with the boy of Hank Williams coming out onstage night after night, dressed like his father and singing his songs to a crowd who seemed to be looking through him to the ghost casting the long shadow in which he stood. But Hank Jr. wasn't just a mimic. He had been soaking up the music of those artists he toured with along with a healthy dose of rock and roll served up by Carl Perkins, Chuck Berry, and Jerry Lee Lewis. He wanted to create his own music, so in the late 1960s he began to break away from his mother, recording albums of original songs. He was becoming a star in his own right by making straightforward country music that fit in with the radio songs of the time.

But within him, that mixture of rock and roll and the influence of his mentors was churning and creating something else. He wasn't the only one to be feeling it either. Those same influences—and others—were pushing other artists to create a synthesis of music. The Allman Brothers Band were coming in to their own, even without their founding guitarist, Duane Allman. Charlie Daniels Band, Lynyrd Skynyrd, the Marshall Tucker Band, Black Oak Arkansas, Wet Willie—they were all blending those influences and making the music that was stirring inside of Bocephus.

Deciding on his path, Hank Jr. went into studios in Muscle Shoals, Alabama, and Macon, Georgia, arguably the epicenter of the new Southern Rock movement, and began to record tracks for a new album. There he was joined by Charlie Daniels, Toy Caldwell of the Marshall Tucker Band, and Chuck Leavell of the Allman Brothers Band to produce an album unlike any he had made before. Rather than shed his hard-core country roots, he stood firm in them and embraced this new Southern Rock sound. He wrapped up recording of the album in July, proud of this new chapter of his life.

Taking a break between recording the album and its release, Hank Jr. went on a vacation to Ajax Mountain located on the Idaho–Montana border. The fresh mountain air was just what he needed, but a misstep sent him plummeting down the mountain. When he awoke in the hospital, surrounded by friends including Johnny and June Carter Cash, he learned his head had been split open and his right eye nearly ripped from his skull. His near-death experience changed his perspective, and now more than ever, he felt, it was time to become the true Hank Williams Jr.

A beard and sunglasses helped disguise the scar that ran across his face as *Hank Williams, Jr. & Friends* was released in December 1975.

The Outlaw Movement was in full swing in country music, and Southern Rock was at its peak. Hank Jr. stood with a foot in each camp. He was the living legacy of country music's most respected star, planting a foot in each style and proclaiming them his. Over the next six years, he scored seven Top Five hits, including four #1s.

Riding high on that success in 1981, in the midst of a heavy pop turn in country music and the near death of Southern Rock, Hank Jr. released *Rowdy*, the fourth in what would become a fourteen-album streak of Top Ten Country Albums. He may have shed the Hank Williams mimicry in the early 1970s, but it didn't mean he was cutting ties completely with his past. Nearly every album from *Friends* on included a song about or by Hank Sr.

For *Rowdy*, he reached back to one of his mentors, Waylon Jennings. Jennings, along with compatriot Willie Nelson and a few others, changed the face of country music with what was tagged the Outlaw Movement. What the movement amounted to was a combination of artists deciding they needed control over their own music, a feat in the record labels' tightly controlled studios, and more attention being paid to them from the rock press and fans. At the height of the movement, while some talked about the negative aspects of the Outlaws—how it wasn't country any-more—Jennings released "Are You Sure Hank Done It This Way" and went to #1 on the Country chart for one week in 1975.

The song was an open-hand swipe at a whole mess of people: the country stars of the day in their rhinestone suits and glitzy shows, the fans talking about the way music had changed, and even those in the Outlaw Movement. The same arguments were still going when Hank Jr. chose to include the song in 1981.

While Waylon's version is built on the loping, phase-shifted boom-chicka-boom sound he became famous for, Bocephus upped the tempo, turned up the crunch on the guitars a little, and turned the song into a bigger barn burner than it already was. Even more, Hank Jr. took the lyrics and personalized them, turning it partly into a biographical story of the break he made from his early years in rhinestone suits to the new sound that had rocketed him to the top of the charts. In the years through-out the 1980s, when Southern Rock had essentially dried up of its country influences, fans made Hank Williams Jr. a superstar and flag bearer for the music.

99. "Two Trains/Orange Blossom Special," Cooder Browne (from *Cooder Browne*, 1978)

After the 1977 plane crash that killed three members of Lynyrd Skynyrd, the term Southern Rock began to wane as a potent marketing tag. Bands that were branded that way began to buck against it, claiming to be not Southern Rock bands but bands from the South. Nevertheless, new bands continued to surface and be tagged as Southern Rock. Such was the case of Cooder Browne.

As this song shows, the band centered around founding member Larry Franklin's extraordinary fiddle. Franklin had grown up attending fiddle contests (competitions held at many local, regional, and state events that pitted fiddlers against one another) with his father, Louis, himself a championship fiddler. At age seven, Larry picked up a fiddle of his own and by age ten was winning contests and being honored as the youngest entry in them. Following in his father's footsteps, he began to compete for the World Championship (competing against and losing to Louis in 1966), capturing the title in 1970 at age sixteen.

Franklin teamed with pianist and vocalist David Haworth, bassist Skip Tumbleson, and drummer Dale Bolin to form Cooder Browne in 1976, a band that local coverage tagged as "progressive country," the kind that had been kicking up dust in Austin for the couple of years before that. Built around Franklin's fiery fiddle playing and Haworth's honky-tonk, boogie-woogie piano, the band made a name for themselves regionally, garnering the attention of a promoter who paired them with Texas icon Willie Nelson for a series of shows. Nelson began to notice that his opening act was receiving standing ovations every night, but instead of being jealous and petty, as many headliners would be, Nelson signed them to his newly formed record label, Lone Star. Soon the band was headed to Macon, Georgia, to record their debut at Capricorn Studios with producer Paul Hornsby. In the course of a year, the band went from sharing weeknight billing with forty-cent tequila night to opening for sold-out Willie Nelson shows in places like Red Rocks Amphitheater in Colorado.

"Two Trains/Orange Blossom Special" opens with Tumbleson's thumping bass as the drums, piano, and fiddle join him softly, building in volume. Franklin lays down some fiddle licks just before Sea Level guitarist Jimmy Nalls joins the band on slide, cutting through just before

Haworth enters on vocals almost a minute into the song. "Two trains of thought running on the same track," he sings, revealing the trains of the title to be metaphorical rather than physical. But what is up in the air is who the two thinkers are. They could easily be lovers heading for disaster with different directions planned for the relationship. They could be business associates, a new young band, and the sharp-toothed record industry sharks looking to devour another income source. Its beauty is in its vagueness, lending a universality to the lyrics.

But that may not be the point anyway. The lyrics exist almost just for the purpose of giving the song a reason to be there and rock. Franklin's fiddle slices and saws throughout while Haworth's piano pounds. Nalls's heavily distorted slide guitar cuts in quickly and then out just as fast. Just over three-and-a-half minutes into the song, the band begins to fade out, mimicking their intro before suddenly changing keys. It's time for Franklin to step into the spotlight and showcase his World Championship fiddling skills with the bluegrass favorite "Orange Blossom Special." It's easy to see why he rose to the top of the fiddle world at such a young age as his sharp fiddle lines fly.

He doesn't hog the spotlight, though, and the band drops out after a minute or so, leaving only Tumbleson's bass, duplicating the thumping rhythm that opened the song. Nalls returns, sans slide, ripping into a string-bending solo before giving way to Haworth's classically inspired piano solo. As his piano builds, it is joined by Franklin's sawing fiddle and Nalls's riffing guitar—sounding like a better-trained bunch of demons from Charlie Daniels's yet-to-be-released "The Devil Went Down to Georgia."

With the combination of Southern Rock's fade and the short-lived nature of Lone Star Records, Cooder Browne was a largely unnoticed band that should have been noticed. Soon the group broke up, only Franklin sticking with the music, first with his own group, then the Texas Swing unit Asleep at the Wheel. The fiddle fire that lit up this song can still be heard on country music songs everywhere by artists like Alan Jackson and Reba McEntire. He's still playing incredible music weekly in Nashville as part of the superstar western swing group the Time Jumpers.

98. "Glitter Queen," Hydra (from *Hydra*, 1974)

Southern Rock was just becoming a category of its own in 1974. The year 1973 saw the Allman Brothers Band breakthrough commercially, landing on the *Billboard* Top 40, followed in 1974 by the Ozark Mountain Daredevils, Wet Willie, and Lynyrd Skynyrd, landing songs and increasing the commercial viability of Southern Rock. As a result, record labels began to look for more southern groups to add to their roster. In other words, it was a good time to be a rock band out of the South looking for a record contract.

Hydra had formed in Atlanta in 1965 and under a series of names began performing regionally, winning battles of the bands and sharing the stage with other up-and-coming acts. By the time the Southern Rock craze was hitting full swing, their manager secured them a contract with Capricorn Records, sharing the roster with the Allman Brothers Band, the Marshall Tucker Band, and Wet Willie. While they shared some influences with those bands and non–label mates Lynyrd Skynyrd, Hydra shared more in common with American hard-rock bands like Grand Funk Railroad and Mountain.

Driven by guitarists Spencer Kirkpatrick and Wayne Bruce and powered by drummer Steve Pace and bassist Orville Davis, the band's first album doesn't fall into what would soon become a Southern Rock formula, sticking to hard-rocking yet melodic songs that fall in line with their rock contemporaries Bad Company or Thin Lizzy. They show their blues influences recording the blues classic "Going Down" and their progressive side on "Miriam," leaving the rest to showcase their rock.

The standout song from their debut is the album opener, "Glitter Queen." Wayne roars out of the gate with a hard-driving lick quickly followed by Kirkpatrick, who provides a counterpoint lick before joining Kirkpatrick with a low harmony, Davis and Pace throwing down a solid backbeat. Playing for years in the bars and clubs of Atlanta, the band was well acquainted with the ladies who liked to spend time with the boys in the band. Some might call them groupies, but to Hydra they were "Glitter Queens" with their rock-and-roll clothes, high-heeled shoes, and diamond rings. Their "sequined smiles suit their style," while their kiss tastes of tequila.

After the first verse, the heavy guitars are broken up by an injection of slightly distorted horns that give the song a bit of a twist with their

surprise entrance. While not often heard in such a hard-rock setting, they add an interesting texture to the song, helping set it apart from the myriad bands that would be making their appearance on the Southern Rock circuit soon.

Hydra's heavier brand of Southern Rock set the blueprint for later bands like Molly Hatchet and Blackfoot, but in 1974 they sounded little like the other bands carrying the tag. Capricorn became the biggest, most important label in the genre, but perhaps because Hydra sounded little like the obviously country-influenced bands on the label, they got lost in the shuffle. Hydra became a favored opening act, doing shows with ZZ Top, Lynyrd Skynyrd, the Charlie Daniels Band, Grand Funk Railroad, and others, but they failed to land a big tour, instead doing small shots with these bands and others. The band went on to record two more albums, 1975's *Land of Money* and 1977's *Rock the World*, before disbanding in 1978.

The success of Southern Rock made an unfortunate footnote of a great band that produced fantastic music that holds up to this day. In 2005, the original members (along with new bassist Tommy Vickery) reunited, recording *Live: After All These Years*, which kicks off with "Glitter Queen," proving the band can still rock as hard as they ever could.

97. "Mind Bender," Stillwater (from *Stillwater*, 1977)

If there is one thing that could stand as a symbol of Southern Rock, it would undoubtedly be the guitar. Sure, it has stood for rock and roll in general ever since Chuck Berry duckwalked his way across music history, so for Southern Rock, let's say, then, that it is dual guitars. The most dominant guitar in the genre was the Gibson Les Paul (which Gibson acknowledged in 2014 with the release of its custom Southern Rock Tribute model). The model's humbucker pickups, influenced by the thick solid body of the guitar, produce a round, thick sound that, when coupled with a bit of distortion from overdriving the amplifier, gives the instantly identifiable sound of Southern Rock.

But there were those who broke away from tradition, choosing instead to arm themselves with Fender guitars, generally the Stratocaster model, most notably Lynyrd Skynyrd's Ed King and the Outlaws Hughie Thomasson. The Strat (and sometimes the Telecaster, used by Dan Baird of the Georgia Satellites and rhythm guitarist Richard Young of the Ken-

tucky Headhunters) has a bit thinner, often brighter tone that sets it apart from the army of Les Pauls that traveled the roadways in Southern Rock's touring heyday.

On their self-titled debut album, Stillwater introduced the story of the melding of the two iconic guitars in "Mind Bender." Vocalist Jimmy Hall (not the same Jimmy Hall from Wet Willie) tells us, over the rhythmic playing of guitarists Bobby Golden, Mike Causey, and Rob Walker, that he walked into a pawnshop one day to make a startling discovery. There on the wall hung an old guitar, the tuning keys "bent and rusted," "its body scratched and scarred." As he looks at the guitar, it begins to talk to him. He was not, he assures us, "stoned nor drinkin'" when he heard the guitar telling its story.

The guitar tells him (and us) that his father was a Gibson and his mother was a Fender and he was given the name Mind Bender. With that, the band takes over with the first guitar solo. In a nice production touch, the rhythm guitars are mixed almost to silence as the solo is accompanied mainly by Sebie Lacey's drums and the throbbing bass of Allison Scarborough.

Once the solo ends, Hall continues. He's taken aback by this suddenly talking guitar, bumfuzzled, in fact. He quickly tells the guitar that people will think he is crazy if they see him talking to the guitar, telling him to hold his tongue. But the guitar doesn't listen and repeats his origin. When the guitar talks, it is with the help of a device known as a talk box. Essentially, the sound of the guitar comes through the device, and the notes are formed by a tube the guitar player holds in his mouth and sings the words. The talk box was created in the late 1930s and was used very seldom and even then mainly as a novelty effect.

In the mid-1960s, steel guitar innovator Pete Drake began to utilize it extensively, recording full albums of instrumentals using the talk box with his steel guitar in 1964 and 1965. In 1969, he was hired by George Harrison to come to Abbey Road Studio to record steel guitar for what became *All Things Must Pass*. On those sessions was a young guitarist named Peter Frampton, who became enamored with Drake's talk box and began using one in his live performances and, several years later, on his massive *Frampton Comes Alive!* Both Frampton, with "Do You Feel Like We Do," and Joe Walsh, with "Rocky Mountain Way," hit the top of the charts using the talk box in their songs in 1976.

"Mind Bender" came the following year and listeners still loved the talk-box sound, pushing the single up the *Billboard* Top 100 chart peaking just outside the Top 40 at #46. Unfortunately, the band couldn't replicate the success with follow-up singles, disbanding shortly after their 1978 release *I Reserve the Right*.

96. "That's Your Secret," Sea Level (from *Cats on the Coast*, 1977)

The world of the Allman Brothers Band has been a tumultuous one throughout the band's history. The band survived the death of two founding members, becoming more successful as they continued. They weathered changing tastes and shifted their style to present a wider representation of their influences. They, at least publicly, endured the effects of drug abuse among their ranks. But it was a breach in the brotherhood that caused the biggest schism.

Gregg Allman's drug use had continually escalated over the years, and when John "Scooter" Herring, a roadie for the band and one of Allman's suppliers, was busted, Allman testified in the 1976 trial against Herring. To his fellow band members, Allman had stooged on their friend and someone who was counting on them to pull him through. In reality, unbeknownst to the band at the time, Allman was given immunity, and not testifying would have sent him to prison. It was a tough spot to be in, and it tore the band apart.

Members of the band went their separate ways, and 1977 saw the release of the Gregg Allman Band's *Playin' Up a Storm* and Dickey Betts & Great Southern's self-titled debut. The rest of the band—drummers Butch Trucks and Jai Johanny "Jaimoe" Johanson, bassist Lamar Williams, and keyboardist Chuck Leavell—began to form an idea for their own group. While jazz had been an apparent influence on the music of the Allman Brothers Band, it had been heavily mixed with blues and country. This new group would lean the other way, exhibiting their jazz side in a more unadulterated fashion.

In the end, Trucks decided to take time off rather than form the new band, but the remaining trio moved forward, playing off of Leavell's name, calling the band Sea Level. The group contacted guitarist Jimmy Nalls, whom Leavell had known since he was sixteen and who had played with Dr. John, Noel Stookey, and Alex Taylor. The band stayed with

Capricorn Records and in early 1977 released their self-titled debut. From the opening notes of the album's leadoff track "Rain in Spain," the differences between Sea Level and the Allman Brothers Band are apparent. The album hit the charts, peaking at #43 on the *Billboard* Top 200 and #35 on the Jazz Albums chart.

To capitalize on the success, the group headed back into the studio to work on a follow-up as the album was still on the charts. For their second, album the band expanded bringing in Randall Bramblett on piano, vocals, and saxophone and second guitarist Davis Causey, who had been playing with Bramblett, and second drummer George Weaver, who had previously played with Otis Redding and Bobby "Blue" Bland. The result, *Cats on the Coast*, improved on the success, peaking at #31 on the Top 200.

Musically, the expanded group allowed the band more flexibility and creativity, as "That's Your Secret" ably demonstrates. The single version, which tiptoed onto and off of the singles chart quickly, clocks in at 2:59 and showcases Bramblett's soulful vocals. While Leavell was a serviceable vocalist on the first album, Bramblett's voice allowed for an extended range in song choices. Where Leavell shines is on organ, providing a shimmering bed for the rest of the musicians. The album version, coming in at just over five minutes, showcases that organ playing to great effect. The album version also includes the fantastic guitar interplay of Causey and Nalls in the second half of the song. Instead of the Southern Rock standard of harmony guitar parts, the two echo and chase one another, coming together at intersections that pass quickly and resolve into each other.

After these initial successes, in 1977 the band went through a few lineup changes but continued on recording three more albums (1978's *On the Edge*, 1979's *Long Walk on a Short Pier*, and 1980's *Ball Room*). In 1982, Leavell began a touring and recording relationship with the Rolling Stones as well as guesting on numerous albums through the years.

95. "Sang Her Love Songs," Winters Brothers Band (from *Winters Brothers Band*, 1977)

Tradition always played a big part in Southern Rock, whether it was thematically with thoughts of home and "the good ol' days" or in song choice with a band picking a country or bluegrass standard to record. For

some, it was a family tradition, as with Hank Williams Jr., and Blackfoot, and it was certainly true of the Winters Brothers Band.

Music ran deep in their blood, starting with the grandfather, who had his own radio shows in Florida in the mid-1950s, playing his music during the popular lunch hour and returning at five o'clock that evening to wrap up the workday. The radio shows allowed him the name recognition to play regionally as "Pop Winters and the Southern Strollers." One member of the Southern Strollers was his son Don.

Don Winters performed with his father, as well as solo when he could, writing and performing his own compositions. Through his playing, he made contact with country-superstar-on-the-rise Marty Robbins, and in 1960, when Robbins had to fire one of his trio singers for drinking too much, Robbins called Winters with an invitation. Winters accepted, and it began a working relationship that lasted twenty-three years. The agreement was that Winters would be part of Robbins's trio of singers (which included Robbins on lead and Joe Babcock as baritone to Winters's tenor), but he would also be his own artist, and though he never had much chart or commercial success, he was able to perform across the country with Robbins's show, his name listed just below Robbins on posters and in ads.

His close association with Robbins brought him frequently to the stage of the Grand Ole Opry, where, as a member, Robbins was obligated to a specific number of performances per year. It became a regular thing for Robbins to close the show and raise the ire of Opry management by always running long (though the broadcast portion of the show would end at its specified time whether he was finished or not). Often hanging out backstage were Winters's two sons, Donnie and Dennis. Being surrounded by the best of the best in country music led them to eye a career in music for themselves. The family lived on a farm owned by Robbins just outside of Nashville where the younger Winters brothers would act as ranch hands, but when they weren't working they would retreat to a bunkhouse on the property to practice their music.

The country music surrounding them mixed with the influences of British bands like Pink Floyd, the Beatles, and Led Zeppelin, coalescing in time for the burgeoning Southern Rock movement to embrace the amalgam they presented. Soon after the brothers assembled their band and began playing around the Nashville area, they were approached by

Atlantic Records and signed a deal to be on their subsidiary ATCO, releasing their self-titled debut in 1976.

The sound of that album hewed closely to what was being released around the same time by their friends in the Marshall Tucker Band and the Charlie Daniels Band (in fact, Taz DiGregorio of the Charlie Daniels Band helped produce their demos and first album). The song from that album that has made the most lasting impact is the ballad "Sang Her Love Songs."

Eschewing the rocking guitars of Lynyrd Skynyrd and the Allman Brothers Band, the Winters Brothers returned to those times in the bunk-house for influence. The song starts with a beautifully lush twelve-string acoustic guitar arpeggiating while DiGregorio plays a soft complementary piano piece behind it. A muted electric guitar gently comes in with subtle string bends introducing the vocals. One of the trademarks of the Winters Brothers was their use of their brother harmony, singing the majority of the song as a two-harmony lead. It is something that sets them apart from their contemporaries and made the band stand out.

The song itself tells a story familiar to many men who, when it comes to love, fall short in expressing what they really feel. "I sang her love songs all night long," the brothers sing, but even so, the protagonist knows he fell short in expressing exactly what he feels inside himself. Even though he feels this way, he can express himself only in song, but for the woman, they are just pretty songs, like the ones he sings from the stage to an audience full of people. In her mind, they are nice, but they only fill the space and are not what she wants to hear from him. As a result, she leaves him, falling in love with "a gambling man" though her guilt and love for him make her leave him as well.

DiGregorio's piano lilts through the song while a Toy Caldwell-esque guitar weaves single notes throughout. In the closing seconds of the song, the acoustic twelve-string returns playing chiming harmonics doubled by DiGregorio's piano ending the song as lushly as it began.

The Winters Brothers failed to hit any commercial targets, recording a follow-up that wasn't released (though it finally was in 2004 as *Southwest Stampede*) before being dropped from the label. Shortly after Marty Rob-bins's death in 1983, they recorded an album of country music with their father. Although they were not in the spotlight, they never stopped performing music around their hometown of Nashville, and in 1995 they began a television show showcasing their music aired in Nashville on

community access television. In 2000, they returned to recording, releasing *Southern Rockers*.

94. "Gambler's Roll," Allman Brothers Band (from *Seven Turns*, 1990)

When *Seven Turns* was released in 1990, several reviewers pointed to "Gambler's Roll" as a standout track that showcased the strengths of the newly re-formed Allman Brothers Band. It showcases the songwriting skills of two new members: keyboardist Johnny Neel and guitarist Warren Haynes. Haynes had written for Gregg Allman's solo project *Just Before the Bullets Fly* as a member of the Dickey Betts Band and cowrote several for *Seven Turns*. The same year, Haynes's song "Two of a Kind, Working on a Full House" was recorded by Garth Brooks and included on his album *No Fences* and became a #1 single in 1991.

It's a mysterious story that is given framework by the song, a story that leaves much to the imagination of the listener. Haynes and Neel open the first scene with the gambler sitting in a dark room, his cards illuminated by his lit cigarette. He's alone and thinking about everything he has lost to the "gambler's roll." In the second verse, we learn there is a girl who has also lost much to the gambler's roll, in fact, on the same roll. It is with that roll that they lost each other. The small breeze of rolling dice "blows a young girl's world apart." With the landing of the roll, with a choice made, she gains her freedom but "lost her soul." It's not to a deal with the devil she has lost it, but instead, by losing this gambler who has become her soul mate, she has perhaps lost her will to continue.

It's a fool's train, the chorus tells us, that the gambler rides on. His wins are outweighed by his losses, but he hopes his luck will change as "times takes its toll." Gregg Allman's voice brims with passion and soul as he tells the story, but as he finishes the chorus he allows his Hammond B-3 to take over, starting softly, playing a round-toned melody while Haynes's guitar stabs add drama to the otherwise subdued sonic texture. But Allman breaks out, soaring to a high register with his right hand as the left reiterates the previous melody. Drifting lower in the mix, the organ fades, allowing Dickey Betts to step up, treading softly into the musical conversation that could stand as a representation of the young girl's voice responding to the gambler's even-keeled but misplaced faith as given voice by Allman's B-3. As Betts continues, the intensity of the

solo increases, punctuated with a quick staccato run that ends with Betts's trademark multistring bends. It is as if the girl is crying out and as if she has lost her voice and allowed another to speak for her. Haynes takes over with a bend before unleashing a flurry of notes. Haynes's intensity nearly doubles that of Betts as he bends the strings, flies up the neck of the guitar, and comes down to meet the band as they hit four times before falling back into the preinstrumental sound of the song.

The pain conveyed by the guitarists leads us into the final verse. Reentering the song, Allman tells us that the dealer knows this is his last game. He also tells us that not even the young girl can know "all the sorrow and pain." What happens next is up to the listener. "As the forty-five deals the fatal blow," Allman sings. But to whom is the blow dealt? Does the gambler go down in a game gone wrong? Does he take his own life? Or does she take her own life, driven to sorrow by shattered dreams that cloud her thinking?

Haynes and Neel have crafted a song that stands among the classics of the Allman Brothers Band with guitar work that sets the stage for the latter twenty-five or so years of their career.

93. "Fox Huntin'," Blackhorse (from *Blackhorse*, 1979)

When something hits big for a record label, other labels, even the original label, start looking for ways to replicate that success. Sometimes it works; sometimes it fails. It doesn't just happen to labels, though. There are times when a promoter or manager will hit with something and they'll look to continue building on what they know. Such was the case with Bill Ham.

Ham had signed ZZ Top in the late 1960s, and the band had continued to grow, becoming a popular concert draw and scoring with blues- and boogie-based records. After their third consecutive Top 20 album and a successful tour in 1976, the band decided to take some time off. In 1978, they were gearing up for a return, recording *Degüello* and preparing to release it the following year. During their time off, Ham went looking for other groups to work with. He first signed Point Blank in the mid-1970s and directed them toward the flourishing Southern Rock scene. Now he found another three-piece hard-rock unit in the form of Blackhorse.

But where ZZ Top reveled in a variety of guitar sounds, blues-soaked riffs, and ramped-up boogie, Blackhorse was a straight-up, in-your-face

hard-rock power trio closer to the Led Zeppelin/Cream vein. The lead track from their debut (and only) album tells you everything you need to know about the band. Drummer John Teague crashes in, his snare cracking and his double bass drum thunderous. Bassist Paul Middleton and guitarist Gary James bear down on a heavy Rush-like riff before James snarls, "All right, turn 'em loose." The sounds of hounds enter as James's guitar descends into feedback while Teague hammers the snare with a straightforward machine-gun beat. James returns to his riffing as Teague subtly switches up the beat to a chugging rhythm, making full use of the drum kit before returning to a solid rock beat.

James's voice falls somewhere between Billy Gibbons and Molly Hatchet's Danny Joe Brown as he growls lyrics about looking for a good time in the club. Just as the title says, he is on the hunt for a fox, and when he finds her, she shares that "feeling deep in our soul," suggesting they "let the good times roll."

Musically, the band shares much more with the nascent British wave of heavy metal that included Judas Priest and Iron Maiden than the "Southern Rock" tag it was given, mainly through their association with Ham and his other bands working within the genre. As heavy as Molly Hatchet and even Blackfoot could get, Blackhorse demonstrated a darker tone.

For whatever reason, the band released only one album on the obscure DSDA label, and while they toured extensively to promote the album, they disappeared from the national stage by 1981. Even so, the band stayed together and continue to play together regularly as of this writing. Their album is a cult hit collector's item that is nearly impossible to find in its original vinyl form and even hard to find in its internationally reissued CD form from 2013.

92. "Rock and Roll Southern Man," Beaverteeth (from *Dam It*, 1978)

The mid- to late 1970s gave birth to several bands that were lumped into the Southern Rock category just as it was beginning to fade and as a result had their careers cut short through lack of marketing—or marketing to a now diminishing audience. Some of the bands who had carried the flag for Southern Rock were now moving into more mainstream waters, playing down their southern roots in favor of a more universal tone both

musically and lyrically. One group that was finding success with that formula was the Atlanta Rhythm Section. Their formation is discussed elsewhere in this book, but their origin is important to another late 1970s rock group, Beaverteeth.

Drummer Robert Nix and singer Rodney Justo were part of Roy Orbison's backing band the Candymen when the group had a surprise hit and soon parted ways with Orbison. A few years later, they teamed with members of other bands to form the Atlanta Rhythm Section. The band, made up of mainly studio musicians, concentrated on what they knew best, recording two less-than-successful albums. Justo, while he had a lot of studio experience himself, enjoyed performing live, having toured extensively with artists like blues guitarist Roy Buchanan. After leaving the group, he received a call in 1975 from BJ Thomas, who was riding the charts with a #1 Country single, asking him to be his band leader and charging him with assembling a band.

To put the band together, Justo reached out to some of his friends in the Alabama studio system, including his ex-Candymen band mate, guitarist John Rainey Adkins. Once the tour with Thomas ended, the ensemble decided to stay together and, calling themselves Beaverteeth, were signed to a record deal with RCA, releasing their self-titled debut in 1977. Just as with the first Atlanta Rhythm Section album, it was met with little fanfare.

For their second album, *Dam It*, they continued the jazzy-pop style of the first album, adding in healthy dose of Southern Rock twin guitars similar in style to the Atlanta Rhythm Section. One of the finest examples of their style comes from this album in the form of "Rock and Roll Southern Man." Although Justo was the band's lead singer, this track featured instead a new addition to the band: keyboardist and vocalist Mike Turner. Turner's vibrant electric piano starts off chording the song when Larry Hunter's drums come down hard on the downbeat. The drums signal in John Rainey and his brother David Adkins on guitar as they play a palm-muted harmony guitar part when Jeff Chesire joins them on bass.

Being a touring musician is a well-worn theme in rock and roll, and here Turner's vocals bring a tender emotion to the lyrics. He downplays the lines about traveling the country performing, "getting drunk and raising hell, breaking out with the Rebel Yell" as a means to get to the heart

of the song, returning home to his love. It is to her he returns, he tells us, when "rock and roll gets him down."

The chorus features a wonderful three-part harmony vocal coupled with the Adkins brothers providing harmony fills while the vocalists re-emphasize the fact that this touring life is like "blowing through like the wind." After the guitars return to the opening riff, Turner returns on vocals, explaining that the reason he continues is that rock and roll is in soul, but "there's an ache in my heart and a blues I can't control." The price for this lifestyle is missing birthdays, holidays, and special occasions.

After another pass through the chorus, the guitars play their riff into the three-minute mark when Turner lets loose a scream and the band notches up the rock, bearing down hard on the main riff, their palms fully off the strings. Both guitars and Turner's electric piano are intertwined in a series of impressive, heavily jazz-influenced harmony runs, ending in an amped-up reprise of the intro, the sound of a swirl Moog synthesizer filling the air around them. Hunter brings the drums to full volume, setting a solid foundation for David's lead guitar solo, which dissolves into the third verse, a restatement of the first.

Beaverteeth, meeting with little commercial success, disbanded shortly after their sophomore release, relegating them to a Southern Rock footnote, though they left some fine songs behind for all to enjoy.

91. "Stonehead Blues," Eric Quincy Tate (from *Eric Quincy Tate*, 1970)

After playing together for several years as the Kings, the quintet that made up the band decided it was time for a name change. Going forward, they would call themselves Eric Quincy Tate. Finding a new band name is never an easy task, so the guys decided to set it up as a tribute to some of their favorites: Eric for Eric Clapton, Quincy for Quincy Jones, and Tate for tater, as in potato. To the band, though, the name sounded suitably English, and they decided to stay with it.

Whether known as Eric Quincy Tate or the Kings, the band was still a popular one around their stomping grounds of Corpus Christi, Texas. They packed in crowds every night at the Rogue's Club and played in as many regional battle-of-the-bands competitions as they could get to, crossing paths with other musicians in the area. One of those was a

younger singer-songwriter named Tony Joe White. In 1968, White finally landed a recording contract, recording *Black and White* for the Nashville label Monument and scoring a Top Ten hit with "Polk Salad Annie." Through his travels, White had become friendly with Otis Redding's former manager Phil Walden, who was in the process of setting up a new record label with backing from legendary producer Jerry Wexler and Atlantic Records. With White's recommendation, Walden decided to check out the band and soon after offered them a management pact.

Capricorn Records was still in its infancy in 1969, releasing mainly 45-rpm singles and ramping up to albums. Since he wasn't ready to take them on himself, Walden got the band an audition with Wexler. Wexler, as it turned out, was in the process of heading up a new label for Atlantic called Cotillion, designed to showcase rhythm and blues, pop, and jazz and building on Deep South soul like that of the label's first signee, Otis Clay (and his version of the Sir Douglas Quintet's "She's about a Mover"). The band was signed to the label and moved to Memphis to begin work on their debut album.

The album's lead track sums up the funky swamp music the band carried with them from Corpus Christi. David Cantonwine starts the song with a funky, stuttering bass line before vocalist and drummer Donnie McCormick unleashes a guttural, James Brown–like "Hey, let's get it here!" His command is met with a blast from the horn section, guitarists Wayne "Bear" Sauls and Tommy Carlisle and keyboardist Joe Rogers following quickly behind. "Stonehead Blues" and, indeed, the rest of their debut album reflect the same swampy roots from which White drew inspiration. Rather than the heavily guitar-driven music of what would become Southern Rock, the horn section is the dominant sound here, accented by the syncopated guitars and punchy organ fills. Lyrically, the song speaks of what the band often saw from the bandstand on a nightly basis: the people moving to the beat, having a good time, and the band being right where they want to be.

As good as the song and the album were, the band couldn't find success with the swamp-rock sound they were using and were subsequently dropped by the label. Fortunately, when that happened, Walden and Capricorn were in a position to catch them, signing them and producing their second album, *Drinking Man's Friend*, in 1972. Changing up their sound a bit, moving closer to other Capricorn label mates, the band was still unable to find commercial success. After parting ways with

Capricorn, the band moved to the short-lived GRC label, releasing their second self-titled album (though more commonly referred to as *Eric Quincy Tate*). After the lack of commercial success, the band released one final try in 1977 with the self-released *You Can't Keep a Good Band Down*, featuring predominantly their versions of old blues and country tunes.

Eric Quincy Tate is another example of a great Southern Rock band that fell through the commercial cracks but that produced some outstanding music that deserves to be heard by a wider audience.

90. "Prime Time," Rossington Collins Band (from *Anytime, Anyplace, Anywhere*, 1980)

Over 10,000 fans packed into Nashville Municipal Auditorium on January 13, 1979, for the fifth Volunteer Jam, the annual concert hosted by Charlie Daniels that drew a variety of musicians who all performed a few songs and then jammed together. The show was always full of surprise guests, and the rumor was that this year would hold one of the biggest. Aside from the overcapacity crowd, the show was being heard throughout the region, broadcast over six Tennessee radio stations that covered the state, plus parts of Kentucky, Georgia, and Alabama. In addition, the six-hour show was being broadcast by WLIR-FM in Garden City, New York.

The show proceeded with the Charlie Daniels Band blazing through a nearly eighty-minute set before taking an intermission. Grinderswitch, John Prine, and Stillwater made appearances in the show's second half before Daniels introduced Teresa Gaines and Judy Van Zant, the widows of fallen Lynyrd Skynyrd members Steve Gaines and Ronnie Van Zant, respectively. The crowd could see band members making their way to the stage, and Daniels turned to the crowd and announced,"The Lynyrd Skynyrd Band." Survivors Gary Rossington, Allen Collins, Billy Powell, and Artimus Pyle (Leon Wilkeson was there but unable to play yet) were joined by Daniels and bassist Charlie Hayward and keyboardist Taz DiGregorio, both of the Charlie Daniels Band, to go through "Call Me the Breeze" (with DiGregorio on vocals) and an instrumental version of "Free Bird" that brought the house down. It was the band's first public appearance, and the crowd's reaction solidified thoughts they had been having in private.

Of the survivors, Powell was the first to get back to work, recording piano parts on two .38 Special albums (*Special Delivery* and *Rockin' into the Night*), but soon the members were back in the studio helping Jacksonville friend Dorman Coburn on a project dubbed Alias. Powell and Pyle played alongside Billy's older brother Ricky on bass (he would later be replaced with Wilkeson when he felt up to the task), while Rossington and Collins, along with another Jacksonville friend, Barry Lee Harwood, provided guitar. Rossington and Collins also helped write some songs and produce the sessions. But after their reception at Volunteer Jam V, they began to wonder why they shouldn't put together a project of their own. Soon, five survivors began to make plans to return to the studio for a new project that came to be called the Rossington Collins Band.

First, they needed a singer, but they knew that anyone stepping up to the microphone would be instantly compared to Ronnie Van Zant. There were only two exceptions to that thought. Comparisons could be avoided if the singer were someone known in his or her own right. Names like Paul Rodgers and Gregg Allman were bandied about, but in the end Rossington and Collins decided they wanted to stand on their own. There was only one other exception to the rule.

While listening to .38 Special's *Rockin' into the Night*, Collins heard the song "Money Honey," a greasy blues number featuring Donnie Van Zant trading vocal barbs with one of the band's background singers, Dale Krantz. Krantz and the Skynyrd crew had crossed paths over recent years, but in that moment Collins was struck by her vocal power and command. He and Rossington decided that a female lead vocalist would be able to escape most comparisons to Van Zant and went to Krantz to invite her into the band. Adding Barry Lee Harwood on third guitar and moving Derek Hess into the drummer stool after Pyle suffered a severely broken leg in a motorcycle accident, the band was complete and went to work.

"Prime Time," the opening track of their album *Anytime, Anyplace, Anywhere*, let everyone know immediately that the band was back and serious about making an impact. "We're alive and well and we're ready," Krantz wails over a rocking rhythm bolstered by the new three-guitar attack. Sonically, the song continued in the vein of "What's Your Name," their last charting single (and borrowing a bit from "Truck Drivin' Man"), fitting right in with the current crop of post-Skynyrd bands. Harwood was given center stage with the solo on the song, allowing him to put his musical voice up front as the first song heard by record buyers. It's not a

deep or profound song, but it accomplishes its purpose: to drive a stake into the ground and declare that the band was back and ready to continue to make kick-ass Southern Rock music.

89. "Levee Blues," Potliquor (from *Levee Blues*, 1971)

Before the tag "Southern Rock" was liberally applied to any band coming out of the South, there were a variety of groups being signed to major labels, and one of the nearly forgotten is the band Potliquor. The band formed in the late 1960s in their hometown of Baton Rouge, Louisiana, and began to play around town under a variety of names. To settle on a name, the band's manager, who also owned the club they were playing in, sponsored a "name the band" contest, and the name Potliquor came out on top.

Once the band signed with Janus Records, they began to play across the country, including venues like the Village Gate in New York and the Whisky a Go Go, West Hollywood. Since the "Southern Rock" tag had not gained widespread use yet, the band was often simply referred to as a boogie-blues band. While they were that, they also carried a heavier sound that brings to mind bands like the Guess Who and Mountain.

A prime example is the excellent title track from their debut album, *Levee Blues*. Guitarist Les Wallace starts the song with a heavily distorted low-end guitar riff before bassist Guy Schaeffer joins in. Schaeffer's bass carries a fuzzed-out tone and doubles Wallace's riff while Jerry Amoroso lands heavy on the drums. The three together give an almost Black Sabbath, heavy sound to the song, which was released just a couple of years after the debut of the pioneering heavy metal band's first album. The similarities end when lead vocalist and pianist George Ratzlaff enters on barrelhouse piano. His upper-register piano tinkling serves as a stark contrast to the heavy sounds surrounding it.

Ratzlaff is a powerful rock shouter whose voice anchors the band between the heavy rhythm and the frenetic New Orleans–style piano. His voice is a perfect fit for the story of a man who has lost at love and has been able to come to terms with it, until he sees her on the levee with someone else. He tells us in the first verse that the affair is over and he is going "down to the river" in hopes he will understand. Once there, he sees her and her friend, telling us, "a long time ago I learned to add." Ratzlaff's guttural growl leaves it up to the listener to decide the outcome

of that encounter as he continues his trip to the river. Did he simply walk away dejected, wallowing in the pain of seeing his former flame with another? Or did the song take a turn into the territory of countless ballads, like "Knoxville Girl" and "Banks of the Ohio," that leave the flame extinguished in the river?

This 1971 debut and the two albums that followed are filled with excellent music (including a fantastic, heavy version of "You're No Good," four years before Linda Ronstadt took it to the top of the charts, and "Cheer," their only single to see any chart action) that is nearly forgotten today. When the band's manager died in a tragic car accident, the band imploded, bringing to the surface years of strife between members. In the late 1970s, to capitalize on the Southern Rock trend, drummer Amoroso and bassist Schaeffer joined with new guitarist Mike McQuaig, re-formed as a trio, but without the powerful voice of Ratzlaff or his piano and organ playing, the band had transformed into something else, adding horns and early synthesizer sounds.

88. "Walk Softly on This Heart of Mine," Kentucky Headhunters (from *Pickin' on Nashville*, 1989)

Gregg Allman famously quipped that the term "Southern Rock" was a bit of a misnomer since all rock came from the South. It's true that most of the originators rose up from the South to bring forth what became rock and roll. At the forefront, at least in the minds of most music fans, was the hillbilly cat from Memphis by way of Tupelo, Mississippi. Sam Phillips released the first Elvis Presley single, "That's All Right," backed with "Blue Moon of Kentucky." The pairing of the straight-up rhythm-and-blues song with a hard-core country song became the defining example of the influences of rockabilly. Presley's version of "That's All Right" doesn't stray too far from Arthur "Big Boy" Crudup's original, but his version of Bill Monroe's "Blue Moon of Kentucky" takes the song from a waltz to a much faster rave-up.

Fast-forward thirty-five years to 1989 and the Kentucky Headhunters's debut album *Pickin' on Nashville*. But first let's talk a little about labels. The "Southern Rock" label, as most of the bands that the term was applied to will attest, was largely a marketing label, something record labels could use as a tool to direct their marketing dollars at people who gravitated to a certain sound. The same is true of any format, including

country music. As Southern Rock was slowing fading away—its remaining practitioners moving toward arena rock or simply playing to fewer and fewer people—country music was beginning to welcome a band called Alabama.

Bands had existed for many years in country music, but they were the backing bands of big-name artists. Ernest Tubb had the Troubadours, and Little Jimmy Dickens had the Country Boys. Buck Owens had the Buckaroos, and Merle Haggard had the Strangers. All of these bands recorded albums apart from their bosses, but they were more of a side project, and most of them contained instrumental versions of the songs they were famous for playing anyway. In the 1970s, Alabama had released three small-label records but failed to get any attention.

That changed with their 1980 release *My Home's in Alabama*. The album went to #3 on the Country Albums chart and produced two #1 singles. Just like every other time something unexpected becomes a hit in the music industry, record labels looked to replicate it. After Alabama's success, more bands were welcomed to country music. What makes a band a country band rather than a Southern Rock band in most cases is really a matter of semantics. Had the Marshall Tucker Band's label decided post-Alabama to pursue a country rather than a pop audience, the band would probably have continued to find success throughout the 1980s. Bands like Southern Pacific, which included a couple of former Doobie Brothers, or the Desert Rose Band, helmed by country-rock pioneer Chris Hillman, found success in the country market during that time.

The bands that did find success leaned heavier on the country-rock template of the Byrds, the Flying Burrito Brothers, and the Eagles than the guitar-heavy work of their Southern Rock brethren—until the Kentucky Headhunters came along. After focusing on a more pop-oriented brand of country for the better part of the late 1970s and early 1980s, country radio was beginning to give more airtime to the "neotraditionalists," such as Clint Black, Randy Travis, Reba McEntire, and Garth Brooks, to name a few. It also opened up enough to include rowdier artists, like Steve Earle, and old favorites, like Alabama and Hank Williams Jr. The Headhunters don't really fit into any of those categories.

As Elvis did before them, they reached into the catalog of Bill Monroe for their debut single, "Walk Softly on This Heart of Mine." Monroe had recorded the song in 1969, and it had been kicked around bluegrass circles for years. When the Kentucky Headhunters sunk their teeth into it,

just as Elvis had with "Blue Moon," they made it their own. The opening chords from Richard Young's distorted Telecaster sound unlike anything it was played alongside on the radio of 1989. Brother Fred Young's snare snaps, and when the drums and Doug Phelps's bass hit, the bottom end is more earthshaking than its contemporaries. Ricky Lee Phelps's Kentucky twang leans more toward the country influences of the band, but that's the only thing. When Greg Martin's Les Paul makes its first appearance, the thoughts of their being a "traditional" country band—or even a not-so-traditional band, like some of the bands around them such as Shenandoah—went out the window.

In 1989, Southern Rock was having a little more light shone on it. The Georgia Satellites were making waves, and both the Allman Brothers and Lynyrd Skynyrd had reassembled and were hitting the road. The crunchy guitars of the Headhunters brought to mind their Southern Rock forefathers, and Martin proved he had the chops worthy of picking up the mantle. When he cuts lose on the solo, his tone is round and buoyant, reminiscent in sound to Dickey Betts.

Whatever their label, the Kentucky Headhunters had found success with country audiences. The single climbed to #25, but on the strength of that song and the next single, "Dumas Walker," the album made it to #2 on the Country Albums chart, showing that there were many country music fans who still prized their Southern Rock roots.

87. "She Talks to Angels," Black Crowes (from *Shake Your Money Maker*, 1990)

For their fourth single from their debut album, the Black Crowes decided to move away from the rocking sounds of their previous singles by releasing the mainly acoustic "She Talks to Angels." *Shake Your Money Maker* had been available for over a year at the time, and the band was continuing to grow in popularity. Just prior to the album's release, the band had been nominated for a Grammy Award in the category of Best New Artist alongside fellow southern rockers the Kentucky Headhunters, Lisa Stansfield, Wilson Phillips, and Mariah Carey (who would sweep the awards that year), and by fall they were nominated in the New Artist category of the MTV Video Music Awards.

By their fourth single, the band's image was of a rough-and-tumble band of brothers from the South who were reluctantly carrying on the

banner of Southern Rock. "She Talks to Angels" showed another side of the band, focusing on the open-tuned acoustic guitar of Rich Robinson. Robinson opens the song with a single-note figure played in open D tuning that resolves into open chords, bringing in brother Chris Robinson on vocals. "She never mentions the word addiction," he sings plaintively over his brother's acoustic strumming. The topic of addiction, he tells us, is something she doesn't mention around "certain company," which perhaps is her family, mentioned in the next line as an illustration of her nature as she tells him she is an orphan though he has just met her family. With that, drummer Steve Gorman crashes in like the realization of just what type of trouble this girl Chris sings about brings with her. With him, Gorman brings along bass player Johnny Colt and the swirling Hammond B-3 of former Allman Brothers Band member Chuck Leavell.

Leavell's B-3 swells in the background, sounding nearly dirge-like beneath Chris's vocals as he returns, describing the girl who paints "her eyes as black as night." She lowers the shade and smiles "when the pain comes," noting that the pain will make everything better. But the pain is a needle breaking the skin; it's a momentary pain, if it can even be felt at all as it moves through the scars of previous usage. Soon the drug moves through her bloodstream, taking her away from everything. Chris then breaks into the chorus, "she talks to angels," he says, and they respond, calling out to her by name. But are they angels calling her away from this doomed life she leads or demons in disguise convincing her to return to them with each prick of the needle?

This life she leads is a one-way, runaway train as she gives herself over to the needle. A lock of a little boys' hair is stored in her pocket, he tells us in the next verse, while a cross hangs from her neck. Chris intentionally leaves the verse vague, allowing listeners their own interpretations. Is the little boy her own? Was he taken in some tragic accident that sent her spiraling onto this path, or is he still around to witness the tragedy to come? And the cross, he tells us, represents someone she hasn't met. "Not yet," he says. But she wears it as if waiting for that savior to step off the cross and carry her away.

"She don't know no lover," he sings, and to her that doesn't mean anything, but to him it means everything. And with that, we are let in a little further. Is the singer a former lover? Or is it possible that the singer is that little boy? She may be an orphan, but he is her family, left to witness things a child should not. Poverty and despair have led her to this,

and it is he who looks for a savior. She tells him, in her drugged state, that the angels call to her by name. And in the last line of the song, he wonders why they would do that. Maybe he wonders because if she answers the call, he'll be alone.

But that's just one interpretation. Chris Robinson has said the character in the song was a composite of people he had met in the clubs of Atlanta as the band played there as Mr. Crowe's Garden. In interviews over the years, as many songwriters do, he has been vague about the exact meaning of the song, leaving it open to the ears of listeners. And listeners latched on to the song, and it became the band's second #1 on the Mainstream Rock Tracks chart and their second-highest charting song on the *Billboard* Hot 100, peaking at #30.

86. "Mail Train Blues," Grinderswitch (from *Macon Tracks*, 1975)

Why one band makes it big over another band is one of the great mysteries of the music business. It is true now, and it was true during the heyday of Southern Rock. Take, for example, the case of Grinderswitch. Made up of a great group of capable musicians with catchy songs, supported by their famous and influential friends, and touring as an opening act in front of crowds hungry for their music, they still never gained the traction to take them too far beyond the name recognition that being name checked by Charlie Daniels in "The South's Gonna Do It Again" would bring in the mainstream.

A fine example of their music is "Mail Train Blues" from their second album, *Macon Tracks*. The song is a catchy addition to the canon of train songs with great vocals by guitarist and singer Dru Lombar. In that fine tradition, the song tells of a moderately successful outlaw who doesn't always come out on top of a card game and needs to ride the rail in the hot sun to get a few more scores before being able to stop.

Throughout the song, guitarist Larry Howard turns in some fine work, punctuating the lyrics with tasty fills. Sawing throughout the song is friend of the band Charlie Daniels on fiddle. When it comes time for the solo, Howard turns in a wonderful, understated solo before sparring with Daniels. The two trade licks and play in harmony while drummer Rick Burnett and bass player Joe Dan Petty lay down the rhythm. It is a song

that stands up with some of the best from the era, standing shoulder to shoulder with their peers.

But it might be that standing with peers was the commercial downfall of the band. Group founder Joe Dan Petty began his musical career playing drums in the Florida-based Jokers with a pre–Allman Brothers Band Dickey Betts. After Betts and the Allman Brothers began to gain in popularity, Petty moved to Macon and joined their road crew (that's him, front and center, on the back cover of *The Allman Brothers Band at Fillmore East*). While hauling equipment with the band, he continued to play music with the goal of getting in a group of his own. Around that time, after the death of Duane Allman, Betts toyed with the idea of striking out on his own and began to assemble a band that included drummer Rick Burnett. When Betts decided to stay with the Allman Brothers, Burnett brought in his old band mate Larry Howard, and along with Petty the three began to form a band. Soon, another old friend, Dru Lombar, made his way to Macon, and the band was formed.

Out of these two stories—Petty the roadie and Betts's backing band—grew the perception by many that the band was simply a second-tier act made up of either Allman Brothers Band roadies or cast-offs of a failed side project. Neither was entirely true, and neither meant they weren't professional musicians wholly capable of sustaining their own creative work. *That* they were certainly capable of.

Once the band was formed and the name Grinderswitch settled on (the fictional hometown of comedienne and Grand Ole Opry star Minnie Pearl), the band went to work on songs. Members lived in Macon and had become friends with nearly all of the area musicians, including producer Paul Hornsby, who had recorded fantastic work with the Allman Brothers Band, the Marshall Tucker Band, and the Charlie Daniels Band. Hornsby and the band became not only friends but musical partners as well, with Hornsby serving as a de facto member of the band, contributing piano and organ to the recordings as well as producing.

On the one hand, this was a great thing, giving the band access to a musical mentor who had accomplished some impressive things in the Southern Rock world. But on the other hand, it seems that they never reached a vision of their own music. While it falls short of mimicry, the band wore their influences on their sleeves, and when those influences are friends and colleagues, it is hard to separate what made them unique in the eyes of the fans.

Even so, the band has become a sort of cult-status band in the Southern Rock genre with their own share of rabid fans and people who fondly remember the great music they released in their relatively short career.

85. "You Can't Get Off with Your Shoes On," Barefoot Jerry (from *You Can't Get Off with Your Shoes On*, 1975)

When you are a session musician, you live the dream of making a living playing music, but often it is not the music you dream of making. When that happens, the solution is to start something of your own. That line of thinking has given birth to great groups like Booker T & the MGs and Southern Rock's own Atlanta Rhythm Section. In 1969, a group of Nashville studio musicians formed the group Area Code 615, led by harmonica virtuoso Charlie McCoy and including Wayne Moss and Mac Gayden on guitar and Kenny Buttrey on drums, among others. The band lasted only a couple of years before McCoy's demanding session schedule led to his leaving the group.

Without McCoy, the band moved forward with a name change and recording original material. Being session players on recordings with Bob Dylan, Simon and Garfunkel, and Joan Baez on the folk/rock side and a list as long as your arm of country artists, the group stood, in 1971, at an early crossroads of rock and country that would come to birth Southern Rock. With the release of their first album, 1971's *Southern Delight*, the band began to carve out a niche for themselves that combined their experiences recording multiple genres. The band was on the leading edge of what was becoming a popular genre, though their music didn't include the bombastic guitars of Lynyrd Skynyrd or later Southern Rock bands, nor did it lean heavily on the country influences that surrounded them daily. They were in a class of their own and enjoying every minute of it.

By the time of their 1975 album *You Can't Get Off with Your Shoes On*, that band was at a bit of a crossroads. Their first three albums garnered little notice, save a few devoted fans of the Southern Rock genre or those who heard them as guests on the single "Boogie Woogie" by McCoy that same year. Moss, the band's de facto leader and spokesman, blamed the lack of recognition mainly on little promotion by the record label, and while there may have been truth in that, the fact is that each of their first three albums were released on three different labels (Capitol,

Warner Bros., and finally Monument, where the band would release its remaining albums), giving little time to gain traction.

Another factor was that the band rarely played live shows. In the five years since their inception, the band had played four live shows. By 1974, Southern Rock bands were dominating the box office, presenting many opportunities for bands within the genre to appear together. Being a band made up of highly successful veteran studio musicians who stood to make much more money staying at home and in the studio put a clamp on any touring plans. But as they released their fourth album, the membership of the band had shifted, and new and remaining members decided to make live performance a priority.

Now with Monument behind them and an increasing number of live performances, the band was beginning to be noticed and finally had a single appear on the *Billboard* charts for the first and only time—though barely. "Can't Get Off with Your Shoes On" carried a titillating title that piqued interest (the band had already raised eyebrows in the conservative country crowd with drug references in their music), and the single made it to #109 on the Pop chart.

Whatever images the title brought to mind, the song is actually a celebration of country living, encouraging listeners to "leave their shoes under the bed," saying "it's good for your feet, and better for your head." Unlike many others in the band's milieu, the song was a look back to the good old days of country living but more of a socially conscious warning about what is lost when "progress" eliminates those areas. Jim Colvard, who joined the band between *Watchin' TV*, their 1974 Monument debut, and the new album, provides the relaxed lead vocal, his understated voice providing the perfect example of the laid-back theme of the song. In contrast to his easygoing vocal, Colvard provides the song's rapid-fire guitar solo, playing against Moss's masterful rhythm playing.

After their brush with commercial success, tragedy struck the band when Colvard took his own life the following year. Other members came and went as the band released two more albums that didn't match the quality of their first four, leading to the band going their separate ways, most back to the studio, including Wayne Moss, who continues to own and operate a popular Nashville studio called Cinderella Sound.

84. "All Over but the Cryin'," Georgia Satellites (from *In the Land of Salvation and Sin*, 1989)

Georgia Satellites's first two albums, 1986's self-titled debut and 1988's *Open All Night*, were four-on-the-floor Southern Rock that, much like Lynyrd Skynyrd had, modeled themselves after their British rock heroes like the Small Faces and the Rolling Stones. The band quickly joined tours, opening for the likes of Tom Petty and the Heartbreakers and Bob Seger and the Silver Bullet Band, as well as their own shows across the United States and Europe.

When the band began to record their third album in 1988, the touring was taking its toll. There was friction between the band members and friction at home. Vocalist and guitarist Dan Baird was going through a divorce as the band began to work on material. With "All Over but the Cryin'," Baird was able to channel his grief, frustration, and anger into a song that is a prime example of the growth of the band.

In the Land of Salvation and Sin showed the band moving away from the full-force rock of their previous two albums and expanding their texture palette. While it still remained in more subtle ways, the band began to move away from their strong Small Faces influence (ironic since Small Faces keyboardist Ian McLagan joined them for half the album) and into other places, like amped-up rockabilly and Little Feat territory.

The biggest move was in their lyrics. They had written songs like "Night of Mystery" on their debut and "Hand to Mouth" on the second album, both of which exhibited some introspection and self-awareness but nothing of the insight and emotion of "All Over but the Cryin'." Baird lays it all out in the open here.

Baird's Telecaster opens the song with a chiming arpeggio as Rick Richards's Les Paul Jr. joins him, lending moral support for what Baird is about to endure. As he begins to sing, his voice sounds weary, worn from the months on the road. Speaking to the woman he had left behind, his words seem almost cryptic to her at first. "There's a fool born every minute," he says, but not him in this minute. "It doesn't take 20/20 to see what I can see," he tells her. It begins to dawn on her, borne of the guilt of always being afraid of being found out, but he cuts her off. He doesn't want to hear her side of the story, the excuses, the reasoning, the lies. Her actions, he tells her, outweigh anything she can say.

"Don't tell me nothing's going on!" he spits out forcefully through nearly gritted teeth. He shuts down her excuses again as she tries to deflect the accusations. He doesn't want to hear what she has to say. "I know the truth and you're lying," he sings with "lying" rising in pitch, his voice rough crescendoing in "It's all over!"—all but the crying, he says as he comes down, Ian McLagan's organ providing a place for him to fall as the band crashes with him.

Richards's guitar sound is a little tougher as he and Baird begin again. This time, she has the floor. Go right ahead "little girl," he tells her; he's just there to listen. "You have my undivided attention," he says, but he's been looking into her eyes, those "Lyin' Blue Eyes" that John Anderson sang about, those "Lyin' Eyes" that the Eagles immortalized. What Baird is going through isn't the first time it has happened, but here, now, it's the most important time. "Don't tell me nothing's going on!" he cries out again. As he repeats the chorus, McLagan's B3 is pushing him along. It's a painful conversation but one that has to happen, so McLagan is there to lean on, providing wisdom and experience.

"All over but the cryin'," Baird repeats, as Richards takes over with his searing guitar licks that echo Baird's cry. Richards then drops to imitate an almost guttural sound before returning to the upper register to sing out. Baird's guitar comes back in with the arpeggios while Richards fades to the back. Baird returns to his conversation, knowing she'll justify what she has done later: call him the fool. His voice nearly to its breaking point, he returns to the anger of the chorus, but as he begins to repeat the title, the anger begins to disappear, and only the pain remains. His strained voice repeating the phrase as Richards's guitar bends echo him, he finally can take no more, his words leave him, and he simply cries out, the cracks in his voice there for all to hear, and Richards takes over the cry until the band slams down together, the sustain of their instruments staring at the door she just closed.

83. "Shout Bamalama," Wet Willie (from *Wet Willie II*, 1972)

It ranks up there with the worst marketing moves in history: 45-rpm records carrying the red, white, and blue stars and bars and proudly proclaiming "Confederate" sent to black disc jockeys at rhythm-and-blues stations all across the South in 1962. More of them probably ended up on trash heaps than on turntables. Those few that put them on heard the

soulful shout of a new up-and-comer, Otis Redding, performing a song of his own called "Shout Bamalama." The song is a novelty song recorded to sound like it was at a party with a raw edge to the rocking band and a clear Little Richard influence in Redding's voice. It was Redding's second pass at the song—his first was called "Gamma Lama" and recorded a year earlier in California for Alshire records—and his manager Phil Walden loved the song and thought it would not only be a hit but also put his client on the road to superstardom with a larger label. Realizing the error of his ways, Confederate label head Bobby Smith changed the name of the company to Orbit and reissued the single, but its time had passed. Redding made the move to Volt and, with "These Arms of Mine," climbed the rhythm-and-blues charts, landing at #20 later that year.

As Redding's star rose, "Shout Bamalama" was being recorded by other hopefuls. Just months before Redding's untimely death in December 1967, soul singer Mickey Murray recorded the track for Shelby Singleton's SSS International label. The song entered the R&B charts at #38 on September 30, 1967. But where Redding's had a frenetic energy, Murray's slows the song down just a bit. But the most important change was to the background singers. Following the Civil Rights Act of 1964, there was a rise in the movement toward desegregation throughout the country and a rise in opposition. In July, major race-related riots broke out in Detroit, Michigan, and Newark, New Jersey, turning protests violent and heightening tensions throughout the country. In Redding's recording of the song, the background singers are buried in the mix, their words barely recognizable. On Murray's version, they are brought closer to the surface and are clearly audible after every line of the chorus, singing "shall be free." Given the atmosphere of the country, those three words sounded a proclamation that rang alongside civil rights anthems like "We Shall Overcome."

Just months after Murray's version peaked on the chart, a plane carrying Redding crashed, taking him from this earth and devastating his friends and family, including Walden. With Redding's death, Walden left soul music and began Capricorn Records and, after meeting Duane Allman in 1969, signed the band and launched what would become a Southern Rock empire.

The traits that attracted Walden to Redding were in full display when a five-piece band called Fox, inspired equally by Walden's past (Redding and his soul compatriots) and future (the Allman Brothers Band), walked

in the door for an audition in 1970. The band was signed and changed their name to Wet Willie. Quickly, the band was put in the studio to record their debut album with the idea that they could be a new Rolling Stones, the label even going so far as to team them with an English producer, Eddie Offord (who became better known as producer of progressive-rock bands like Yes and Emerson, Lake & Palmer). Their self-titled debut was critically noted, and the band returned to the studio with Offord to begin work on their follow-up, *Red Hot Chicken*, though they settled on naming it *Wet Willie II*.

Kicking off the album, the band wore their influences on their sleeve, diving headfirst into Redding's "Shout Bamalama." In 1972, civil rights were far from a dead issue, but progressive bands such as Wet Willie were multiracial affairs. Here, the band returns the song to its party roots, perhaps as a way to celebrate progress or maybe just as a way to escape the realities of the world. Either way, the shouts of vocalist Jimmy Hall convey a strong sense of joy, even euphoria. The band pumps and jumps like the best juke-joint jumpers in the business. John Anthony pounds the keys of his electric piano while bassist Jack Hall percolates, moving the rhythm forward in tandem with drummer Lewis Ross. Guitarist Ricky Hirsch slides into the chords, chopping their arrival with fine funk fashion. Jimmy Hall gets in a short solo on saxophone before returning to the vocals. At 2:15, background singer Ella Avery steps forward, and she and Hall trade vocal licks in a celebration of integration all their own, with a gospel-style call-and-response that rises and falls like a Sunday morning service.

82. "In America," Charlie Daniels Band (from *Full Moon*, 1980)

Standing before Congress on January 23, 1980, President Jimmy Carter delivered his State of the Union address. A pall hung over the proceedings as the thoughts of the nation and its leaders were directed elsewhere. Nearly two months earlier, on November 4, 1979, fifty-two Americans were taken hostage in Iran. The seeds had been planted almost a year from the time Carter was giving his speech, when the shah of Iran, after a revolt by his people, fled the country. Seeking refuge and medical treatment for cancer, the shah made his way to the United States. The people of Tehran wanted him returned to them and, in an attempt to force America's hand, stormed the U.S. embassy, taking the Americans there hostage.

America was a country dealing with its own inner turmoil throughout the 1970s. As the decade opened, the war in Vietnam caused a division in public opinion. By 1973, President Richard Nixon had ordered the withdrawal of American troops, but the Watergate scandal had taken its toll on American trust in the government. The situation in the Middle East came to a head for many Americans with the energy crisis that dealt a blow around that same time. But on that January evening as a new decade dawned, President Carter noted that the country had never come together in such great unity during peacetime as it had right then, in the shadow of the hostage situation.

"Together as one people, let us work to build our strength at home, and together as one indivisible union, let us seek peace and security throughout the world," he said, wrapping up the address. "Together let us make of this time of challenge and danger a decade of national resolve and of brave achievement."

The year 1979 was a breakout year for the Charlie Daniels Band. Their album *Million Mile Reflections*, powered by the blockbuster single "The Devil Went Down to Georgia," went multiplatinum, boosting their career. The band toured the country nonstop, and in doing so, Daniels came into contact with people of all walks of life across the country. It became evident to him that the Iranian hostage situation was drawing them together. In his State of the Union address, President Carter said, "Our position is clear: The United States will not yield to blackmail." As Daniels saw it, the American people agreed.

"In America," the first single from the band's new album, *Full Moon*, put Daniels's observations to music. A rolling drum fill signals the song's start as Daniels and lead guitarist Tommy Crain serve up a staccato twin-guitar riff before paying heed to the drums one more time, letting their guitars ring out the last note. "Well the eagles been flying slow, and the flags been flying low," Daniels says, noting the speculation that some said that the country was going to fall. The weight of war, government distrust, and crisis had taken a toll on the citizens, but Daniels reminds the doubters, most pointedly the Russians, that the country has never fallen and wasn't going to now.

"And you never did think that it ever would happen again," Daniels says of the wave of unity that was sweeping the country in light of the foreign threat. Daniels notes the different people who have been brought

together from coast to coast, "the cowboys and the hippies and the rebels and the Yanks."

The song was a declaration of unity, a song about patriotism in a time when an outside force looked to further divide a country already showing cracks. Released seven months after the beginning of the hostage crisis (and seven months before its end), the song grabbed listeners who identified with the song immediately. While not rising to the level of "Devil Went Down to Georgia," the song peaked at #11 on the Top 40 chart and #13 on the Country Singles chart.

In 2001, following the terrorist attacks of 9/11, the song experienced a bit of a resurgence as fans used it as a rallying cry, again bonding under the unity the song upheld.

81. "Heard It on the X," ZZ Top (from *Fandango!*, 1975)

No matter how you define Southern Rock, there are a few traits that form a common thread through the music that fit under that moniker. One of them is paying homage to the music that came before it, whether it is through recording a version of an old standard or singing about those times in the lyrics. With "Heard It on the X," ZZ Top give a pretty good summation of their inspirations.

Released on 1975's *Fandango!*, the song is one of the shortest in the ZZ Top catalog, clocking in at 2:25 and containing only two verses and a short chorus. But there is a lot about the band packed into those two verses that showcase the beginnings of the trio. That's highlighted by the fact that bassist and vocalist Dusty Hill and guitarist/vocalist Billy Gibbons trade couplets through the verses.

Hill brings up the year 1966 in the first couplet, three years before ZZ Top was formed. In 1966, Gibbons was going through a string of bands, leading to his formation of the psychedelic-inspired Moving Sidewalks, while Hill and drummer Frank Beard were knocking around Texas as American Blues.

"Country, Jesus, hillbilly, blues," Gibbons sings in the second couplet, telling us that's where they learned their licks. The music the band was soaking up included a little of everything: gospel, country, blues, and rock and roll. Hill returns with a line that the music was heard coast to coast and in every county, and Gibbons clarifies that it was the "outlaw

X" that was "cuttin' through the air." Anywhere and everywhere, they say in the chorus, they heard it on the X.

But what is the X? They get to that in the second verse and open up for a little history. First, they thank "Doctor B," who crossed the line, and "with lots of watts he took control." There is a lot behind those few lines. In the early days of radio, the watts allotted to power a station were kept low by the governing organizations in charge of this new medium. Stations were kept at between 500 and 1,000 watts (and some even lower), keeping their broadcast range to a limited area. In 1928, Cincinnati's WLW became the first station to be granted a license to broadcast at 50,000 watts, becoming "The Nation's Station." Soon, they were joined by other stations, including Chicago's WLS and Nashville's WSM, all becoming clear channel stations, meaning that no other station could broadcast on their frequency.

In the mid-1930s, WLW began to campaign to increase frequency to 500,000 watts and was granted an experimental license to broadcast at that frequency. After an unsuccessful attempt by WLW and other clear channel stations to persuade the Federal Communications Commission to make 500,000 watts the standard, WLW rolled back to 50,000 watts in 1939. But the power and capability had been exhibited on a national scale, so in 1941, Doctor John R. Brinkley of Kansas went to Mexico and set up the station XERA on the border and began broadcasting at 500,000 watts. Broadcasts could be heard into parts of Canada and all across the United States. Legend has it that if you were fairly close to the station, you could even hear it on fence wire.

What "Doctor B" began was continued with other border radio stations, like XERF and other stations whose call letters began with X. The general format of these stations was to have no format. Music of all kinds was played one after another, giving the listener, like the three kids who would eventually make up the Little Ol' Band from Texas, a wide variety of music.

The members of ZZ Top were able to take the stew of influences that floated on the night air and combine them with a solid boogie base, sprinkled with the crunch of the evolving guitar sound of the time, to create a signature sound like no other. *Fandango!* was the band's fourth release and their second Top Ten album.

80. "Comic Book Hero," Wet Willie (from *The Wetter the Better*, 1976)

Standing in the middle of the Fortress of Solitude, Superman is motionless; a strange, alien plant called a Black Mercy clings to his chest. Batman, Robin, and Wonder Woman see him as they enter with gifts to celebrate the day he arrived on Earth. The Black Mercy, given to him by the interplanetary conqueror Mongul, attaches itself to its hosts, placing them in a catatonic state as they travel, in their mind, to the happiest circumstance they can image. For Superman, that means never having left the planet Krypton, which never exploded, marrying and raising a family. As his subconscious fights the effects, his happy place begins to crumble. Driving his son into a deserted area, he explains to him that he doesn't really exist, as he fades into the night. When he awakens in reality, Batman having removed the plant, tears fill his eyes as he demands to know who did this to him. This 1985 story by Alan Moore, titled "For the Man That Has Everything," examines the inner thoughts of a character noted for his invincible body and superhuman strength.

One collection that includes this story includes a two-part story also written by Moore called "Whatever Happened to the Man of Tomorrow?" In it, Lois Lane recounts to a reporter the last adventure of Superman, in which he battles and defeats all of the main villains of his mythos before subjecting himself to gold Kryptonite, a substance that strips him of his powers. As Lane is talking to the reporter, her husband, whom she introduces as Jordan, enters, puts down Superman a bit, and then leaves the room. As the reporter leaves at the end of the story, Jordan reappears with their child. Once the reporter is gone, Jordan sits the child down, who begins to play with what turns out to be small chunks of coal. As his parents talk, the boy squeezes them into diamonds. The last panel shows "Jordan" breaking the fourth wall, winking at the reader.

How to deal with the world's most incredible superhero is something writers have struggled with for years. Moore, who built his reputation on deconstructing the superhero with works like *The Watchmen*, provided a sharp left turn for the character as the company was gearing up to reboot the franchise into something more grounded. Various aspects of his life have been dealt with in pop culture in the years since his creation in 1938. But before Moore took a crack at it and two years before the world would

believe a man could fly with 1978's *Superman: The Movie*, Jimmy Hall and the boys of Wet Willie were busy thinking about the same questions.

John Anthony's unadorned electric guitar begins the song, quickly giving way to Jack Hall's bass, Michael Duke's synthesizer, and Ricky Hirsch's bluesy guitar. Wasting no time, Jimmy Hall enters ten seconds in, introducing the story of a comic book hero who lives in a "red and blue book" and spends his days caring for people and his nights fighting crime. Helping people gives him joy, and he knows "crime just don't pay." "Just don't pay," Hall repeats as Hirsch ascends the guitar neck before Hall commands "Get it down." At that command, the song goes from the happy-go-lucky pluck of the first verse to a pulsating bass line, Lewis Ross pounding out a march-like beat on the drums as Hirsch punctuates with quick guitar stabs.

The music matches the lyrical mood shift as Hall reports that what he's recounted in the first verse is simply what is seen by the average person when in reality our hero is miserable, always on call for the next person in trouble, and when in fact he'd really just like to raise a family. But because the world still needs him, Hall tells us, "he's alone forever." Hirsch repeats his ascending guitar figure as Hall sings an elongated "yeah." The band then drops into a boogie rhythm as the story shifts to Lois Lane, who is driven crazy by Clark Kent and Superman because neither one can commit. "They keep playin' on and on," Hall repeats.

The music near silences as Hirsch's guitar trills signaling a return to the happy-go-lucky rhythm of the first verse as Hall says "meanwhile." The crux of the issue, Hall tells us, is that Superman just "needs a little acceptance," reminding us that though he's called the *man* of steel, he's actually an alien who was sent here and had to deal with being a Man of Steel in a world of paper. But he will continue to fight for humanity, battling whatever comes against it.

With that, at nearly the three-minute mark, the band drops out, and Hirsch returns to the riff that separated the first movements. "Turn it on!" Hall shouts as one by one the rest of the band joins in playing the riff. Playing out the rest of the song, Hirsch and Hall trade vocal and guitar riffs, Hirsch turning in a scorching solo, egged on by Hall's "Get it! Get it!" In under five minutes, Wet Willie captures the struggle that every writer approaching Superman faces—and they rocked their way through it.

79. "Uncle Ned," Point Blank (from *Second Season*, 1977)

When ZZ Top hit the scene in the early 1970s, they immediately grabbed the ears of listeners and became a popular touring act. Their star only continued to brighten as they moved toward supernova in the 1980s. A record promoter out of Houston named Bill Ham was the man behind the band who had signed them, continuously promoted them, and produced their early work. By even the early 1970s, ZZ Top, as a business entity, was self-sustaining, allowing Ham to pick up other artists under his Lone Wolf Productions company and, it was hoped, replicate that same success. During that time period, he signed Jay Boy Adams and Point Blank (with Blackhorse to follow later in the decade).

Just as he had when he signed Billy Gibbons with the aim of assembling a band around him, Ham signed guitarist Rusty Burns to a management deal, and the rest of the band came together afterward. The band began playing regionally in Texas and soon branched out, opening shows for Grand Funk Railroad, ZZ Top, Lynyrd Skynyrd, and the Marshall Tucker Band. Such high-profile gigs brought them to the attention of Arista Records, and the band signed with the label, producing their self-titled debut.

Centering on the guitar work of Burns and second guitarist Kim Davis, the band crafted hard-rocking songs heavy with blues influence. One of the best examples is a tribute to a fan who attended their pre–record deal gigs at the Old Cellar Club in Dallas. Leading off with a solid groove from drummer Peter "Buzzy" Gruen, Davis, Burns, and bassist Phillip Petty join in with a crunchy, bottom-heavy riff as heavy as any in hard rock. Around the thirty-second mark, singer John O'Daniel begins the story of "Uncle Ned," telling us that every evening Ned stands in the "very front row," describing him as a "lead man with a pea coat on his back." Ned "hitchhikes every morning from the railroad track," and no one can understand a word he says, requesting "someone say good-bye for Uncle Ned."

While seemingly unimportant details, they soon come into context in the second verse, where Uncle Ned stands on the street telling others of the Cellar Club, where he'll meet the band. "Uncle Ned's a good boy," O'Daniel proclaims before telling us he was a war hero in his time, a "natural-born lover, a killer in his prime," then repeating that no one can understand a word he says. With this context, the song ceases to be about

a down-and-out hobo who enjoys seeing the show and reveals itself to be about the luck and shabby treatment a veteran receives on returning to civilian life. Not knowing Uncle Ned's age and the song coming in 1977, it is easy to imagine that Ned was one of the thousands of Vietnam veterans who served their country under no choice of their own, only to return home damaged (physically and emotionally), cast aside, and even looked down on by others, much like the lead character in the Charlie Daniels Band's "Still in Saigon."

As the second verse ends, O'Daniel lets out a series of escalating "yeahs" that sound less like exhortations to party and more like a mounting frustration from within, perhaps channeling the inner turmoil of Ned, until at around the 1:40 mark, he sustains the last yell as the band sustains behind him. As he begins to fade, Gruen taps the high hat in a straightforward beat as Burns shifts into an angry-sounding riff that continues to channel Ned's frustrations as the band slams behind him, accenting the downbeat. After the band joins back in full force, Davis roars out a midrange moan on the fretboard before launching into an aggressive solo that gives way to Burns. Burns, a left-handed player who plays with a flipped-over right-handed guitar (meaning that the high-end strings are on the top as opposed to the bottom part of the neck), scorches through a solo of his own. When he finishes, O'Daniel returns with his anguished cries, leading the band into a proto–heavy metal beat, culminating in a harmony ending.

The song did not receive any particular success at the time of the album's release, and on subsequent albums the band moved to a more arena-rock sound before scoring a minor rock hit in 1981 with "Nicole." Soon after that, the band disbanded but reunited in 2005, and, as of this writing, the band continues to tour and record new music.

78. "Hand Picked," Richard Betts (from *Highway Call*, 1974)

By the time of his death in 1971, Duane Allman was already considered a guitar god. His command of the blues and his extraordinary slide playing abilities had drawn the attention of both wannabes and fellow guitar gods like Eric Clapton. But standing beside him, lick for lick, was Dickey Betts. Their relationship was built on mutual respect and admiration for one another's playing, with a sibling-like rivalry thrown in. Allman encouraged Betts's talents not only in guitar playing but also in singing and

songwriting. After Allman's passing, though, his shadow hung over the band—and Betts's in particular—like a specter that he couldn't escape. Betts's breakthrough moment came with 1973's *Brothers and Sisters*, when his creative vision became the guiding force in a band that was devastated by loss. But often critics and fans alike would wonder at the licks they heard Allman playing on a record, though he was gone and they had been played by Betts.

At the height of the popularity that the album brought, both Gregg Allman and Betts recorded solo projects. Gregg's solo album *Laid Back* served as an altered extension of the Allman Brothers Band circa *Eat a Peach*, even drawing from *Idlewild South* for the album opener "Midnight Rider." But Betts took a slightly different tack in an attempt to assert his own identity outside the band and beyond the shadow of Duane.

When discussing a solo project with Capricorn vice president Frank Fenter, they struck on the idea of paying an homage to one of Betts's guitar influences, the gypsy jazz guitarist Django Reinhardt. The idea was for Betts to record with a frequent Reinhardt collaborator, violinist Stephane Grappelli. The problem was that Grappelli refused to fly and would travel to the United States only via steamship, which would take more time than could be allotted to complete the project. While plans were being mulled over to instead send Betts to Paris to record, Betts attended a bluegrass festival in Florida where he met fiddler Vassar Clements. After a few jam sessions, Betts had found his foil. Clements had played with Bill Monroe and the Blue Grass Boys and recorded with John Hartford, Steve Goodman, Gordon Lightfoot, and J. J. Cale but had developed his own style incorporating jazz, western swing, blues, and bluegrass, just as Betts had on guitar.

Bringing in session players Stray Straton and David Walshaw on bass and drums, respectively, Betts rounded out the ensemble with Allman Brothers Band pianist Chuck Leavell and steel guitarist John Hughey, who was working with Conway Twitty. The album amps up the country influences that Betts had brought to the fore on *Brothers and Sisters*, delving deeply into his country and western swing influences. The second side of the album consists of two instrumentals: "Hand Picked" and the Clements-penned "Kissimmee Kid."

"Hand Picked" as an incredible example of Betts as musician and band leader. In a project designed to showcase his skills outside of the Allman Brothers Band, the album is remarkably free of ego as Betts

shares the spotlight with the incredible pickers he has brought together. Betts often cited western swing artists like Bob Wills and the Texas Playboys as influences, sprinkling their melodic sensibilities into songs like "Blue Sky" and "Ramblin' Man," but on "Hand Picked" he lays it all out.

Bringing immediately to mind the raw Tiffany Transcriptions–era triple threat of electric mandolinist Tiny Moore, electric guitarist Eldon Shamblin, and steel guitarist Herb Remington, Clements, Betts, and Hughey open the song on fire. Nearly fifteen minutes long, this high-octane romp gives each band member a place to stretch out and showcase his incredible ability in turn. Hughey's steel guitar is given a place to run free, something the constraints of radio-friendly country scarcely allowed, while Clements offered up a preview of the groundbreaking fiddle style he would soon produce on his self-titled solo album and *Hillbilly Jazz*, both released the year after *Highway Call*. (Ten years later, he would record his own album with Grappelli.)

Powered by the Allman Brothers Band's successes, *Highway Call* peaked at #19 on the *Billboard* 200, though the album is credited to and marketed as Richard Betts. The whole album is fantastic, giving a look at a side of Betts that he never fully returned to in future work.

77. "Still in Saigon," Charlie Daniels Band (from *Windows*, 1982)

Charlie Daniels hit platinum in 1980 with the album *Full Moon*, powered in large part by the lead single "In America." He wrote the song as he observed the wave of unity sweeping the country in the face of the Iranian hostage crisis. In 1981, on the day that Ronald Reagan replaced Jimmy Carter as president of the United States, the hostages were released, and the country rejoiced. The Charlie Daniels Band had become a bona fide star attraction with both rock and country audiences. Two other singles were released from *Full Moon*, but neither made much impact. Nevertheless, the band continued to tour and ended the year recording the next album, *Windows*.

Where the lead single of *Full Moon* was about unity, the lead single of *Windows* put the spotlight on one of the most divisive subjects in the country's history: the Vietnam War. But these weren't the observations of Daniels. Instead, this song was from an outside songwriter, only the fifth time a song had been pulled from outside the group in eleven albums.

The songwriter Dan Daley had been a professional songwriter since 1975 when he was touring as steel guitarist for the band Free Beer, recording three albums for RCA. In 1981, Daley began writing a song about what combat must have felt like. The exercise began to take form and after a few drafts became "Still in Saigon." Rather than choose sides, the song comes from the point of view of a soldier who survived, only to be continually haunted by both what he saw and experienced and the opinions of others. After performing the song for his publishing company, the decision was made to record a demo and shop the song. Two artists who had publicly spoken out about Vietnam veterans were on the top of the list: Bruce Springsteen and Charlie Daniels. Both of them passed on the song.

But the song stuck with Daniels. Although he never served in Vietnam, he could clearly see the plight of veterans whom the country had essentially turned their backs on even though many of the soldiers had no choice in serving. So Daniels began to talk to veterans whom he knew, some of them members of his road crew, listening to their stories and showing them the lyrics of the song. They not only loved the song but also encouraged him to record it. So he did.

At the time of its release, the nation's treatment of Vietnam veterans wasn't a subject that was openly or easily discussed. Vietnam Veterans of America was formed as a nonprofit in 1978 to help veterans reestablish their lives in the United States, but it was a sensitive issue tied to a lot of political baggage—so much so that when Daniels released the song as the lead single, headlines questioned how Daniels could release such a patriotic song as "In America" and then turn around and release something as critical as "Still in Saigon." The answer was easy for Daniels: both were patriotic songs in his eyes.

The song reached #22 on the Top 40 singles chart (perhaps tellingly, in the conservative climate of the 1980s, the song didn't even chart on the Country singles chart) and became a fan favorite. Dan Daley pledged a portion of the song's royalties to the Vietnam Veterans of America.

76. "Georgia Rhythm," Atlanta Rhythm Section (from *A Rock and Roll Alternative*, 1976)

Everybody wants to be a rock star. Every day is a party, pretty girls and handsome dudes mill around backstage, and days and nights are filled

with nothing but good times. If the extracurricular activities aren't enough, there's the music, the nonstop party fuel that brought you to the dance in the first place. After the show, you can spend your night jamming or having, as the Atlanta Rhythm Section called it in 1978, a "Champagne Jam."

As the song from the album of the same name tells it, the band is going to hang out all night playing music, but they are not hanging out sipping whiskey or swilling beer. No, this group is living the highlife (and not the Miller kind), so they want only Dom Perignon. It's just the music and champagne; all else is superfluous.

Sometimes there's the story we tell ourselves, the one that we want to portray to those around us, and then there is the real story. In 1978, the Atlanta Rhythm Section had finally made it to the top of the charts after years of struggle, but in 1976, it was a struggle where they sat right in the middle.

Formed by a group of studio musicians at Studio One in Doraville, Georgia, in 1971, the band had gotten off to a rocky start. After their first album, vocalist Rodney Justo left the band. Replacing him with smooth-voiced Ronnie Hammond, the band went back into the studio to record a new album. The studio was a place with which they were all familiar, a place comfortable. By the time their fourth album was failing on the sales and airplay charts, the band knew they had to hit the road. Being a group of studio musicians, the road was something they hadn't experienced. Reviews were mixed, but in a short time they found their footing and were able to start winning over crowds.

But the lack of the album's success was taking its toll. As guitarist J. R. Cobb told a reporter just before the release of their sixth album, "If this new record doesn't put us over the top, I'm gonna go home and forget about the thing."

"Georgia Rhythm," from that sixth album, *A Rock and Roll Alternative*, captures the feelings they were struggling with long before it became the easy days of a "Champagne Jam."

Cobb opens the song with a gentle acoustic guitar, picking out a rhythm as guitarist Barry Bailey rings in with a distorted electric guitar. The glamour of playing all night sipping champagne isn't the picture drawn here as Hammond lists the daily realities: suitcases as dressers, hotel rooms, rental cars, airport bars, and hot, boring days waiting for the show. But he's quick to remind us that even though his job as a musician

makes him a little crazy, he wouldn't change a thing. In fact, he sings in the chorus, the steady backbeat and Gibson guitar sounds have him "lovin' the life we're livin'," and playing this music makes him feel something nothing else ever has.

Those moments onstage playing that music are broken up by bits of real life, like waiting on an airplane at four in the morning. It's not champagne they're shooting in the airport bar to pass the time, hoping to dull the pain. The ray of sunshine that parts the cloud is the crowd's reaction to the band during their brief time each day in the spotlight.

With the release of A Rock and Roll Alternative, the spotlight grew a little brighter. Cobb didn't have to go home and give up his dreams, as the album climbed the charts, landing at #11.

75. "Twice As Hard," Black Crowes (from Shake Your Money Maker, 1990)

Most of us have been there. You are with someone for an extended period of time, and then things end. A few months pass, and the next thing you know you're driving halfway across the country in a borrowed pickup truck to fetch a girl and her earthly possessions from Rhode Island, only to have to end it again a month later. It's tough enough to end things the first time, but the second time, as Chris Robinson sings, is "Twice As Hard."

Rich Robinson's fully distorted Fender Telecaster, tuned in open G, opens the song playing a short riff and repeating it four times before letting an open-chord ring, followed by another just before unleashing his built-up emotion by bringing out the slide. As he does, the band joins in, and guitarist Jeff Cease begins a call-and-response as Rich uses the slide and Cease answers with bending double-stops. Since the release of their first album, comparisons to the Rolling Stones and the Faces dogged the band, and they admitted drawing more influence from them than the Southern Rock bands with which they were often associated. The dual interplay of Rich Robinson and Jeff Cease (and Marc Ford after Cease left the band after the first year) did owe more to Keith Richards and Mick Taylor (and later Ron Wood) than it did to Duane Allman and Dickey Betts. Rather than the noted riffing of the Southern Rock bands like the Allman Brothers, Lynyrd Skynyrd, or even .38 Special, the Black

Crowes depended more on open tunings, slide guitar as a rhythm instrument more than a lead voice, and slashing call-and-response guitar parts.

On this, the band's third single, their hard-driving rhythms pushed Chris's lyrics, driving home the emotional impact he was singing about. The relationship had ended, and it is never easy when one does, but something brought them back together. Before long, those same problems that drove them apart return to do it again. In his mind, he had worked through those problems, put them behind him, and forgave and forgot. But here they are, to be dealt with again. The pain of ending a relationship is accompanied by the embarrassment of being burnt twice by the same old flame. Chris and Cease continue their back-and-forth throughout the song, using it as an introduction to the solo break provided by Cease after the last verse.

The single hit the Album Rock Tracks chart (later known as the Mainstream Rock Tracks chart) at the end of June 1990, just as their second single, "Jealous Again," was heading off the charts and the album was continuing its climb up the Top Pop Albums chart. On its second week, *Billboard* designated it a "Power Track," making it one to watch. The song continued to move up the chart, peaking at only #11, though it became a crowd favorite in the band's live sets.

74. "Knoxville Girl," Outlaws (from *Outlaws*, 1975)

Southern Rock was exploding in the early 1970s as the Allman Brothers Band topped the charts with "Ramblin' Man" and the debut albums of Lynyrd Skynyrd and the Marshall Tucker Band were breaking through. This triggered a gold-rush mentality among record labels. Among them was Clive Davis. Davis had been fired from his longtime post at Columbia Records and picked up by the unrelated Columbia Pictures, which gave him his own label, which he named Arista. As he surveyed the landscape, he was hearing about a band that was making a lot of noise out of the South. Looking to get in on the Southern Rock action, Davis decided to give the band a look.

Hughie Thomasson had begun putting together his band in 1967, and as the years went on he assembled a group of fine players known as the Outlaws. The band boasted three guitars, which seemed standard issue for Florida-based rock acts, but what set them apart was the fact that they also had four very good vocalists. The Outlaws started playing as much as

possible and eventually found themselves opening for Lynyrd Skynyrd. Ronnie Van Zant came away impressed with the group and encouraged Skynyrd manager Alan Walden to take a look at the band. The band already had a manager, Charlie Brusco, and had been planning to record an album for Bell Records with Bob Johnston, who had produced ground-breaking albums with Bob Dylan and Johnny Cash. Once Walden saw the band, he didn't hesitate to pick it up, joining forces with existing manage-ment and putting out the feelers for a record deal.

Those feelers had reached Davis, who made arrangements to see the band open for Lynyrd Skynyrd in Columbus, Georgia, in 1974. After a set that had impressed Davis, Skynyrd took the stage, and during their time Van Zant addressed the crowd. Looking out into the audience, he called everyone's attention to the fact that Clive Davis was in the audience and then, talking directly to Davis, said, "If you don't sign the Outlaws, you're the dumbest music person I've ever met." After the show, in their band's hotel room, Davis told them he wanted to offer them a contract, making them the first rock band signed to the label.

The first order of business was to get them in the studio with producer Paul Rothchild, a Los Angeles–based producer well known for his pro-duction work with the Doors. Removing themselves from the South, the band went to Los Angeles in March 1975 to record their debut album. Carrying in songs that had been rigorously road tested, the band was ready to make a name for themselves. The band had spent so much time on the road that the theme pervaded the album.

One of the most interesting ways in which it did was in "Knoxville Girl." The song had grown over the years from an old English ballad called "Wexford Girl" and into a country music standard recorded by acts like the Blue Sky Boys and several years later the Louvin Brothers (who had the most enduring hit with it), Jim and Jesse, and the Wilburn Broth-ers. But here, Outlaws vocalist and guitarist Henry Paul writes new verses to the song, relating how much he misses his girl who waits for him while he is on the road. Strummed electric and acoustic guitars form the back-ground before the band stops after the first verse. At that point, Thomas-son coaxes a few squeals from his Stratocaster as the band takes off, leading Paul into the chorus of the older versions of the song, telling about his girl with the "dark and rovin' eye" who'll "never be his bride." In his next verse, Paul borrows the first two lines from the traditional arrangement ("I met a girl in Knoxville town, a town that I knew well")

before telling us about the loving times he and his girl shared. After the band returns to the familiar chorus, guitarist Billy Jones takes a guitar break as Thomasson plays a few intertwining fills before taking over the lead, full of chicken picking. Paul returns to the chorus a third time before jumping into the third verse, where he makes it clear that the girl's dark and rovin' eye has found someone else. Jones and Thomasson then take off in a twin-guitar race that closes the song in a blaze.

Paul's take on the song—that his girl he has left behind on the road has found someone else—is a departure from the song's original story. In the original telling, as relayed through the years, the singer finds his girl's dark and rovin' eye troubling, and instead of leaving her, resigned that she has found someone else as Paul seems to, he beats her to death with a stick and then goes home and goes to bed. It's interesting that a band called the Outlaws, in a genre known for its rough-and-rowdy ways, decides to take a little higher road when it comes to dealing with a broken heart, but nonetheless they put their stamp on the song.

73. "Am I Losin'," Lynyrd Skynyrd (from *Nuthin' Fancy*, 1975)

MCA was in a hurry to follow up the success of Lynyrd Skynyrd's first two albums as the band was finishing up the song "Saturday Night Special" for Burt Reynolds's 1974 vehicle *The Longest Yard*. As the film grew in popularity, the record label pushed a little harder. Unlike their previous trips to the studio, Skynyrd was unprepared, with next to no songs worked out or ready. The band had been touring relentlessly, leaving little time for anything beyond the hard-core partying that followed the shows. On top of that, their original drummer, Bob Burns, had decided to leave the band. He was later diagnosed as bipolar, but at the time he was just seen as unstable, and the road and the parties were too much. On the suggestion of Charlie Daniels, the band brought on drummer Artimus Pyle, whose style was more aggressive than that of Burns.

The songs for the album, with the exception of "Saturday Night Special," were written in the studio. Ronnie Van Zant had always been the band's lyric writer, pouring his thoughts and feelings into the songs and giving them a workingman's touch and insight. The feelings that came out during the writing of "Am I Losin'" were close to the surface. After two huge albums, even people in his hometown of Jacksonville, Florida,

treated him differently—and mostly not in the roll-out-the-red-carpet kind of way.

Van Zant's writing style was unique. One of the guitarists, in this case cowriter Gary Rossington, would have a riff or chord progression, and as they played through it Van Zant would sit or stand with his head bowed, gently nodding it to the music. If he hooked on an idea, he'd signal for the guitarist to continue to play as the lyrics formed in his mind, where they would stay. Van Zant never wrote his lyrics down, believing that if they were good enough and the guitarist didn't lose the groove, they'd come back to him. Once the lyrics were finished, the rest of the musicians filled in their parts.

Rossington's acoustic guitar starts the song off, strumming through the pattern Van Zant uses as a springboard, before the rest of the band comes in together. The bright chords and straightforward beat belie the sad tone of the lyrics as Van Zant remembers the good times he had with friends when he had no money. But now that he has a little money, those same friends say he's changed because of it. Is it jealousy on their part? Is it that this hardscrabble singer from a working-class family made the determination early to get out and make something of himself and that his friends only see their own failures reflected back at them, echoing as Van Zant sings to them, "It's you, my friend, that has really changed."

Allen Collins joins Rossington on acoustic guitar, showing another side to two-thirds of the guitar trio that came to define the band's sound. Leon Wilkeson's bass takes a lot of the lead space throughout the song, playing in and out of Pyle's solid rhythm.

But the star here is guitarist Ed King, who straps on the sole electric guitar in the song. Playing subtle rhythm figures and fills behind the vocals and acoustic guitars, King weaves in and out of the music sur-rounding him. When the solo comes, King switches from the Stratocaster to his Gibson SG for a completely off-the-cuff solo that King calls his tribute to the Marshall Tucker Band's Toy Caldwell. The soulful feel of the solo, with the bent notes crying out after being released from the syncopated short phrases that defined Caldwell's style, serves as a perfect homage to the South Carolina thumb picker. Forty-five seconds into the solo, the Caldwell tribute ends as King switches from the rounded tones of the neck pickup to the brighter tone of the bridge pickup. Instead of a regular pick, King uses a small seashell, and the unique tone and harmon-ics it gives off are King's alone. The short syncopated phrases become

shorter and even more syncopated as King lets loose. Even when Van Zant comes back singing, King goes on soaring behind him, though you will have to strap on the headphones to hear the master at work.

72. "Fancy Ideas," Rossington Collins Band (from *This Is the Way*, 1981)

Anytime, Anyplace, Anywhere had proven to be a critical success for the survivors of Lynyrd Skynyrd. Released in June 1980, the album was certified gold by August. The band was selling out auditoriums and had their sights set on arenas. But tragedy was never far from the band and would exert its will again soon. Internal strife, centered between Allen Collins and Dale Krantz, that led to temper tantrums onstage, shouting matches in the street, and canceled tour dates strained the idea of the band's future. After one such fight, the band canceled a tour date and took three days off before resuming, only to have bad news from outside the band delivered in a one-two punch. While on the road, Collins's wife Kathy, pregnant with their third child, suffered a miscarriage, resulting in the death of her and the unborn child. Months of tours dates were canceled, and Collins, already known for his self-destructive bent, sunk deeper. Eventually, the band began to work on a follow-up, though the discord within the band and Collins's state of existence threw out any pretense of working together to create a cohesive album. This meant that much of the work fell to other members of the band. Barry Lee Harwood took the reins and began to work to make the project a success.

Harwood had known the guys from Skynyrd since their days playing local Jacksonville clubs and had played Dobro and mandolin on songs from three albums. He had gone on to work as a studio musician around Atlanta and began playing with pop-rock acts like Lobo and Melanie. One day in 1975, he was finishing packing his bags to leave the next day on a European tour with Melanie when his phone rang. It was Dean Kilpatrick, old friend and Skynyrd's road manager. "Ed just quit the band," Kilpatrick told him, referencing guitarist Ed King, who got up one night on the bus and left in the cover of darkness. They wanted Harwood to join as his replacement, but being a man of his word Harwood was already committed to the tour. So he left, and the band found Steve Gaines.

Now Harwood was back in the studio with the guys trying to make this project a worthy follow-up. Whereas on the first album he contributed to four songs as cowriter, on the new project he was the sole author of three songs and cowriter on one. Collins's absence also left room for Harwood to contribute more guitar work to the album. "Fancy Ideas" is Harwood's tour de force. Contributing all of the guitars and the vocal, as well as having written the song, it shows the talent that attracted them to Harwood.

From the muscular opening riff, "Fancy Ideas" is also the band's toughest-sounding song, something along the lines of what Molly Hatchet and Blackfoot were building on to reach heavy metal audiences. Harwood's layered guitars build and thunder down as heavy as anything this or the members' previous band produced. Harwood delivers the vocals with a knowing sneer, a warning to those who try to take advantage. "Your fancy ideas are just lies in disguise," he sings with authority. "I ain't nobodie's fool," he snarls later, leading to a drum break by Derek Hess before layering guitars form a march to the end of the song. Hess and Leon Wilkeson make a solid foundation as Harwood's guitars roar over Billy Powell's shimmering B-3.

The follow-up, *This Is the Way*, was critically acclaimed and sold well, but the internal stress took too big a toll on the band, causing them to break up soon after its release. Rossington married Krantz, and the two went on to form the Rossington Band and, later, Rossington. The rest of the band, along with vocalist Jimmy Dougherty and guitarist Randall Hall, formed the Allen Collins Band. Collins's self-destruction claimed that band as well, scattering the musicians after its fall. Tragedy would again stalk Collins, though it could be said that he courted it when, while driving under the influence, he wrecked his car, killing his girlfriend and paralyzing himself.

71. "Fall of the Peacemakers," Molly Hatchet (from *No Guts... No Glory*, 1983)

The first Molly Hatchet album moved past gold to platinum, and their second album raced straight to platinum. The band was on fire and moved quickly from an in-demand support act to a headliner. Then front man Danny Joe Brown started to act as if the spotlight were his alone, and the band had to fire him. As they were doing that, Epic Records, their label

home, wanted a follow-up to their two huge successes. So the band brought in a new singer and rushed into the studio to record the album to be called *Beatin' the Odds*. There was no announcement that Brown had left the band and been replaced by Jimmy Farrar, but from the first notes of the album it was obvious that Hatchet's distinctive voice was gone. Brown had come to believe himself the most important element in the success of Molly Hatchet and was going to prove it, so he formed the Danny Joe Brown Band and released an album that was in direct competition with his ex–band mates. But the sum was greater than its parts. *Beatin' the Odds* was steady, but as people heard the voice, they knew it wasn't the same, and their sales went from platinum to barely gold. Brown's album didn't even reach that, as he had the voice, but the other elements were gone. Brown didn't make a second album, and Molly Hatchet released only one more with Farrar in the lead, 1981's *Take No Prisoners*. At the suggestion of Epic Records, the two parties mended fences and reunited to record a new album.

No Guts . . . No Glory marked a new start for Molly Hatchet. Original drummer Bruce Crump left and was replaced by Barry "B. B." Borden, who had played with funk-rock pioneers Mother's Finest, and original bassist Banner Thomas left to be replaced by Riff West, who had been playing with glam rockers White Witch. Whether it was the influence of these new players or simply musical growth, the album made use of a wider variety of textures in the music, including keyboards and piano (supplied by session player Jai Winding and soon-to-be-member John Galvin from the Danny Joe Brown Band), and more prominent use of acoustic guitar. The prime example is the album's crowning jewel, "Fall of the Peacemakers."

Cowritten by guitarist Dave Hlubek and bassist Riff West (though who wrote how much has been a point of contention for years), the song is a reflection that centers mainly on John Lennon, who was killed just two years before, but touches on the loss of Martin Luther King Jr. and John F. Kennedy. The song marks Hatchet's first attempt at a true ballad, or at least it starts out that way. After Lynyrd Skynyrd built the Southern Rock template with "Free Bird," other Southern Rock groups laid down their own ballad to rockers, and this was Molly Hatchet's.

From the first notes of Duane Roland's twelve-string acoustic guitar, the song sounds different than any Hatchet song that came before it, as piano sprinkles throughout, leading to Hlubek's first short solo as the

introduction reaches 1:15 before Brown enters. Over a bed of the twelve-string, subtle electric rhythm guitar, and organ, the first verse speaks to the deaths of both Lennon and King before Roland enters with a piercing electric solo. Brown returns with a verse on the funeral of Kennedy and the sobering of a nation as the song crescendos at the halfway mark.

It's there that the riff becomes heavier and the tempo quickens. Hlubek and Roland are joined by third guitarist Steve Holland for a nearly minute-long three-part harmony guitar solo before Hlubek steps forward with his own break. Roland then takes the spotlight with a raucous lead and then bows out, opening a hole for Holland. As he finishes, they again join together for a three-part harmony part until Hlubek takes the lead again as the song fades out. The song is a powerhouse example of the three-guitar attack of the band and became a mainstay in their live sets.

Although it remains a popular Molly Hatchet song, it couldn't restore the band to its former platinum selling glory. The band soldiered on, releasing new music and touring for many years with various lineups.

70. "Please Be with Me," Cowboy (from *S'll Getcha Ten*, 1971)

The strands that made up Southern Rock were as varied as the influences that informed the genre. While many easily remember the rock-, blues-, and country-influenced artists, there were also artists influenced by more current singer-songwriter and folk origins, chief among them the group Cowboy. Formed by Scott Boyer and Tommy Talton, the band focused more on lyrics and harmony vocals than many of the Southern Rock groups, paving the way for bands like the Eagles, which came on their heels.

While their catalog is filled with great songs, perhaps their most enduring song was "Please Be with Me," written by Scott Boyer and recorded for their second album. With lyrics of pure poetry, the acoustic song is an introspective look at how being in love can change how a person looks at the world and one's place in it. Its lines sum up the feelings we have all felt, like the first time we say "I love you" to that special person in our lives or that feeling of fear, humility, vulnerability, and exhilaration. Boyer sings of lying in his bed wondering what he said "that made me think I'd lost my head when I knew I lost my heart instead."

With those words uttered, he hopes she'll "read his signs" following him, becoming a gypsy, living free. He asks her to tell him what he hopes to find deep within him, knowing she sees more in him than he sees in himself. He tells her, "Because you can't find my mind, please be with me." By speaking those potentially devastating or endearing words, he has, as he told us, lost his mind, but his heart she already has. The song is a tender and introspective entry into the Southern Rock song catalog, showing a side of the music that was rarely seen.

Aside from its lyrical qualities, the song is also remembered as Duane Allman's last non–Allman Brothers Band studio session. Allman had got into the business as a studio player, which led to his being able to form the Allman Brothers Band and sign with the fledgling Capricorn Records. He had been friends with Talton and Boyer since their early years in Florida, and it was through his recommendation to label head Phil Walden that the band was signed to the label. In this acoustic track, Allman showcases his Dobro prowess, adding tender lines that wrap around Boyer's voice. Fans of Allman who might have missed the original release picked up on it with the following year's *An Anthology*, which presented several cuts of Allman's studio works.

Music fans in general may remember the song from Eric Clapton's *461 Ocean Boulevard*, his 1974 rebound from heroin addiction. On it, he re-creates Allman's Dobro parts, though some reviewers at the time questioned the move, wishing to hear more Cream- or Derek and the Dominos–style guitar work.

69. "Uneasy Rider," Charlie Daniels (from *Honey in the Rock,* 1973)

When Charlie Daniels began his solo recording career, he was known mostly for his studio session work with Bob Dylan and Leonard Cohen, and while his country influences were obvious, he drew heavily on these artists when recording his first album in 1970, the self-titled *Charlie Daniels*, for Capitol. The album, filled with songs carrying a heavy Band influence, did little, and Daniels soon left Capitol for Kama Sutra, where he released *Te John, Grease, & Wolfman* in 1972. Daniels pulled a few songs from his debut, including the lead track "Great Big Bunches of Love," added some new ones, and the album as a whole shows an artist working toward a style for which he would later become known.

That style came into sharper focus on his 1973 album *Honey in the Rock*, with the deep groove of "Funky Junky" and the country soul of "Big Man," showing Daniels exploring a wider sound palette while still retaining his folk and country roots. Those roots are laid bare on the album's breakout track "Uneasy Rider," where the music places Daniels and band firmly in a country sound leaning on the folk tradition of the talking blues.

Told from a first-person perspective, Daniels tells listeners he's taking a trip to Los Angeles, "toking on a number and digging on the radio." Just as he crosses the Mississippi state line, his tire blows out, and he eases down the shoulder until he reaches a roadside bar, "kind of a redneck lookin' place called the Dew Drop Inn." Before going in, he tells us, he is sure to tuck his long hair under his hat. In the early 1970s, the last place a long-haired man wanted to be stuck in was a rural area of the country. Once inside, he calls for a tow truck and sits down for a beer, content to wait it out and look inconspicuous while doing it.

That plan fails when a local comes in asking who owned the car sporting a peace sign. Taking that as his cue to leave, Daniels lays his money on the bar and heads for the door, only to be met by five more locals and "one old drunk chick and a feller with green teeth." One of them "requests" that Daniels tip his hat to the lady, and when he does, his hair falls down. When it does, the guys begin to laugh, and, perhaps having been in this position before as a long-haired country boy in the South, Daniels knows that a fight is about to follow. So as a preemptive strike, he kicks "Green Teeth" and grabs a chair. But instead of swinging the chair or continuing the losing path of violence, he begins to tell the man's friends that he's not who they think he is. Instead, he's an "undercover agent of the FBI" on assignment to infiltrate the Ku Klux Klan. He continues to cast dispersions while backing toward the door, "laying it on thicker and heavier" as he went. Finally, "Green Teeth" begins to defend himself as his friends are looking at him with great suspicion. By then, Daniels is out the door and jumping into his just-finished car. He chases them a bit before hitting the road, wondering if next time he should reroute his trip—through Omaha.

The song showed Daniels as a masterful storyteller, spinning a yarn that got laughs and had an edge of social commentary, and it was the song that broke Daniels through in public recognition. In a *New York Times* profile, Daniels told writer Ian Dove that the song was an "anti-redneck"

song. In the context of the song, the rednecks are the ones who instantly judge (perhaps even condemn) the man who has long hair and a peace sign. They become suspicious of a lifelong friend who is a member of the John Birch Society when the stranger tells them he was part of a plan to take down the Ku Klux Klan and was caught tearing off bumper stickers promoting avowed segregationist George Wallace, not to mention voting for George McGovern and hanging a communist flag. These rednecks are the stereotypical kind that breed hate and fear from things they do not understand or like.

People, then as now, affixed various meanings to the term "redneck," sometimes depending on where they were from or who they were aiming it at. The song hit the charts in late July 1973, and as it was continuing its ascent on the Pop chart, Johnny Russell's "Rednecks, White Socks, & Blue Ribbon Beer" entered the Country charts. Whereas Daniels's characterization of "rednecks" as bigoted, ignorant country boys held the song to #67 on the Country chart, Russell's song, which characterized rednecks simply as working-class people, rose to #4 on the Country chart. Even though country audiences may not have loved the song at the time, mainstream audiences took Daniels's song to #9 on the Pop chart, and it even spent some time on the Adult Contemporary chart, peaking at #37.

Within country music and Southern Rock, the term "redneck" crossed between both meanings, depending, again, on who was saying it and to or about whom. Reviewers who might not be big fans of the genre were apt to use "redneck" as a derogatory term, while others simply applied it to working-class listeners. In 1976, being a "redneck" was being officially reported in newspapers across the country as the newest fad, egged on perhaps by the explosion of Outlaw Country, and was viewed as a "nostalgia movement."

In 1988, coming on the heels of his Top Ten smash "Boogie Woogie Fiddle Country Blues," Daniels released "Uneasy Rider '88," about two guys on a road trip who happen into a gay bar, but it failed to appear on any chart.

68. "So into You," Atlanta Rhythm Section (from *A Rock and Roll Alternative*, 1976)

Before there was an Atlanta Rhythm Section, its members were studio musicians and members of regional bands. One of the bands, Classics IV,

ascended the regional scene, taking the song "Spooky" to #3 on the Pop charts in 1967. Guitarists Buddy Buie and J. R. Cobb left the band soon after the hit and moved to Doraville, Georgia. Shifting from musician to manager, Buie decided to assemble a group, picking up ex-members of Roy Orbison's backing band—the Candymen singer Rodney Justo, drummer Robert Nix, and keyboardist Dean Daughtry—along with two studio musicians—bassist Paul Goddard and guitarist Barry Bailey—forming the nucleus of the Atlanta Rhythm Section. After their first album, Ronnie Hammond replaced Justo on vocals, and the band worked to become a live act.

The band worked to come up with a sound of their own, but commercial success was still out of reach as the group grew and matured as a unit. After their second album, the band left Decca Records for Polydor, a move that the band felt put them in the big time. Three albums later, they still struggled for success. Fortunate to have been recording at a time when record labels allowed a group to slowly cultivate an audience and not immediately discard them after one or two tries, the band finally found success with their sixth album, *A Rock and Roll Alternative*.

The single that drove the success of the album was a groove-filled song of conquest that saw the band tweak their sound from the raucous driving rock of their early albums to something smoother, more mellow. It was a slight departure for the Atlanta Rhythm Section, but at the same time it harkened back to their origins, borrowing from both "Spooky" and another Classics IV song, "Stormy," though not consciously, said Cobb, who cowrote all three songs.

Carried by the rhythmic guitar interplay of Cobb and Bailey, the song carries a seductive swagger, like a rock-and-roll Love Unlimited Orchestra. Hammond's smooth croon grounds the song, carrying it effortlessly. The drums drive a solid rhythm that leaves little doubt to Hammond's intentions, while Goddard's bass highlights the band's deep rhythm-and-blues influences.

The confidence brought out by Hammond perfectly fits the lyrics as the singer watches a beauty walk into a club. It's lust at first sight for him, and his singular goal becomes being with her. He stands, "captured" by her style, captive to the "voodoo in the vibes." Although he has fallen deeply into lust for her, he is unable to attract her attention. His yearning powers the line "Now I stand here helplessly" as he hopes she'll take notice of him and return the primal feelings that well inside him.

As the song enters its last minute, with Hammond repeating his plea, imploring deeper each time, Bailey's guitar licks and Daughtry's electric piano intertwine to exemplify Hammond's seductive quest. In the song's final seconds, Bailey breaks free for a smooth, understated guitar solo as the song fades out.

A Rock and Roll Alternative was their breakthrough album, landing the band at #11 on the Pop Albums chart and the single landing at #7, making it the band's only Top Ten single.

67. "Come and Go Blues," Hank Williams Jr. (from *Whiskey Bent and Hell Bound*, 1979)

It would be hard to pull into question the fact that Gregg Allman possesses an innate ability to write insightful lyrics that blend so incredibly well with his guttural and soulful voice and that they transcend genre and even time. Just the songs that made this list, let alone the others in his catalog, bear witness to the man's skill. "Come and Go Blues" is an outstanding example.

Allman originally recorded the song with the Allman Brothers Band for the 1973 album *Brothers and Sisters*. Musically, the song is upbeat, with the piano and organ taking center stage while Lamar Williams makes his debut on bass with a funky bass line that bubbles under the song. As good as the music is, it is incongruous with the lyrical content of the song as Allman sings to a woman who has him under her spell even though only hurt awaits him in the long run. He took another swing at the song on his 1977 solo album *Playin' Up a Storm*, this time featuring more acoustic guitar and less keyboards. While he mixes a bit more melancholy into his voice, the song retains much of the same upbeat tempo that distracts from the lyrics.

By 1979, the Southern Rock subgenre was fading as bands who once flourished under the tag headed for more mainstream waters of arena rock and many of the country aspects of the music were being assimilated into mainstream country music by way of bands like Alabama and Hank Williams Jr., who had dabbled in Southern Rock and operated in the same musical circles. Just two years removed from his own reinvention, where he brought his Southern Rock friends Toy Caldwell, Dickey Betts, and Charlie Daniels alongside for *Hank Williams, Jr. & Friends*, Williams

included "Come and Go Blues" on his late 1979 album *Whiskey Bent and Hell Bound.*

By the time he cut the tracks for *Whiskey Bent and Hell Bound*, he had, encouraged by producer Jimmy Bowen, thrown caution to the wind, recording the kind of songs he wanted to with the sound he wanted to record. The album, as *Family Tradition* had before it earlier in the year, was filled with a wide variety of songs, from the hard-core country of the title track to the rocked-up version of the J. P. Richardson–penned, George Jones–associated "White Lightnin'" to the laid-back celebration of "Outlaw Women" to the edge of "OD'd in Denver." Heavily distorted guitars cut their way through the rock-edged songs of the album, but when it comes to "Come and Go Blues," the song's past is forgotten.

Featuring just an acoustic guitar and Williams's voice, the soul of the song is laid bare. "People say," he sings, "you're no good," as if he's ashamed for her and himself, knowing he wouldn't let her go even if he could. Floating in indecision, the woman cannot decide whether she wants to stay with him or leave him but instead changes her mind quickly and often. But the spell she has over him has him unable to side with either decision, regardless of how it makes him appear to those outside of the relationship. "Maybe I'm a fool to care," he sings, stretching out "fool" to almost a sob. It's Williams's delivery that finally marries the lyrics with an emotional musical arrangement that conveys the downtrodden state in which the singer finds himself.

Williams's mix of Southern Rock into his country turned out to appeal to a larger audience, and *Whiskey Bent and Hell Bound* was the second in a string of seventeen Top Ten albums (six of which were #1s).

66. "Railroad Steel," Georgia Satellites (from *Georgia Satellites,* 1986)

Songs about trains reach back as far as the history of trains themselves. Early country and folk music is filled with songs that tell true stories involving a train or the use a train as the main vehicle of leaving one's troubles. There are even such songs on this very list. There's something about the power of a locomotive and the lonesome sound of the whistle that captures the imagination of many songwriters.

Johnny Cash had a list as long as the Louisville-Nashville line of train songs that he performed over the years. Daughter Rosanne Cash scored

her second #1 single, in 1981, with Leroy Preston's "My Baby Thinks He's a Train." In that song, she likens her man to a train in that every time he hears the whistle, he's gone. While he's gone, she knows he'll be back around eventually after giving "some tramp a ride."

With "Railroad Steel," the Satellites give us the man's side of that story. Dan Baird's twangy, loose Telecaster pounds out the first few bars like the steel wheels of an iron horse coming to life before the band—Rick Richards on guitar, Rick Price on bass, and Mauro Magellan on drums—join him, hammering the beat as the engine gathers speed. "Some men like to ride that train," Dan Baird starts. "I like it better when the train rides me." In the first line, we know instantly that this train is powered not by steam or coal but by a healthy dose of machismo, alcohol, and lust. That train whistle is the sound of another girl calling out to him, reminding him to move on.

When the lust begins to fade, the narrator turns to stronger stuff, saying he has Dixie Crystals flowing through his veins. Although Dixie Crystals is a brand of pure cane sugar, it's also another name for methamphetamine. With that, he's, like Cash's "baby," gone, "two tire tracks disappearing in the pouring rain." But he has to keep on the move. He has to keep working for what he has in life because nothing worth having comes for free, even the love of his girl.

But maybe it isn't the girl's love he has to work for. Maybe he has to keep working to keep that loyalty, to stay true to her. After all, it isn't only the tracks that are made out of railroad steel but also his heart: "cold, hard, true, and mean." She has to know how he feels, he tells himself as he is headed out of town again. Just like Rosanne waiting at home for her train to return, Baird's girl should know he will return. Whether he will be in the same condition he left in is up for debate.

Here, Richards's guitar fills in the gaps, reeling off a blistering solo to be met by Baird's rolling pull-off run leading to the question, "Are you listenin' baby?" He speaks directly to her, telling her he feels her pulse pounding before he orders a drink for the road, a Coke mixed with Ronrico 151, a high-proof rum, to take the edge off the Dixie Crystals before heading out full-steam ahead. After repeating the chorus, as a reminder to her of what she signed up for, he lets loose a bellow to mimic the train whistle as the guitars slam forward, fading out the song.

65. "All I Can Do Is Write about It," Lynyrd Skynyrd (from *Gimme Back My Bullets*, 1976)

Lynyrd Skynyrd had cultivated a reputation as a band of hard-knock southern rockers who would fight anyone who stood between them and a good time. It was a well-deserved rap that they rolled with easily. It made for good press, and the magazines of the time enjoyed playing up their antics. But the press often liked to also play up the redneck stereotype, going as far as printing interview answers that dropped all the "g's" (such as "droppin'" instead of "dropping"). This one wasn't deserved—by Skynyrd or any other Southern Rock band. Both combined caused Ronnie Van Zant to do very few interviews toward the end of his career, preferring instead to let his music talk for him. And "All I Can Do Is Write about It" says plenty.

Skynyrd's third album, *Nuthin' Fancy*, had become their highest-charting album, though it produced only one single, but the rushed recording schedule and merciless tour schedule had taken their toll. Al Kooper (who had produced their first three albums) and the band came to the decision to go separate ways. Guitarist Ed King came to his breaking point mid-tour and walked away in the middle of the night. The partying was consuming some members of the band. Altogether, Van Zant felt the band had stopped progressing in many ways.

But they had a Top Ten album, and the record company wanted a follow-up, so nine months after recording the rushed and ill-prepared-for third album, the band was in the studio recording tracks for a new release, *Gimme Back My Bullets*. In the producer's chair was noted producer Tom Dowd, but he didn't have much to work with: songs that were gems of ideas at best and a band that was burning out. Somehow they pulled out of it enough to produce nine tracks (eight originals and one cover). "All I Can Do Is Write about It," the brightest gem among them, put Van Zant's feelings front and center, bared among acoustic guitars rather than the roaring crunch of their best-known songs.

Gary Rossington and Allen Collins layer strummed acoustic guitars over gently picked electric guitar intertwined with Billy Powell's organ to create a lush bed for Van Zant's vocals, his voice worn but hopeful as he tells us that this traveling life has taken him everywhere. Barry Harwood, a longtime friend of the band, punctuates the point with a soft Dobro flourish as Van Zant finishes the first lines of the song, ushering in a still-

unidentified fiddle player, Leon Wilkeson's bass, and Artimus Pyle's percussion.

The song is part homesick remembrance as Van Zant tells us "there's no place like home" and part lament of the encroaching urban sprawl he had seen taking over areas the band passed through in their travels. Both cause him to reminisce about "the hills of Carolina," "the grass in Tennessee," and a she-gator protecting her young. He feels the creep of the concrete, something he sang about in the more defiant "I'm a Country Boy" from *Nuthin' Fancy*. Here it is mixed with more sentimentality, a heartfelt longing to hold on to the simple pleasures in life rather than give them up for more corporate stores and parking lots. The song swells—with pride, with happiness—as Powell takes a short solo, Harwood now adding mandolin in the backing.

A touch of fatalism is woven into the lyrics as Van Zant continually hopes that the Lord will take him and his family before the concrete—or the rushed and hard-edged lifestyle it represents—comes. In the context of the music and the proud thoughts of better things, the lyric plays as a down-home saying—until the song nears its end. As the song enters its final minute, all of the instruments playing their parts, Van Zant offers up the lament one more time, but this time, as he sings those words one last time, he ends on a minor note, the band following him into the melancholy, as if he turned around to find the time was not coming—it was here.

64. "Jealous Again," Black Crowes (from *Shake Your Money Maker*, 1990)

The new decade was just a couple of months old when the Black Crowes made their debut. Pop starlets like Paula Abdul and Janet Jackson and heavy metal rockers like Whitesnake and Skid Row topped the albums charts. Just a few months earlier, in November 1989, the Georgia Satellites had released their third and, unfortunately, final album: the diverse *In the Land of Salvation and Sin*. When the Crowes debuted, there were few comparisons to their home-state compatriots but instead to their shared influences in the Rolling Stones, Humble Pie, and the Faces. Heavy metal, at least what made the airwaves, had become largely a collection of power ballads and party songs, so the songs of the Satellites and the Crowes were a reminder of the glory days of what was fast

becoming known as "classic rock," Aerosmith's late 1980s revival not-withstanding.

By the time of the Satellites's third album, the band was varying their material, including more ballads and even acoustic numbers, breaking the hard-rocking mold set by their previous two albums. It was a sign of a maturing band and maybe partially even an attempt to gain a wider audience. But the Black Crowes came out swinging. "Jealous Again" was the warning shot signaling what was to come. From Rich Robinson's opening riff to Steve Gorman's snare drum snap, the song was a rocking example of the new album just appearing on record store shelves.

The Crowes grabbed attention not only with their music that recalled another time but also with their wardrobe, which consisted largely of 1960s-era jackets and frilly shirts. Front man Chris Robinson attracted comparisons to Mick Jagger with his rail-thin body and strutting mannerisms. But "Jealous Again" and, indeed, the rest of *Shake Your Money Maker* proved that the band was more than just a tribute act. The catchy melody of the single instantly drew listeners in, and the dual guitars reminded people, as the Satellites had, just how good straight rock and roll really was. In turn, listeners drove the song to #75 on the Hot 100 and #5 on the Mainstream Rock Tracks chart.

63. "Searchin' for a Rainbow," Marshall Tucker Band (from *Searchin' for a Rainbow*, 1975)

By the time the Marshall Tucker Band released their fourth album, *Searchin' for a Rainbow*, in 1975, the band was on fire. Their first three albums had all gone gold, the band was burning up the roads touring constantly, and their new album was their most popular yet. Led by the first single, "Fire on the Mountain," the album was climbing the charts as the title track was released. The single would stall out at #104 on the Pop chart (#82 on the Country Singles chart), but the album would make it to #15 on the *Billboard* Top 200. It was also their first of four albums to chart on the Country Albums chart, landing at #21. Critics acclaimed the album though often claiming that the album had a decidedly more country feel to it even though nothing had really changed in their trademark sound.

In "Searchin' for a Rainbow," George McCorkle's acoustic guitar downstrokes layer over Toy Caldwell's understated pedal steel guitar.

Not his primary instrument, of course, Caldwell never attempts to take his steel playing into the realm of Buddy Emmons or Lloyd Green but rather uses it to add color and a new texture to the band's already eclectic sound. As the song begins to get its feet, the song's first guest, Charlie Daniels, enters on fiddle, echoing Caldwell's pedal steel licks.

Recording at Capricorn Studios left the door open, quite literally, for other artists floating through town to guest on others' recording sessions. After the second time through the chorus of the song, Daniels enters again with a fiddle solo before the second guest of the song, Dickey Betts, appears with a signature guitar solo. This collaborative spirit was an example of the camaraderie within the bands labeled as Southern Rock.

Something that set the Marshall Tucker Band's songs apart from others was that many of them focused not on the South or southern concerns but instead on the West, either in a figurative way or in a literal one. "Searchin' for a Rainbow" takes the western theme of heading out for a gold rush and tells the story of one cowboy's search, missing home and losing his horse along the way. But the story is only partially about that. Caldwell, the band's primary songwriter during their prime, implants a lot of subtext into the song. Instead of your standard road song, something like Blackfoot's "Highway Song" or Bob Seger's "Turn the Page," this is a metaphorical tale that can be taken as a literal western story or as the story of the toll exacted on a band by being on the road.

"I rode into town today, in my mind I said, Lord, I'd like to stay," Doug Gray sings with a weary quality to his voice, conveying the mood of the lyric. But with that, though, he's on to the next thought, having to leave town in this continual and seemingly never ending search. But, he sings, there is someone waiting at the end of the road who is more important than the pot of gold, and when he reaches her, "to Hell with that pot of gold"—not that he'll ever reach the end of that road, even if he wants to. This wanderlust is in his bones; it prods him along whenever he tarries, making it impossible for him to stay in one spot. He says to hell with the prize, but it's a hollow sentiment, something to placate the loved one he's left behind. He'll continue on the road until it claims him.

62. "Bounty Hunter," Molly Hatchet (from *Molly Hatchet*, 1978)

Southern Rock was changing dramatically by 1978. The Allman Brothers had disbanded. Lynyrd Skynyrd had been torn apart in a violent plane

crash, and the survivors had yet to regroup. The Marshall Tucker Band was feeling the stress of the road and pressure to produce more pop-oriented hits. The Charlie Daniels Band and Wet Willie were continuing on with their unique brands of the genre, while bands of lesser fame were dropped from their labels. Into this landscape a few new bands made their entrance, two of which had ties to Lynyrd Skynyrd. One of those bands was Molly Hatchet (the other being the band of Ronnie Van Zant's little brother Donnie, .38 Special).

The members of Molly Hatchet grew up near Skynyrd's hometown of Jacksonville, Florida, and founding guitarist Dave Hlubek grew up across the street from the Van Zants. After all of the stress of living on the road, Ronnie Van Zant was, in 1976, working on shedding his hard-partying ways and concentrating more on his music and his family. One of the things he was looking to do was get into the producer's chair for another band. It would be a path that would allow him to be completely immersed in music creativity outside of his band but also, more importantly, off the road more often. When he was introduced to Molly Hatchet, he made plans to produce their debut album. He and the group entered Lynyrd Skynyrd's small 8-track rehearsal studio to record a few demos that they could shop around. After a few were down, Van Zant left for a tour to support Skynyrd's new album, *Street Survivors*. He would never return from that tour.

Now the band was left without one of their biggest supporters and a friend. Even so, their demos made the rounds, and they were signed to Epic Records by producer Tom Werman, who was at the time both producer, working with acts like Ted Nugent and Cheap Trick, and Epic's A&R man. Werman took the band into the studio and began working on eight songs written by the band (plus the Allman Brothers Band's "Dreams").

Of all of the most popular Southern Rock bands, Skynyrd had a sound that stayed closer to their British rock influences while the majority of others leaned toward other influences (the Marshall Tucker Band and Charlie Daniels to country, Wet Willie to soul, and the Allman Brothers, an island of their own). With the help of Werman and his rock credentials, Molly Hatchet dug down to an even grittier place, something more akin to the hard-rock acts like Nazareth that are forefathers to heavy metal. Southern Rock's regional pride and blue-collar lyrics melded with a harder edge than previous Southern Rock bands, giving Hatchet an

opening to a different audience than .38 Special or other touring Southern Rock acts.

The difference was set off by the album cover, which utilized a 1973 painting by artist Frank Frazetta called *Death Dealer*. Red-orange eyes glow from underneath a horned helmet as the Death Dealer is mounted on a sturdy black steed. Vultures circle in the background as the fresh blood drips from his axe, the shield he holds bearing the scars of those that tried to defend against him. Judging a book by its cover would lead you to believe you've just picked up something in the wrong bin. Flipping the album and checking out the band's picture would offer little help. Except one detail: the T-shirt that reads "Redneck Power." Dropping the needle on the first cut brings forth sharp, distorted guitars and vocalist Danny Joe Brown's guttural "Hell yeah."

As the guitars—three of them: Dave Hlubek, Steve Holland, and Duane Roland—rock behind him, Brown assumes the role of the song title's character, "Bounty Hunter." As the dust swirls on the trail, the bounty hunter begins to rethink this life he has chosen. It is, after all, "one hell of a way" for him to earn his pay. He begins to wonder what the men feel like when they die, wondering when his turn will come. His moment of empathy doesn't last long as he restates his purpose: to stop the outlaws who are running from the noose.

Hlubek takes the first guitar break of the album, dealing out some melodic double-stops before Brown's whistling throws him into overdrive. As he winds down, Brown's gruff drawl asks us, "Did you know $500 will get your head blown off?" followed by a dismissive laugh.

This album, this song, introduces Molly Hatchet to the world—a world they came to claim as their own regardless of the consequences. And fans responded positively. They soon began to tour with some of the most popular rock acts of the time, capturing fans worldwide with their brand of redneck metal.

61. "Travelin' Shoes," Elvin Bishop (from *Let It Flow*, 1974)

Everyone can more or less agree that "Southern Rock" was little more than a marketing tag, something to identify a music that shared a similar style, similar influences, and musicians of a similar background. No one exemplifies that more than Elvin Bishop, who came to be identified as a

southern rocker during the tag's heyday, more by association than anything else.

Bishop was born in California but soon moved with his family to Iowa, where he was raised until age ten when the family moved to Tulsa, Oklahoma. His time on the farm was spent with no electricity, but the family owned a battery-operated radio on which they occasionally listened to the popular songs of the day. Once the family moved to Tulsa, the radio became an increasingly important part of his life. Their home was located in a large, flat area, and he tuned into blues coming from Nashville's WLAC, and this new music called rock and roll, coming from other scattered stations. But it was the blues that fascinated Bishop as a young boy, and at age fourteen he began to play the guitar. At age sixteen, he was awarded a National Merit Scholarship, which enabled him to attend school anywhere. Knowing there was blues coming out of Chicago, he decided that was where he needed to be.

Soon after landing in Chicago, he met another young white blues lover, Paul Butterfield. Butterfield, along with Bishop, guitarist Michael Bloomfield, and the rhythm section of bluesman Howlin' Wolf (drummer Sam Lay and bass player Jerome Arnold), formed the Paul Butterfield Blues Band. The group initially played pure Chicago blues but soon began to expand their sound, using Eastern modal scales and incorporating the jazz work of artists like John Coltrane and Cannonball Adderley. The 1966 album *East-West* included a Nat Adderley song ("Work Song") and closed with the just-over-thirteen-minute title track that explored the modal music and experimental jamming. This album (and, in particular, this song) is often credited as the starting point for the extended jam music of the late 1960s, including the Grateful Dead and the Allman Brothers Band.

After *East-West*, Bloomfield left the group, and Bishop stepped into the lead guitar slot for the band's next two albums: *The Resurrection of Pigboy Crabshaw* and *In My Own Dream*. *Resurrection*, taking its name from a nickname of Bishop's, saw the band move in a more rhythm-and-blues–influenced direction, adding horns and minimizing the jamming aspects. In 1969, Bishop decided to strike out on his own and moved to San Francisco to dive into the burgeoning rock scene there, quickly becoming a regular at the Fillmore, where his group, the Elvin Bishop Group, opened for and jammed with many of the bands that came through, including those that the Paul Butterfield Blues Band influenced,

like the aforementioned Grateful Dead and the Allman Brothers Band. When Fillmore owner and promoter Bill Graham formed his own label, one of the first acts he signed was Bishop.

Fillmore Records released two Elvin Bishop Group albums: 1969's self-titled album and 1970's *Feel It!* The music featured a strong mix of blues, country, rhythm and blues, and rock, a type he would stick to throughout his career. The label folded in 1972, and Bishop, now under the name the Elvin Bishop Band, did a brief stint on Epic Records before finding themselves without a label again. The band had been playing the Fillmore, both West and East, regularly and doing a series of dates with the Allman Brothers Band. At a party one night, Dickey Betts brought Capricorn Records label head Phil Walden over to hear some of Bishop's music. The next day, Bishop was added to the Capricorn roster, the center of the Southern Rock universe in many ways.

Bishop kept his San Francisco base, switched out a few players (dropping the "Band" from his moniker), and headed south to record. One of the new additions to his band was guitarist Johnny Vernazza, whom he had met through his friend Gideon Daniels. The band settled into the Capricorn Sound Studios in Macon, Georgia, to begin recording with producer Johnny Sandlin. This being ground zero of the Southern Rock universe, other players making their way through the studio stopped by to add to the recording. Charlie Daniels, Dickey Betts, Paul Hornsby, Randall Bramblett, Toy Caldwell, and even non–southern rocker Sly Stone make appearances on the resulting album, *Let It Flow*.

Although it was recorded in the South, at Capricorn, and for Capricorn, with several southern rockers on hand, the music on the album doesn't deviate greatly from the music Bishop was already making, and included one blues tune (written by Lightnin' Hopkins) and two country tunes (one by Hank Williams and one by Merle Haggard)—the rest straight Elvin Bishop music.

"Travelin' Shoes" is a prime example of what exactly is Elvin Bishop music. Borrowing thematically from decades of blues songs, the song talks about the desire to get away from his nagging "old lady." Musically, the song shines as a showcase for the guitar work of Bishop and Vernazza. Rather than the flurry of notes that often served as a musical statement from other, often more hard-rocking bands, the guitars here swing. The opening twin-guitar lines sound more inspired by Bob Wills's Texas Playboys than the Allman Brothers Band. After the first verse, the duo

reprise the twin guitars, this time both of them using a slide before Vernazza takes a break that often returns to the melodic theme of the riff. It might be Bishop's band, but Vernazza takes the bulk of the solos here, with Bishop coming in as a second to double up parts, as the pair do throughout the song. Consciously or not, at around 2:55, the duo play off a slight variation of the Allman Brothers Band's "Blue Sky" for a little over twenty seconds.

The song draws from another strain of influence not as often so close to the surface of Southern Rock: gospel. The upbeat tempo is underpinned by fine piano work from Phil Aaberg, who breaks out a solo of his own four minutes into the song, bantering with the guitars forty seconds in, before returning to his own solo work, until Bishop returns for the final verse at 5:20. Aaberg's piano walks a balance of boogie-woogie, honky-tonk, and gospel that continues to lift the song. In the same vein, Vernazza, who had come to Bishop through his work in the progressive gospel group Gideon and Power, brings something akin to the sacred steel tradition in the solo slide guitar passages in the song. Finally, the song ends with Bishop and the backing vocalists diving into an extended stretch of "ohh's" that bring to mind the wordless vocalizing of many traditional gospel performances. In live performances, that feeling was escalated in often extended piano and the vocal sections. Search out, for example, the 1977/1978 clip of the band performing on *Don Kirshner's Rock Concert* with pianist/organist Melvin Seals in the band.

Supported by the popularity of Southern Rock and Bishop's association with it (often joking it was the only time music writers could find a classification to stick him in), the song became a breakthrough for him on FM radio, even flitting about the lower regions of the Hot 100. It would soon be eclipsed by his biggest hit, but this remains a truly overlooked and often nearly forgotten Southern Rock classic.

60. "Don't Misunderstand Me," Rossington Collins Band (from *Anytime, Anyplace, Anywhere*, 1980)

When the Rossington Collins Band unleashed itself on the world, they were determined to make one thing clear: This was not Lynyrd Skynyrd II. When the airplane that ended the band went down, the members of the band were only in their mid- to late twenties. They had plenty of music left inside them, and they wanted to get out and play it. In interviews,

both Rossington and Collins talked about how easy it would be to reclaim the old name, but instead they were determined to make it on their own. "We're determined to be a new band," Leon Wilkeson told a reporter. The band hired Dale Krantz so that the powerful female vocalist could set the band apart from their former band. In concert, only one Skynyrd song was included in the set list, as "Free Bird" served as the closer, performed as an instrumental tribute to their fallen friends.

Their determination to form a sharp delineation between then and now makes the choice of "Don't Misunderstand Me" a curious one, seeing as it is the only song on the debut featuring a male voice up front, although it is alongside Krantz as a duet. Nevertheless, the song is a fine example of what the new band had to offer. Barry Lee Harwood serves as Krantz's vocal sparring partner on the song, showcasing that the band now had two strong voices.

The opening riff, with Rossington's feedback, brings an echo of the past before Harwood comes on strong with the first verse. After a string-bending fill from Rossington, Krantz makes her first appearance, demonstrating her powerful voice. The band then drops the tempo for a quick riff before things go quiet, and Billy Powell offers a soft, melodic keyboard part that gives way to Harwood's frantic, stuttering guitar break, leading to the third verse. As Harwood and Krantz trade lines and double up on the chorus, all that the Rossington Collins Band has to offer has been previewed within this track.

It was the first single released from the album, giving listeners a chance to hear what the new album was made of. Critics took notice of the band, respectful that they weren't just trying to trade off of their previous incarnation. The single peaked at #55, but fans of Lynyrd Skynyrd had found something to latch on to, albeit a different type of group. Whether it was from curiosity or true fandom, the band sold out shows everywhere, including a successful run in New York City. As good as it was, the band still lived in the shadow of their former lives, a shadow that would continue to grow and eventually envelop the band, eclipsing any attempts to distance themselves.

59. "Four Walls of Raiford," Lynyrd Skynyrd (*Legend*, 1987/ *Lynyrd Skynyrd*, 1991)

This was recorded exactly as you hoped it would be, just like any number of classic blues tunes: in the Deep South, late at night, two chairs facing each other, a microphone and a bottle of Jack Daniel's the only things between the guitarist and the singer. Vocalist Ronnie Van Zant had the lyrics in his head, where he kept all of his lyrics, never writing them down. But he needed to get them out before they went away. He didn't have time to wait for a member of his band to be around to help, so after an impromptu recording session at Lynyrd Skynyrd's demo studio had broken up, he asked .38 Special guitarist Jeff Carlisi to hang out a while and help him out. Carlisi grabbed a nearby Dobro and, between swigs of Jack, the two hammered out an arrangement.

Carlisi starts the song out by sliding into the opening note, letting it ring before playing the hook. Van Zant comes in, his voice intimate and close to the mic. The effects of the late hour and the whiskey's burn bring the character in the song vividly to life. That character is spending time in Raiford, a state-run prison in Skynyrd's home state of Florida, for armed robbery. Two years into his three- to five-year sentence, he can't bear to wait for the parole board to decide his fate. Driven by thoughts of his wife and children, he makes a break for it.

The verse gives away to the chorus, where Van Zant turns the song to a prayer, asking Jesus for mercy, knowing that when the guards find him, there is no way he is going back. Instead, he'll make his stand and they won't take him back alive. In the second half of the chorus, it is revealed that the protagonist is a veteran. He served his country proudly in Vietnam, but when he returned to the United States, there were no jobs. With a wife and two kids to feed, his back is against the wall.

Van Zant wrote and recorded the song in 1976, just a few years removed from the withdrawal of troops from Vietnam. Maybe he didn't mean it as a political statement, but it serves as an illustration of how veterans are often (mis)treated on returning to civilian life. It was something he surely witnessed in his hometown of Jacksonville. He acts here as reporter as well as storyteller, crafting a song that shares both a compelling narrative and a cautionary tale. After recording the song, it sat untouched until it was released in 1987.

Legend, released to commemorate the tenth anniversary of the plane crash that took Van Zant, pulls together B-sides and rare tracks from the history of the band. Considering that no member of Skynyrd other than Van Zant appeared on the song, it was decided to take it into the studio and allow three of the surviving members—Gary Rossington, Leon Wilkeson, and Billy Powell—to overdub new parts. They weren't needed. Although Rossington adds acoustic guitar and Wilkeson acoustic bass to fill out the song, Powell's dated and way-too-far-up-in-the-mix synthesizer takes away a lot of the impact of the song.

The year 1987 also saw the debut of the Tribute Tour, with a reconstituted version of Lynyrd Skynyrd fronted by Ronnie's baby brother Johnny. The new band released a live album, *Southern by the Grace of God*, and in 1991 they released an album of new material. Their sights were set on the future. But, as they do, the record label was ready to make some money off the past, promoted by the present. To do that, they released *Lynyrd Skynyrd*, a three-disc boxed set collecting the best of their catalog along with demos and rarities. One of them is the undubbed version of "Raiford." It's the version that Van Zant and Carlisi laid down in the wee hours of the morning in Jacksonville in 1976. It's the only way it should be heard.

58. "Rockin' into the Night," .38 Special (from *Rockin' into the Night*, 1980)

Before he was taken from this world in the 1977 plane crash, Ronnie Van Zant had his sights set on moving to the producer's chair, and the first two bands he had in mind were Molly Hatchet and .38 Special. The Hatchet boys had grown up in the same neighborhood, but .38 Special's lead singer, Donnie, being Ronnie's younger brother, had grown up in the same home as Van Zant. The band included bassist Larry Junstrom, who had played on some of Skynyrd's earliest demos, and guitarist Jeff Carlisi, who had recorded the song "Four Walls of Raiford" with Ronnie Van Zant. The middle Van Zant brother, Donnie, had assembled the band in 1974 along with Junstrom, Carlisi, guitarist Don Barnes, and drummers Steve Brookins and Jack Grondin, and they had been playing regionally in the clubs preparing for their big break. The band was becoming a solid unit—the Skynyrd connection didn't hurt—and the band was signed to A&M.

Their 1977 self-titled debut shows the heavy Skynyrd influence, and it carries over into their second album, 1978's *Special Delivery*. With the loss of their mentor, the band was adrift. While the music of those first two albums certainly isn't bad, it's somewhat unremarkable. The band was in a tough position with Donnie being a living link to Southern Rock's biggest band, but on the other hand, Southern Rock as a genre was fading in commercial appeal. Molly Hatchet had chosen to go for a heavier boogie sound, while .38 Special leaned a little more toward the pop side of the genre. They stood at a crossroads trying to decide their fate, looking to record their third album. They knew they needed to choose a direction.

At the same time, a Chicago-area band named Survivor was working on their debut album in a Los Angeles studio. During one session, they presented their producer, Ron Nevison, with a song that they had recently begun playing in concert to a great reaction. Nevison recorded the demo but thought the song didn't fit in with what the band had already worked up for the album. The band was disappointed since they had seen the crowd's reaction to the song and felt it could be a hit. But Nevison was an experienced producer who had worked with UFO, the Babys, Dave Mason, the Rolling Stones, and Led Zeppelin, so they followed his instinct and decided to leave the song alone. Since they weren't using it, their A& R man John Kalonder asked Nevison for a copy of the demo. Knowing the song could find a home elsewhere, he played it for manager Mark Spector, who was working with .38 Special at the time. He in turn played it for the band.

The band loved the song and thought it could be a hit—everyone except Donnie. On the previous two albums, Donnie had provided all of the lead vocals. But now, presented with a song with hit potential, he didn't like the song, and, furthermore, the band wasn't sure if his voice was right for it even if he did like it. Since Don Barnes had sung in bands prior to .38 Special, the band asked him to give it a try, and it turned out that he had the range that the song called for and needed. In the studio, Donnie gave it a try but after hearing Barnes agreed he needed to take the lead. The song itself was different than anything the band had done before, eschewing the regionalism and themes of the genre. Where their first two albums had been full of "gators and whiskey and swamps," this took them in a more general direction.

The band and label believed in the song enough to title the album after it and issue it as the album's first single. The hunch paid off, and the fans quickly noticed the new direction of the band, rewarding it with their highest-charting album, hitting #57 on the *Billboard* 200. The song barely missed the Top 40, landing at #43, but it has gone on to be one of .38 Special's most recognizable numbers. "Rockin' into the Night" laid down the foundation on which the band would continue to build.

57. "Hard to Handle," Black Crowes (from *Shake Your Money Maker*, 1990)

The commercial resurgence of Southern Rock kicked off in 1986 with the release of the Georgia Satellites's self-titled debut. The next year saw the return of Lynyrd Skynyrd in their tribute configuration, and the year after that, the Allman Brothers Band re-formed, releasing an album in 1990. Against this backdrop, the Black Crowes screamed out of Atlanta, twin guitars blazing. Their sound drew comparisons to some of the finest British rock bands, but their location led many journalists to lump them in the Southern Rock category.

In interviews, guitarist Rich Robinson was quick to minimize the connection, noting the obvious influences of other prominent bands. In a *Billboard* interview, he criticized people who believed that any band coming out of Georgia had to sound like R.E.M. or the Georgia Satellites, asking why people can't just comment that they are a good rock-and-roll band. Brother Chris took a different approach with critic David Fricke in a *Rolling Stone* interview, drawing a line from the Allman Brothers to the sounds that came after to the Black Crowes, noting it was "what I'd like Southern rock to become."

It was an astute observation in that one of the most enduring bands from the Southern Rock category is Lynyrd Skynyrd, who admittedly sounded little like the Allman Brothers Band and instead expressed the goal of becoming the American Rolling Stones. Skynyrd's influences were deep in the British hard-rock blues bands of the Rolling Stones and Free, much as the Crowes were. Rather than the country influence that many greats capitalized on, the Crowes, as Skynyrd had before, sought out the blues and soul influence filtered through the British bands that had also influenced bands like Skynyrd and others.

Intentionally or unintentionally, the choice of including "Hard to Handle" on the album (and as a single) gave the Black Crows an anchor to the soul tradition and to the roots of Southern Rock. The original version of the song was recorded by Otis Redding in his last recording session before his untimely death in 1967. It was released as a single from the 1968 *The Immortal Otis Redding* album, peaking at #51 on the *Billboard* Hot 100 and #38 on the Hot R&B Singles chart. After that, the song was recorded by a wide variety of artists, including Tom Jones, Tony Joe White, the Grateful Dead, New Riders of the Purple Sage, Brenda Lee, and Toots Hibbert. Of course, Redding's manager, Phil Walden, became the founder of Capricorn Records, the launching pad for much of the Southern Rock universe.

Previous singles had displayed the band's brand of rock; "Hard to Handle" added the swagger. Steve Gorman starts with a heavy beat, soon joined by the rest of the band, with Rich and Jeff Cease on guitars, taking the place of the original's piano and horn introduction. Johnny Colt on bass and ex–Rolling Stones sideman Chuck Leavell on organ and piano fall in behind them, adding rhythmic support. Chris Robinson's soulful tenor drives the swagger up a notch as he belts out the lyrics. (A hard-to-find promo remix was distributed to radio stations prior to the single's release and features a horn section. The 1998 boxed set *Sho' Nuff* includes a bonus EP of live cuts recorded at New York's Beacon Theater and features the Dirty Dozen Brass Band on the song.)

The song entered the charts toward the end of 1990 and soon peaked at #26 on the *Billboard* Hot 100, making it the band's highest-charting single, and hit #1 on the Mainstream Rock chart, becoming their first #1.

56. "Jim Dandy," Black Oak Arkansas (from *High on the Hog*, 1973)

Black Oak Arkansas was one of the earliest bands to be caught up in the "Southern Rock" tag without purposely aiming for that audience. In fact, their first album was released before the tag had risen too far from its marketing origins. From their debut, they were capturing the ears of fans and critics alike, most drawn to the gravel-throated wild man that fronted the band, Jim Mangrum, better known as Jim Dandy.

Mangrum was born in 1948, and eight years later rhythm-and-blues songstress LaVern Baker hit the Top 20 with the song "Jim Dandy." With

the song high on the charts, Mangrum's father began to call his son "Jim Dandy," and the name stuck. Several years later, his son, a natural-born entertainer, began to form a band with childhood friend Rickie Lee Reynolds. Bringing in other friends along the way to form Knowbody Else, the band was signed to Hip, a subsidiary of Stax, but the gig didn't last long and the band broke up, though Mangrum and Reynolds stuck together. Soon they had assembled musicians to form Black Oak Arkansas.

Bands often come by what becomes their signature song by some machination of fate that brings the right song at the right time. For Black Oak Arkansas, fate used Elvis Presley to prod them to their most recognizable song and biggest hit. As the band had spent some time in Memphis, they became friends with a local disc jockey named George Klein. Klein was a big supporter of the band and promoted their music on the air every chance he got. He also happened to have grown up with Presley. As the story goes, Klein called the band one day and told them they should expect a call from Elvis any time. To their disbelief, he did call them, encouraging them to continue to make great music. Always a student of music, he also suggested the band record Baker's 1956 hit, especially given Mangrum's nickname. The boys weren't going to turn down the suggestion of Elvis, so they decided to record the song for their next project, what would become their fourth studio album, *High on the Hog*.

Perhaps in part as homage, the guys wanted to feature a female voice on the song, and they had just the voice. As the band had grown in success, they decided to try to use some of the money and experience to help a new band or two. Their first project was a petite bombshell with a mane of red hair named Ruby Starr. With a blues-soaked voice many times larger than her body would suggest, Starr made an instant impression on the band when they ran across her in a bar in Evansville, Indiana. Before long, she was traveling on the road with them singing background vocals and preparing for her big break. Part of that break is her immediately identifiable voice on "Jim Dandy."

The song, a rough-and-rowdy copy of the original that has become a quintessential party song, was released at a time (January 1974) when the *Billboard* Pop chart was seeing a revival of sorts with current artists recording older songs, including Donnie Osmond and Bob Dylan recording versions of Elvis hits "Are You Lonesome Tonight" and "A Fool Such As I," respectively; Marie Osmond's "Paper Roses"; Ringo Starr's "You're Sixteen"; and Bette Midler's "Boogie Woogie Bugle Boy." Al-

though it was the lowest charting of that crop, peaking at #25, it became the band's signature tune.

55. "Country Side of Life," Wet Willie (from *Keep on Smilin'*, 1974)

Although they mixed in a variety of influences—from rock and roll to gospel to blues— the most dominant influence in the music of Wet Willie was soul, and "Country Side of Life" stands as a prime example. After years of hectic touring, vocalist Jimmy Hall decided that when their rare downtime came around, he wanted to spend it not in a city but in a more secluded area. Drawing from those thoughts, guitarist Ricky Hirsch put them into a song that became the band's second charting single.

"You can have your buildings," Hall sings over the band's syncopated rhythm. He has no need for the busy city streets or "city slicker tricks"; instead, he just needs the freedom to move around uninhibited, someplace where he can "look down at my toes" and see the ground instead of concrete. With that line, the Willettes, background singers Donna Hall and Ella Avery, join in as they go into the chorus. "Gimme that country side of life," they sing. It's a place where he can stretch out and not be uptight.

As they sing the chorus, bassist Jack Hall punctuates the lines with a funky extended bass run that is the star of the song. Muted horns steadily rise beneath them, bringing to mind the classic soul hits of the 1960s, a direct influence on the band.

Verses 2 and 3 expand on the virtues of country living: going fishing just to clear your mind, it's a place where "laid back lovers" can play their games and never worry about getting out of bed, and people live by the golden rule, never trying to get what is yours.

The theme of staying out of the city crops up in other Southern Rock songs, most notably in two Lynyrd Skynyrd songs that came after "Country Side of Life." Comparing the three shows both the diversity of Southern Rock bands and the essence of Wet Willie.

"I'm a Country Boy," released on 1975's *Nuthin' Fancy*, and "All I Can Do Is Write about It," from 1976's *Gimme Back My Bullets*, lean on the same theme as "Country Side of Life" but differ greatly, even from each other. "Country Boy," with its Free-inspired riff and piercing slide guitars, contains huge amounts of swagger, holding the city life at arm's

length with sneering disdain. "All I Can Do" is a more nostalgic take mixed with a dose of melancholy for a way of life that was quickly losing ground in many places.

These outlooks—disdain and melancholic nostalgia—are in sharp contrast to Wet Willie's overarching presence of joy, an emotion that shines through so much of their catalog. Instead of sneering at the city slicker with arms folded, Jimmy Hall sounds as if he is standing in his front yard, surrounded by tall pines, arms outstretched to welcome visitors from the city. He's not defiantly blowing them off but rather showing them what surrounds him and asking "how could you want anything different than this?"

54. "Gator Country," Molly Hatchet (from *Molly Hatchet*, 1978)

As we'll discuss later in this book, the Charlie Daniels Band released "The South's Gonna Do It Again" in 1975, and the song became both a hit for the band and a song forever identifying the Southern Rock genre. It was a song of solidarity, name checking many of the bands who were friends of Daniels, and represented the cream of the Southern Rock crop. Three years later, on their debut album, Molly Hatchet decided to do their own song of name checking. But this time, instead of raising a glass to their compatriots, they raised a middle finger.

Dave Hlubek's guitar kicks off the song with a short but searing solo before Danny Joe Brown begins to sing, first about Alabama and Lynyrd Skynyrd followed by Charlie Daniels, but Brown isn't extolling their music. Instead, he is dismissing their outlooks, saying that Alabama doesn't look that great to them and that the "good Lord" doesn't live in Tennessee. Instead, the band will just make their way back to Florida. It's their home, where "the wine and the women are free." No matter where they travel, it calls them back.

Hlubek returns, reprising his earlier guitar lead, just before Brown returns to push back on the Allman Brothers, Dickey Betts specifically, and Elvin Bishop, both named in Daniels's song of brotherhood. Brown then returns to that voice calling him home. In his mind, it takes the form of a gator that hides in the bushes and calls his name. Steve Holland then steps forward, delivering a tasteful and melodic solo, joined at the end by Duane Roland with a little extra harmony.

When Brown returns, he gives a little guff to the Marshall Tucker Band in the first half of the third verse. The second half is reserved for the only band who doesn't earn his ire, the Outlaws. The reasoning is simple: they are from Tampa, "a mighty fine place to be." Hlubek returns like a siren, his guitar blistering and joined by Roland for a few lines of harmony as Holland plays beneath them, utilizing the three-guitar attack to its most effective.

One of the hallmarks of Southern Rock as a genre was the regional pride the groups had. Even when they didn't agree with being tagged "Southern Rock," they agreed that they shared a similar background and upbringing. The majority of the bands branded as Southern Rock indeed hailed from the South. It was something that was identifiable to both record buyers and the musicians themselves.

"Gator Country" marked a shift. Molly Hatchet came as part of the second wave of Southern Rock bands. Even the liner notes of their first album, dedicated to Ronnie Van Zant and featuring the members of Lynyrd Skynyrd, .38 Special, and Grinderswitch, proclaim, "This ain't Southern country/rock." A few years later, .38 Special, themselves part of the second wave, would also work to distance themselves from the "Southern Rock" tag. It wasn't enough, if it ever had been, to be proud to be from the South as a rock band.

But here, instead of aiming for a wider audience as other southern bands would soon do, Hatchet moves from regionalism to a hyperregionalism, proclaiming their allegiance not to the South but, more specifically, to Florida. It is a playful swipe at their fellow Southern Rock bands, many of which were influences on them, but it is the first of the bands from that genre to come out and say in song, "Look, if we are proud of being from anywhere, it is from our home state." It was an attempt to separate themselves from the marketing tag of "Southern Rock" and any negative connotations that came with it.

53. "This Ol' Cowboy," Marshall Tucker Band (from *Where We All Belong*, 1974)

There was no slow burn for the career of the Marshall Tucker Band once their debut album was released by Capricorn in 1973. The album sold quickly, and the band was in the studio while the record was still climbing the charts. The band's concert schedule ramped up, putting the band

on the road for three hundred dates a year. Still looking to capitalize on their growing success, Capricorn had the band in the studio just as the release of their second album was beginning to sell. Since the band was becoming a headlining act, the label decided their third album, *Where We All Belong*, would be a double album, with sides 3 and 4 made up of live tracks.

The first half of the album contains new original material, continuing to expand the soundscape the Marshall Tucker Band built their career on. While other bands in the Southern Rock club were exploring blues or a harder rock sound, the Marshall Tucker Band were drawing on more varied styles of country. "This Ol' Cowboy," for example, draws heavily on western swing, like that of Bob Wills and the Texas Playboys.

Opening with a descending figure played by Toy Caldwell that swings upward with a jazzy run, the band joins with Jerry Eubanks on flute, and Andy Stein and Charlie Daniels on fiddles launch into the song's recurring riff. A couple of seconds in, Toy joins in, and the foursome lock together to deliver the riff with Toy playing variations branching from the fiddles and flute. Tommy Caldwell's bass bubbles over the top of George McCorkle's funky acoustic guitar chords as Paul Riddle, who began his career as a jazz drummer, creates a cymbal-heavy pocket for the band.

The lyrics, written and sung by Toy on the record (though by Doug Gray in concert), tell of a man who has just been left by his woman. At first, he seems dazed, talking about going to Dallas to "tie up a few loose ends," then getting a job to earn a little money before hitting the road again. As the verse wraps up, he tells her he doesn't want her to worry— this is not the first time this has happened to him. The fiddles, flute, and guitar enter with the song's main riff, giving the singer time to collect his thoughts. When he comes back, his attitude has shifted from blasé to regret that he ever let her into his life. But then he's quick to let her know that once he kisses another woman, she'll be a faint memory.

With this thought, the twin fiddles separate for a little back-and-forth. Charlie Daniels, by now an honorary member, begins with a run before Stein, a member of Commander Cody and His Lost Planet Airmen, answers back with a run of his own. The two trade improvised licks, each time shorter than the one before it, before giving way to producer Paul Hornsby, who provides a piano break before Toy enters on guitar. His Wes Montgomery thumb-picking–style solo is a glorious syncopated romp through the musical themes of the song. After a minute of Toy's

solo, Eubanks enters on flute, taking the song to another place. As his solo comes to an end, he mimics the vocal melody, and overdubbed flutes serve as a harmony to wrap up. Caldwell returns, telling the listeners not only that this woman meant nothing to him but also that none of the women he had been involved with previously meant anything to him. His vocal never veers one way or another emotionally, leaving us to wonder if he's being dismissive or putting on a brave face as he heads back out on the road.

The single served to show the diversity of the band and separated them from the Southern Rock pack early on, reaching #78 on the Hot 100, though their greatest commercial successes lay ahead.

52. "Long Haired Country Boy," Charlie Daniels Band (from *Fire on the Mountain*, 1974)

In the early 1970s, particularly in conservative communities in the South and Midwest, a man who wore his hair long—and "long" in many of those places meant touching the collar—was looked down on as a sissy, something less than the manly ideal. Many young men wore the style regardless, some as a fashion statement, some out of protest. It was a way for them to instantly and outwardly show separation from the out-of-date thinking. But it was in many cases that the person wearing the style didn't actually disagree with someone who didn't wear the style. There were musicians, even those within the traditionally conservative country genre, who began to wear their hair longer. Artists like Willie Nelson and Waylon Jennings identified with the growing youth-led counterculture, and their style reflected it. With "Uneasy Rider," the hit that gave Daniels national exposure, Daniels was identifying with the counterculture, siding with them in opposition to the actions taken against the character in the song.

Fire on the Mountain (1974) was the album that put the Charlie Daniels Band permanently in the national spotlight. It was in large part due to the leadoff single, "The South's Gonna Do It Again," but the album's follow-up single became a sing-along anthem for a generation of fans who instantly identified with "Long Haired Country Boy."

Daniels sympathized with many of the concerns of the youth movement, including their beliefs on the Vietnam War, even going as far as to participate in several rallies against the war. But though he had long hair,

he also wore other fashion identifiers of his old southern culture, including the large cowboy hat, boots, western shirts, and large belt buckles often identified more with rednecks and shitkickers than peaceful protesters. As he stood in Central Park at one particular rally, surrounded by groups like the Socialist Party, the Communist Party, and others, the thought dawned on him, "I'm a darn fool. I'm not a Communist. . . . Me hating the war don't make me love the Viet Cong."

Once he returned to Nashville, he began to put his thoughts into lyrics. For him (and the many who identified with the song), he was stuck in the middle. His long hair and rock music put him on the outside of a lot of the conservative culture that he identified with, but his often conservative views put him outside of many who identified with his long-haired-musician looks and agreement on some subjects, like marijuana and the Vietnam War.

In the end, he decided he could hold this duality of identity and summed it up in the chorus: "If you don't like the way I'm livin', you just leave this long haired country boy alone." In the verses, he identified with the stoners, with his desire to "lay around in the shade," damned the duplicity of televangelists, who were rising in popularity, and brushed against the issue of class divisions before deciding that none of it mattered, so he'd take another toke.

Led by a syncopated acoustic guitar riff, the song featured Dobro flourishes by Allman Brothers Band guitarist Dickey Betts and rose to #27 on the Country charts, though it didn't touch the Top 40 chart.

The song became a staple in the Charlie Daniels Band's live shows, with the crowd singing along night after night. In 1980, six years after the song's release, music publisher Acuff/Rose filed suit against Daniels claiming he had stolen the melody and structure of "Long Haired Country Boy" from the song "Bad News" written by John D. Loudermilk and administered by the company. Loudermilk had recorded and released "Bad News" in 1963, but it was Johnny Cash's 1964 version that landed at #8 on the Country chart. In 1982, Daniels was called on to prove his case and brought a guitar into the courtroom, strumming the chords to "Long Haired Country Boy" and singing the song, along with lyrics from "Old Dan Tucker," "Proud Mary," "Honky Tonkin'," and, ironically enough, "Folsom Prison Blues," arguing the generic nature of the song. In 1983, a judge dismissed the case (though musically the songs don't share much, melodically it's easy to see where the case stemmed from).

In 1988, Daniels made news when he dropped the crowd favorite from his live set list. His reasoning centered on two lines from the song, both having to do with drugs and alcohol. In interviews, he noted that times have changed and that where once those were relatively harmless activities, the recent popularity of harder drugs among young people was alarming to him. He felt that leaving the lines in might send the wrong message to young listeners. The self-imposed embargo lasted just over a couple of years, after which Daniels decided to bring the crowd favorite back with altered lyrics removing the drug references. Crowds still eat the song up and can sing whichever lyrics they like.

51. "Honky Tonk Night Time Man," Lynyrd Skynyrd (from *Street Survivors*, 1977)

Of all of the bands wearing the "Southern Rock" label, Skynyrd was perhaps the most obvious in wearing their British blues–rock influences on their sleeve. They were quick to cite bands like Free and the Rolling Stones, and their concerts featured a near note-for-note rendition of Cream's take on Robert Johnson's "Crossroads." But like others under the "Southern Rock" tag, their music also carried a country influence. Another live staple was a rocked-up version of Jimmie Rodgers's (the "Father of Country Music") "T for Texas," turning it into a guitar showcase.

Ronnie Van Zant had name checked Rodgers in "Railroad Song" from *Nuthin' Fancy*. In the same song, he name checks The Hag, the nickname of one of Van Zant's heroes, Merle Haggard. The Bakersfield-based country music superstar had been recording hit songs since the early 1960s, and just a year before the 1974 release of *Nuthin' Fancy*, he released the album *Merle Haggard Presents His 30th Album*.

Entering the studio, reinvigorated by the addition of new guitarist Steve Gaines, Van Zant and band decided to do more than name check The Hag and record one of the songs from the *30th Album*. Stirring together Van Zant's and Gaines's love for the Oklahoma-born singer (Gaines was also from Oklahoma) and Gaines's high-energy fingerpicked guitar, the band decided to take "Honky Tonk Night Time Man" into the studio for their 1977 album *Street Survivors*.

Artimus Pyle leads the charge with a locomotive-style snare beat, quickly joined by Gaines's ultraclean fingerpicked guitar popping into

earshot. Van Zant announces "little bits of Bakersfield" before the band jumps in, led by Barry Lee Harwood's rolling Dobro. Leon Wilkeson's bass thumps with authority as Billy Powell's barrelhouse piano jumps and rollicks.

Unlike their take on Rodgers's "T for Texas," the band plays this one as the straight honky-tonk rave-up it is in the hands of Merle and his band, the Strangers. As Gaines gets about halfway through his string-popping solo, Van Zant proclaims, "sounds like Roy," a shout-out to Strangers guitarist Roy Nichols and Telecaster master, whom Gaines pays tribute to with his solo. Skynyrd nearly doubles the length of the song with Powell's energetic piano solo, which gives way to Harwood's barrage of notes, expanding the song's original Dobro lines laid down by Norm Hamlett.

Just before his untimely death (along with Gaines) in October 1977, Van Zant had expressed enthusiastic interest in recording a solo project with Haggard. Listening to this song leaves you wondering just what the world missed out on.

50. "24 Hours at a Time," Marshall Tucker Band (from *A New Life*, 1974)

Even before their debut album, the Marshall Tucker Band was playing a lot of local and regional shows, opening for bands like the Allman Brothers Band and Wet Willie. Once their debut album broke through, the band's schedule increased even more so, now as a national touring act. Although it was a dream come true for the band members, they were family men who enjoyed their time at home. The theme winds its way through many of the band's songs, including this crowd favorite from their second album, *A New Life*.

The contrast between "24 Hours at a Time" and "This Ol' Cowboy," from their third album, *Where We All Belong*, is an interesting look at Toy Caldwell's songwriting. Both center around the main character being in Houston, Texas, a long way from Caldwell's actual home of Spartanburg, South Carolina. Where "Cowboy" is a kiss-off song, "24 Hours" is a song about longing to get back to the woman he loves. Where the former shows Caldwell's imagination, the latter shows his heart.

Gray's vocal expresses both the longing to be home and the exuberance of looking forward to the trip. The music gallops along, moving the

theme ahead at a determined pace. The combination of the band and producer Paul Hornsby is on full display in the arrangement of the song. Tommy Caldwell's bass thumps into the opening, bringing Paul Riddle's drums along, countered by Hornsby's piano and George McCorkle's acoustic guitar. Toy thumbs his way over them, opening for Gray's vocals. Once the verse is started, Charlie Daniels enters in behind Gray, prodding him along. At nearly three minutes, McCorkle plays a short twelve-string acoustic lick that Toy responds to with a string-bending response. McCorkle and Toy continue, with McCorkle repeating the lick and Toy responding with string bends or bursts of notes. Daniels begins to saw the fiddle, cuing synthesized strings to swell underneath Toy as he continues to play short bursts of notes, then laying off. McCorkle returns playing the previous lick as the synthesizer strings swell, leading to the end, where he plays a closing acoustic fill to end the song.

Coming in at 5:03 on the studio album, the decision was made to also include it on the next album in a live version. Designed to show audiences what they were in for when they made it to one of the band's many shows, the live version on *Where We All Belong* amps up the tempo, making the trip home that much faster. Gone are the acoustic guitars and piano, though Charlie Daniels does show up with fiddle in tow. This live version comes in at 13:31, giving Toy and Daniels solo space while allowing for Tommy Caldwell to take a bass solo and Jerry Eubanks to add a fine sax solo. Near the 11:00 mark, Eubanks and Toy begin to play dual lines before the tempo ramps up again and Eubanks goes on his own. Bringing it back home, Toy takes another ride before Toy, Daniels, McCorkle, and Eubanks lock together to restate the main riff.

Throughout recent years, other live sets (from 1973, 1977, 1980, and 1995) have been released featuring extended editions of the song, showing that even through personnel changes in the band, the song remained a showcase and a crowd favorite.

49. "Hurry Sundown," Outlaws (from *Hurry Sundown*, 1977)

After two successful albums produced by Paul Rothchild, best known for his work with the Doors, the Outlaws decided to make a move, snagging producer Bill Szymczyk to produce their third album. Szymczyk, who had produced albums by artists including BB King, Albert Collins, Rick Derringer, and fellow southern rocker Elvin Bishop, was one of the hot-

test producers on the rock scene. By 1974, Szymczyk had produced several albums with Joe Walsh, going back to the James Gang to his 1973 Top 10 album *The Smoker You Drink, the Player I Get*, and at that time Walsh shared a manager, Irving Azoff, with the Eagles, who were looking to change producers and move away from their country-rock sound. Over the course of the next three albums (*On the Border*, *One of These Nights*, and *Hotel California*), the band moved to more of a harder-edged rock mixed with pop sound.

Szymczyk's experience with that West Coast multiguitar, multivoice band was certainly a strength, though the Outlaws drew heavier on their rock roots than on their country roots. The bands shared the intrinsic vocal harmonies, as featured on songs like "Breaker, Breaker" from their second album *Lady in Waiting*. A shining example of their collaboration is the title track, "Hurry Sundown," which features their tight vocal harmonies on the melodic chorus.

The song is also an example of guitarist/vocalist Hughie Thomasson's imaginative songwriting. While in a hotel room one day, he had the television on but the sound down. When he looked up at the screen, he saw an episode of *Bonanza*, the 1960 episode "Dark Star," in which a beautiful young gypsy girl is convinced by a man trying to separate her from her family that she is a witch. Her family had also become convinced of this, and as the episode nears its end, the matriarch of the group begins to cast out the spirits. As she does this, some of the gypsy women dance around her with tambourines waving. The image struck Thomasson's imagination, and out came the story written in "Hurry Sundown."

Building from the brief scene he had watched, Thomasson constructed a story of a ceremony where the gypsies were calling on the spirit of a fallen outlaw, Sundown. As the witching hour approached, they awaited his return, their hope that he would avenge the death of the girl with "hair as black as darkness, eyes of emerald green." Sundown, we are told, had "hands as fast as lightning" and "silver devils in his holsters," and he would come to avenge the girl, putting her killer in his grave. As the song ends, the gypsies and the listeners still await his return.

Musically, the song showcases the collaboration of the band and producer, starting with a strong twin-guitar opening riff featuring Thomasson and Billy Jones. During the verses, acoustic guitars play a muted boom-chicka-boom rhythm that sounds like the clip-clop of horseshoes. After the first run-through of the chorus, Billy Jones brings his Les Paul in with

a melodic recapturing of the opening riff before Thomasson's Stratocaster comes in with his trademark intensity and on-the-verge-of-chaos tone, leading back to the chorus. As the song rounds out its last forty-five seconds, Thomasson returns for a few seconds before bending the strings to meet Jones, who then takes over the solo briefly before the two join together in repeating the opening riff as the song closes out.

Although hopes were high, the album didn't chart as highly as their previous effort (#51 versus #36). It also marked the last album for vocalist, songwriter, and guitarist Henry Paul, who struck out on his own with the Henry Paul Band. The vivid storytelling, the seamless interplay of the guitars, and the vocal harmonies of "Hurry Sundown" serve as a 4:06 summary of what the band was about.

48. "Trudy," Charlie Daniels Band (from *Fire on the Mountain*, 1974)

With a few exceptions, most notably "Uneasy Rider," the early work of the Charlie Daniels Band bore little obvious country music influences, relying more on their rock and blues influences. That notable exception is an example of what type of main influence the band could and would draw—that of storytelling. While there are songs in rock and other forms that tell stories, it has long been a hallmark of country music to tell a complete story within the song. "Uneasy Rider" did that, but within the blues-rock formula used throughout the band's first three albums, it was rarely found.

Producer Paul Hornsby was able to pull the band away from the Allman Brothers Band mold they had found themselves in and help them infuse a bit more of their country roots on *Fire on the Mountain*. Hornsby, who had found success blending the country roots into the rock elements of the Marshall Tucker Band, was able to bring Daniels's fiddle playing to the forefront on the song "The South's Gonna Do It Again" and the laid-back country sound to "Long Haired Country Boy." But he didn't strip away their blues-rock elements to remake the band completely. Instead, they remained and were infused with a new energy. One of those new energies was Daniels's storytelling. As "Uneasy Rider" had shown, he possessed the ability to craft a well-told story that captured the attention of the audience. *Fire on the Mountain* contained two: "Caballo Diablo," the Mexican-tinged tale of a wild bronco, and "Trudy."

In "Trudy," Daniels sings of a Cajun working in Dallas, Texas. We can surmise he is Cajun because he tells us his home is in Louisiana and he refers to himself as a "coon-ass boy," a term applied to Cajuns (some feel this is a derogatory term, others feel it is a term of endearment). As he finishes up his six-month stint in Dallas, he decides to stop in a bar on the way out of town. Loaded with cash, he runs into a "peroxide blonde" for whom he shows off a little bit, downing whiskey and pumping money into a slot machine. In the back of the bar, he can see a card game in progress.

Our protagonist sits at the table for a game and quickly begins to win, "raking in chips like Grant took Richmond." In that moment of triumph, Johnny Lee Walker enters the scene.

Johnny Lee Walker's reputation is widespread, and the protagonist knows he likes his whiskey and his women and that he's the "luckiest man in Dallas County." He also knows he's a gambler who is good at what he does, evidenced by the "big, long black limousine" he drives, the townhouse he has in Dallas, and the hotel suite he keeps in New Orleans. Packing a knife and a gun, he deals with cheaters swiftly. But there's something about the way Daniels says that Walker is the "luckiest" man that tells us he might believe that there is something a little more than luck involved.

Walker, a card shark, takes control of the game, winning all of the singer's money. He immediately accuses Walker of cheating. When Walker reaches for his gun, the singer hits him with a chair and makes a run for it. He's quickly pursued by the police, who apprehend him, though it "took half the cops in Dallas County" to get him in jail, he brags.

So there he sits in the jail, begging the jailer to call Trudy or send her a letter to let her know where he is and that he's "just about to lose" his mind wondering what Johnny Lee Walker is going to do when he gets out.

While Daniels and Hornsby brought in the storytelling, they didn't take out the blues-rock jamming that made up much of the early band's work. Daniels and second guitarist Barry Barnes combine here on licks that they come back to repeatedly as a turnaround throughout while the loping rhythm moves the story along. The combination of elements is what becomes the trademark of the Charlie Daniels Band's sound and a foundation that they built on throughout their long career.

47. "Southbound," Allman Brothers Band (from *Brothers and Sisters*, 1973)

After the success of their third album, *At Fillmore East*, the Allman Brothers Band existed in a balance of tragedy and triumph. Shortly after the album was released and made it to #13 on the albums chart, their highest peak to that point, group founder Duane Allman was killed in a tragic motorcycle accident. Their next album, *Eat a Peach*, featured All-man on guitar, and the album made it to #4. A few months later, bass player Berry Oakley was killed in a hauntingly similar way as Allman. The following year saw the release of the band's most popular album, *Brothers and Sisters*.

The band was changing in sound and direction as the nascent Southern Rock scene was sprouting up both around them and from them. Even the lyrically melancholic songs like "Come and Go Blues" and the blues song "Jelly Jelly" carry an air of gaiety that shows the band moving, as best they could, past the hard times and sorrow. That gaiety turns to downright exuberance on "Southbound," written by Dickey Betts and sung by Gregg Allman.

Kicking off with a call-and-response between the band and Betts's lone guitar, the funk is turned up quickly as the band makes way for Gregg's vocals. In the vein of so many great Southern Rock songs, it is a road song about the feeling one gets when returning home after being gone for an extended period of time. In this instance, that joyous reunion is a sexual one as he tells her, "You'll have your hands full now woman, just as soon as I hit the door."

Aside from a great shuffling honky-tonk piano solo by Chuck Leavell, the song features several guitar breaks from Betts, increasing in fire as they go. His opening guitar part screams with abandon as he calls back to the band. After Gregg's first verse, the band shifts into a boogie rhythm that Betts punctuates with short guitar fills until the band crashes down, leaving only his wailing guitar to bring them back up. The band returns to that rhythm once the second verse is completed, but this time Leavell's piano comes in for his solo, performing as a counterpoint to Betts's excited feel. When Betts returns, the feeling of excitement has risen to a fever pitch, culminating in a big finish. Being the sole guitar in the song allowed Betts to express himself freely and openly, his Les Paul the lone voice.

"Southbound" became a crowd favorite, and the band often performed it on televised performances, such as *Don Kirshner's Rock Concert* and *Saturday Night Live.*

46. "Cheap Sunglasses," ZZ Top (from *Degüello*, 1979)

There are songs that stay with you because their lyrics are deep and penetrating, making you look deep within yourself. There are songs that stay with you because they remind you of a lost love or cause a nostalgic trip down memory lane. Then there are songs about something as simple and common as sunglasses that reach out and grab you with a groove that you can't shake.

Degüello was released three years after the Top Twenty 1976 album *Tejas* and showed the boys were back and ready to go. Their last three albums had charted well, but the band decided it was time to take a break. During that time, their beards grew out (even drummer Frank Beard sported one, but he soon shaved it), and they got caught up in the punk music scene. It wasn't that the band geared their sound in a more punk direction with their new album as much as they adopted a little of the attitude, deciding that they weren't going to chase the chart success if it meant not playing exactly what they wanted.

One of the things they wanted to do was expand their musical palette a bit, including using synthesizers (which is maybe a little ironic given the punk inspiration). Their later success with the songs from *Eliminator* were criticized by some fans as a sellout, but long before that, "Cheap Sunglasses" was their first go at using them. Here they are used more for atmosphere and emphasis, sounding more like an electric piano than their later synthesizer work would.

The band also relied a bit more on multitracking to fatten the sound of the three musicians, as showcased in the opening of the song. With a fairly clean tone, Billy Gibbons slides the chord in, accompanied by Dusty Hill's echoing keys volleying to Gibbons's fuzzy tone and Hill's solid bass as they pop out the distinctive seven-note riff. The interplay continues under the first section of the verse until all of the instruments punctuate the lyrics with a variation of the riff topped off by the synthesizer.

The lyrics were written in a short amount of time as the band was driving through Texas. Every stop they made, they saw cheap sunglasses

for sale. The first section of the verse tells us we need some cheap sunglasses to get out in the world and get to work. The second section tells us about the girl he was following the night before, the one with the "West Coast strut," and how her choice in economy eyewear was the cherry on top.

The riff variation returns as Gibbons lets loose a few "oh yeahs!" before the synthesizer begins to play a simple rhythm figure while Gibbons's guitar "whoos" in the background. For the song about cheap sunglasses, he chose to use a cheap Stratocaster knockoff that was running through an effect called a ring modulator. After twenty-five seconds of mellow groove, Gibbons fires the faux Strat through an amp with one of its tubes blown. The understated groove of the next nearly thirty seconds is a prime example of the kind of tasteful playing for which Gibbons has become revered. The whole solo is played with essentially fewer than seven notes, syncopated and finessed and repeated in varying orders. The synthesizer and modulated guitar return for another mellow cruise before Gibbons returns, this time slightly more aggressively, using the same notes but unleashing some of his distinguished artificial harmonics that squawk out in joy.

The band then returns to the song's riff, giving way to Gibbons's vocals, telling us, again, that we need to pick up a pair of sunglasses but to know that they come in two varieties: "rhinestone shades or cheap sunglasses." After a few more "oh yeahs," the band breaks into a slightly more syncopated groove while Gibbons playfully noodles over top. Between notes, he mutes the strings, using it as a form of percussion. In unison, under Gibbons's percussive hits, the band begins to slow down and play more quietly as the song slows, ending with a short, sweet run from Gibbons.

While the album returned them to the album charts, as a single "Cheap Sunglasses" barely cracked the Hot 100, but it remains a favorite of fans of the band even today.

45. "Rock Bottom," Dickey Betts Band (from *Pattern Disruptive*, 1988)

Supporting the lackluster 1981 album *Brothers of the Road*, the Allman Brothers Band appeared on *Saturday Night Live* on January 23, 1982, and once they walked off the stage, they wouldn't perform on the same stage

for over four years. The wear and tear of being on the road had taken a toll on everyone, and it was time for an extended and perhaps final break. As the years passed, Gregg Allman assembled the Gregg Allman Band and Dickey Betts the Dickey Betts Band, both hitting the road separately.

Rather than pull from the existing pool of Southern Rock musicians or members of his older groups like Great Southern, Betts assembled an impressive ensemble of virtual unknowns, bringing together Nashville studio keyboardist Johnny Neel, bassist Marty Privette, drummer Matt Abts, and guitarist Warren Haynes. Haynes, perhaps the largest standout in the group, had met both Betts and Allman in 1981 when playing with David Allan Coe, who had opened a show for the Allman Brothers Band. The band toured for a couple of years before entering the studio for their debut album *Pattern Disruptive*.

"Rock Bottom" kicks off the album with a powerful dual-guitar riff before opening into a chopping rhythm that exhibits the influence of blues greats like John Lee Hooker's "Boogie Chillen." Neel's organ playing pulsates in the background like a spotlight on the guitars on top of it, while the bass and drums set a bedrock foundation for the song. "Once I had the good life," Betts sings before describing the "gypsy woman" who took him to incredible heights, only to throw him down to "rock bottom." The betrayal came out of nowhere for the singer, though his friends warned him it was coming. At the end of the second verse, the band reels with Betts as he repeats the phrase.

With that, the band hits on eight solid beats before the guitars simulate the fall. Once they hit bottom, Neel's B-3 organ makes his solo debut with a bluesy run. Betts mimics the run with a jazzy one of his own. Neel answers, Abts playing a high-hat heavy jazz rhythm behind them as Neel and Betts trade licks. Their jazz-inflected interlude lasts less than a minute, evoking the freewheeling nature of the singer's love affair, before Haynes and Betts join together for a harmony run that ends the illusion of peace. As it does, Haynes takes over with a screaming multistring bend that harnesses the pain of betrayal. Haynes leaves behind the jazz of Neel and Betts for pure blues rock, culminating in Betts joining him to reprise the opening riff.

The pain of her leaving freshly out into the open, his emotions laid bare as he is in his darkest moment, Betts still holds out hope that she will return. His misguided optimism has left him alone: "I've pissed off all of my friends," he laments. Rather than pick up and move on, he longs for

her to return, knowing that if she does not, "they'll find my remains, right here at rock bottom." As he repeats the lyric, the band slams the emotion home. In the background, mixed low, a screaming guitar echoes, Betts entering above it with a blues run of his own. Haynes joins him, and the two enter into an Allman Brothers Band trademark harmony guitar dual, but it isn't the brightly colored harmony of their classics like "Blue Sky" or "Jessica" but rather a darker-toned harmony of pain as the song fades out.

The album barely entered the charts, peaking at #187 on the *Billboard* 200, but it signaled a return to form for Betts. "Rock Bottom" was released as the album's first single and peaked at #11 on the Mainstream Rock chart. The music on the album served as a foreshadowing of things to come in the Allman Brothers world.

44. "Brickyard Road," Johnny Van Zant (from *Brickyard Road*, 1990)

It was a gradual process, beginning in 1973, for the descriptor "southern rock" to become the marketing tag "Southern Rock." The Allman Brothers, Lynyrd Skynyrd, the Marshall Tucker Band, Wet Willie, and a host of others were lumped into the category soon after. Although none of the bands stood up and claimed the label, none of them denied it at that point either. In interviews, they talked about brotherhood and shared backgrounds, often showing up on each other's albums. When the plane carrying Lynyrd Skynyrd went down in October 1977, things changed in more ways than one. Suddenly in interviews, artists like Charlie Daniels, Marshall Tucker band drummer Paul Riddle, and .38 Special guitarist Jeff Carlisi were brushing the term off, denying there ever was such a thing as "Southern Rock," offering up the variety of music that fell under the term as evidence. Newer bands like Molly Hatchet and Blackfoot identified more with the rising wave of heavy metal, claiming to be a rock band from the South, not a southern rock band. By the mid-1980s, Charlie Daniels was lamenting the change, as he did in a 1984 newspaper interview, saying, "It's kind of sad to me. It's not like it was." Around the same time, .38 Special, having huge hits and tours by moving into a more accessible arena-rock sound, were actively dissuading interviewers from using the term to describe their music.

In a post-Skynyrd world, it wasn't as profitable to be called a Southern Rock band. But just as the end of Lynyrd Skynyrd marked that shift, their rebirth marked its resurgence. The former members of the band had tried to do other things in the time since the crash, including the Rossington Collins Band, the Allen Collins Band, Rossington, the Artimus Pyle Band, and even the Christian music outfit Vision. But none of them connected with fans like the music of Lynyrd Skynyrd had. As the ten-year anniversary of the plane crash approached, rumors of some sort of reunion began to circulate. The first reunion of the band—the reunion that led to the formation of the Rossington Collins Band—had taken place in 1979 at Volunteer Jam V, so it was only fitting that the next reunion would also take place at Volunteer Jam XIII, held on September 6, 1987. The appearance kicked off the yearlong Tribute Tour, where a reconstituted band featuring Gary Rossington, Billy Powell, Leon Wilkeson, and Artimus Pyle were rejoined by Ed King and augmented by guitarist Randall Hall. Selections recorded during the tour were released in 1988, marking a return of the "Southern Rock" tag.

Groups like Georgia Satellites and the Wild Seeds, two bands that shared little in common other than both released debut albums in 1986, were suddenly tagged as "Southern Rock." Gregg Allman's solo career gained a boost, as did Dickey Betts's new album with the Dickey Betts Band, both leading to a reunion of the Allman Brothers. But it was Johnny Van Zant who benefited the most.

Johnny had begun his career in the late 1970s, releasing his debut album, *No More Dirty Deals*, in 1980, though neither it nor its subsequent follow-ups—1981's *Round Two* and 1982's *The Last of the Wild Ones*—garnered much attention. In 1985, as a sort of last attempt, Johnny, the youngest of the Van Zant brothers, teamed with brother Donnie for *Van Zant*. Although the album crept into the *Billboard* 200 (resting at #170) and landed two singles—"I'm a Fighter" and "You've Got to Believe in Love"—on *Billboard*'s Mainstream Rock chart, it quickly faded away.

When the Skynyrd team were putting plans together for the Tribute Tour, they approached Johnny about fronting the band. It was a daunting offer for him. He had essentially given up on music and had resigned himself to staying home and leasing out trucks for a living. In the end, he decided there was no better way to honor his fallen brother than to keep his music alive in any way he could. The tour proved a smash, packing in

crowds and increasing the sale of both Skynyrd's back catalog and their new archival releases. It also put Johnny in a different light with labels.

After the Tribute Tour ended, he signed with Atlantic Records to produce a new solo album. Unfortunately, the music was unremarkable and fell into a generic mainstream rock formula. Except one song: song 2, side 1.

The title track opens with a soft organ that evokes both a southern Sunday morning and the opening of "Free Bird"; a piano tinkles, opening the door for a brief acoustic guitar run. Johnny comes in with a wistful vocal that strengthens with each line. By the time he reaches the line "Oh Lord can you help me find my way," the sound of his defiantly overcoming the lump in his throat is evident. Written with collaborator Robert White Johnson, the song is about the last day the three Van Zant brothers spent together. References to their parents' house on Brickyard Road, including the 1955 Chevy in the driveway and Ronnie's little daughter Melody, are sprinkled throughout the song, bringing it to life.

But let's be honest here. There are songs on this list that are here because of their technical brilliance—some for their good-time, party vibe. There are songs here for their historical importance to the genre and the genres they borrowed from or those that would borrow from them. But this one, "Brickyard Road," recorded in a typical-of-the-time power ballad style, is here strictly for emotional impact.

The Tribute Tour had brought fans a little piece of the music back through a nostalgic stroll through the Skynyrd catalog. No one thought it was going to go on forever. It was a moment in time that many feel was taken advantage of in the following years, as the band still continues to trade on the once-glorious name. And much of the time, the blame for subsequent decisions is put, wrongly or rightly, on the shoulders of Rossington and Johnny.

This song came before all that, when Johnny was seen mainly as a man trying to honor the memory of a brother who left too soon. It is the most emotionally raw and powerful performance he has put down on wax, a lasting tribute to the brother who gave the world so much great music.

43. "I'm No Angel," Gregg Allman Band (from *I'm No Angel*, 1987)

After the breakup of the Allman Brothers Band in 1982, Gregg Allman took a little time off to regroup. When he decided to return to music, he put together a band to back him, pulling from previous Allman Brothers associates drummer David "Frankie" Toler and guitarist Dangerous Dan Toler, former Gregg Allman Band roadie Bruce Waibel on bass, and former Dapps keyboard player Tim Heding. The band headed to the studio for Allman's first recording in five years and his first with his new label, Epic, which had signed him in 1986.

Although Allman had written some of Southern Rock's greatest songs, for the album's leadoff track and first single, he picked up a song written by Phil Palmer and Tony Colton, "I'm No Angel." Musically, the song moves Allman away from the country and blues sounds of the Allman Brothers Band and closer to a mainstream rock sound with a southern edge, much like the music being released at the same time by .38 Special. Lyrically, though, it was a perfect fit to Allman's rough-and-tumble persona. Dan Toler's opening guitar riff gives the song a little bounce setting an almost playful tone for Allman's gruff and gritty vocals.

"No, I'm no angel," he sings, telling this woman, whom he's just met, exactly what she is getting in the deal. "Let me start a fire in your heart," he sings to her after telling her that he may steal her diamonds but that he'll bring her back some gold. It's not the best pickup line, but for someone with the reputation of Allman, it is probably the most honest. That reputation preceded him into the release of the new album. He had a high-profile and tabloid-covered marriage to Cher, endured the wrath of friends who believed he had betrayed them, sunk into the depths of addiction, and came out the other side. "I'm no angel," he sings as an understatement to this young girl he's chasing.

Admittedly, the song is lighter fare in the catalog of Allman, but it is significant as a return to music and put him on a path that would eventually lead to the re-formation of the Allman Brothers Band. Epic believed in him, pushing his work relentlessly, and it paid off. The album reached #30 on the *Billboard* 200 while the single reached #49 on the *Billboard* Hot 100 and #1 on the Mainstream Rock chart. The album also charted two other mainstream rock singles, "Anything Goes" and "Can't Keep Running."

42. "Fire on the Mountain," the Marshall Tucker Band (from *Searchin' for a Rainbow*, 1975)

Three albums into the Marshall Tucker Band's recording career, guitarist Toy Caldwell carried the songwriting burden completely, with only two exceptions: their recording of the blues standard "Everyday (I Have the Blues)" and "Now She's Gone," a cowrite with brother Tommy, both recorded for their third album, *Where We All Belong*. As they headed into recording their fourth album, his writing was showing no signs of weakening, but the confidence in other band members had grown. As such, Tommy brought in the song "Keeps Me from All Wrong" to the group as his first solo piece. Guitarist George McCorkle then brought a song that would become one of the band's signature songs, though it wasn't even intended for the Marshall Tucker Band.

With the sharing of often similar backgrounds and worldviews, there was a loose kinship between members of Southern Rock bands. One of the tightest relationships was the one developed between the members of the Marshall Tucker Band and Charlie Daniels. The two shared concert stages across the country, and Daniels had played fiddle on their second and third albums. Daniels had just teamed up with Paul Hornsby, who had produced the records of the Marshall Tucker Band, in an effort to focus the sound of the Charlie Daniels Band into something different than their earlier records. The first of several projects would be called *Fire on the Mountain*. For McCorkle, the title conjured up vivid images, and a story began to unfold in his mind. Putting pen to paper, he drafted a mysterious tale of a man who strikes out from his "Carolina home," heading west in search of gold. Once done, he gave it to his friend for his new album, though, ultimately, Daniels decided not to record the song, encouraging McCorkle to take it to his band.

The Marshall Tucker Band's songs always carried a strong sense of home, that being South Carolina, though Toy would often place that center in points west, telling stories that brought to mind western themes, such as their fourth album's title track. So this song of westward travel fit right in with what the band was already doing.

Toy's pedal steel opens the song with lush, gliding chords, drawing inspiration from the Everly Brothers' "Let It Be Me," before McCorkle joins with a syncopated rhythm, raised up by Paul Riddle's loping drums and Capricorn session percussionist Jerome Joseph's congas emulating

the steps of the travelers' horses. Doug Gray takes McCorkle's words and conveys them with the determination of someone who is taking their family on a cross-country journey into mystery. He sings of a six-month trip, his eye constantly on the prize represented by that fire on the mountain. At each chorus, Charlie Daniels provides a fiddle set low in the mix that adds a buoyancy to the lines, and after Gray's first run through the chorus, McCorkle enters with a descending, double-tracked acoustic part that adds an air of foreboding to the story, which Gray picks up with them, reaching the gold-rush town and sifting through their stake. Toy enters this time after the chorus. Where McCorkle's stripped-down acoustic guitar gave a sense of the barren and dangerous trip, Toy's steel lilts upward with chords bringing to mind the saloons of those towns where travelers congregated. As his last note sustains, Jerry Eubanks enters on flute, foreshadowing a more heavenly end, as Gray returns with a description of the rough-and-tumble city of lawlessness that serves as the western outpost, including women of ill repute, murderers, and general displays of violence. Once more through the chorus, his eyes again look to the fire on the mountain—maybe not the same mountain as before but perhaps beyond it. McCorkle's acoustic guitars return with the same descending run, but this time it isn't representing the tough journey west, as Gray returns to describe the scene: "Now my widow, she grieves by my grave." This now disembodied voice tells us he was gunned down by a "gun that carried fame," all for a claim that didn't amount to anything. This time, the chorus brings to mind another home as Gray sings over Toy's sustaining steel guitar chords.

The song, with its western theme that could have stood as an analogy for the life of the band, was the first single from the new album and struck a chord with fans, reaching #38 on the Top 100 and making it their most commercially successful song to that date.

41. "Good Clean Fun," Allman Brothers Band (from *Seven Turns*, 1990)

When the Allman Brothers Band broke up in 1982, it appeared to be for the last time. After taking a little time off, both Gregg Allman and Dickey Betts had formed new bands. Those who hoped for a reunion were in for a roller-coaster ride when the respective bands joined for a short tour in which they came together at the end of the show to perform five Allman

Brothers Band classics. At a June 1986 show in Macon, Georgia, the two bands converged onstage and were joined by Allman Brothers Band drummers Butch Trucks and Jai Johanny "Jaimoe" Johanson and keyboardist Chuck Leavell, marking only the second time in the past four years the band had reunited. Betts was quick to warn, though, that neither he nor Allman was ready to lay aside their bands to re-form the Allman Brothers Band, saying, "It's fun to reunite for special occasions. We don't do it for the money; we do it for the fun." Fun hadn't been on the agenda at the end days of the Allman Brothers Band, so solo careers, where they could occasionally play together but not have to be constantly together, remained the way to go.

Michael Caplan, a new A&R man for Epic Records, found a cassette of demos made by Allman and went to work signing him to the label. A year later, he signed the Dickey Betts Band to the label. A "longtime, serious Allman Brothers Band fan," Caplan had his sights set higher than just helping along the careers of the principals of a band he admired. Allman recorded two albums for the label. The first, *I'm No Angel*, was a surprise hit, but its follow-up, *Just Before the Bullets Fly*, didn't live up to its predecessor, while the Dickey Betts Band's *Pattern Disruptive* climbed the charts. With both Allman and Betts out on the road promoting new projects, their previous label, Polydor, issued *Dreams*, a four-disc retrospective that also included two songs from Allman's two newest projects and one from Betts's.

The success of the boxed set and the growing popularity of the "classic rock" radio format were pushing the Allman Brothers Band into the ears of old and new fans alike. This was where Caplan's long game came into play. Having the two principals on the same label eliminated the possibility of legal obstacles to a reunion, and they all entered talks to do just that. Soon the band was re-forming with Allen Woody, previously of the Artimus Pyle Band, taking up the bass, and Dickey Betts Band keyboardist Johnny Neel and guitarist Warren Haynes joining the group. The result was *Seven Turns*, and it proved that the band was back in full force.

"Good Clean Fun" leads the album and brings the band back to their most basic roots of hard-driving blues rock. It's also symbolic in that it is the only song in the band's long history that was cowritten by Allman and Betts. From the opening riff, the band powers through the song with unbridled intensity. In Haynes, Betts found someone to both play against and push him forward, the young guitarist taking the slide parts and

harkening back to the band's original incarnation without falling into mimicry. The song incorporates the great things of the Allman Brothers Band's history—harmony lines, expert slide playing, and Allman's soulful vocals—with a new harder-edged sound and newfound enthusiasm.

Fans took to the album immediately, sending it to #53 on the *Billboard* 200 and the single to #1 on the Mainstream Rock chart. After nearly a decade apart, the newly re-formed band would continue recording and touring, with some personnel changes along the way, for another twenty-five years.

40. "Dixie Rock," Wet Willie (from *Dixie Rock,* 1975)

"Southern Rock" at times has been a pretty nebulous term that even those who were branded with it didn't always fully understand. Gregg Allman famously said all rock comes from the South, so the term "Southern Rock" was redundant. Others simultaneously spurned and embraced it, as was the case with Charlie Daniels, who gave valid points for why the term was useless while at the same time producing a genre-defining song in "The South's Gonna Do It Again."

Wet Willie was there at the beginning of the whole shebang, releasing their debut album just two years after the Allman Brothers released their debut and just as the Brothers were really breaking through with their third album, the live masterpiece *The Allman Brothers Band at Fillmore East.* As a result, Wet Willie's rise paralleled that of the subgenre. But it wasn't until their fourth studio album, *Dixie Rock,* the follow-up to their breakthrough album *Keep on Smilin',* that the band took a stab at defining the genre for themselves with the title track.

Two homages are paid in the beginning of the song. First, we hear one of the background singers say a few words amid background noise before someone counts off the song, sounding very much like Otis Redding's recording of a song Wet Willie also recorded, "Shout Bamalama." It's a quick and perhaps unintentional link to both the band's recent past and one of their strongest influences: the party songs of soul music.

When the band kicks in, the second homage, perhaps also unintentional, is the sound of the music, particularly the guitars of Ricky Hirsch and John Anthony, who, instead of their regular clean and funky sound, here mimic something closer to the Marshall Tucker Band. In a song looking to define Southern Rock, it is appropriate that the band highlights their

past and also tips the hat to one of the subgenre's most popular bands, a band that had opened for Wet Willie and prompted vocalist Jimmy Hall to encourage them to contact Phil Walden, leading to their signing with Capricorn.

Before getting into what the music is, the writers—guitarist Ricky Hirsch, bassist Jack Hall, and vocalist Jimmy Hall—instead set the stage with how they were feeling beforehand: tired, troubled, down and out, lost in the shuffle, and full of pain and doubt. In the mid- to late 1960s, music had begun to shift away from the party songs of soul and rock, the shimmering beach songs of the Beach Boys, and the teenyboppers pining for adult love. The world was changing. The battles of civil rights were daily. The United States was getting involved in foreign conflicts that would divide generations. The "generation gap" was growing, and the optimism that had once been widespread was fading quickly.

As the 1970s dawned, young people wanted to put it behind them. When asked by a reporter why the band didn't play more issue conscious songs in 1975, Lynyrd Skynyrd's Ronnie Van Zant answered, "I don't think young people want to get involved so much anymore with the daily events of the world. We've played in the North and in the South, and it seems like the young people around America just want to feel good now."

Feeling good became a higher precedent than activism in the lyrics of much of the music of the times. As Wet Willie put it, when looking for a remedy to all of those things they were feeling, they "heard the jukebox jumpin' / with a silly melody." The music had a "real good beat" and a "whole lotta soul."

In describing Dixie rock, the songwriters offer up another, more inten-tional homage. They request that someone play more "good-time music" the way it used to be played, paraphrasing Chuck Berry's 1957 "Rock and Roll Music," saying, "Any old way you choose it / You know you just can't lose." Offering up another tribute to those who came before them, they also request "some nasty pickin' / some blues on a black guitar."

Rather than pointing out other bands that play Dixie rock, Wet Willie instructs listeners that if "they're gettin' tired of trouble" or "feelin' down and out," they need to listen to the "smokin' shuffle" being played down south in Alabama, Tennessee, Georgia, and Louisiana. But more impor-tant than geography, the band defines the music as the kind that makes you forget your troubles, whether personal or global, and makes you feel

good. Whether the definition fits all of Southern Rock, it certainly fits the music of Wet Willie.

39. "Freeborn Man," Outlaws (from *Lady in Waiting*, 1976)

On this very list, there are eleven songs that were originally recorded by someone other than the artists who made this list with the song. The Outlaws have a total of six songs on the list, and three of them are songs that have been recorded multiple times by multiple artists before the band got hold of them. But when the Outlaws recorded such a song, they put their indelible stamp on it. Take, for instance, this song from their 1976 album *Lady in Waiting*.

Before the Outlaws put their version on record, the song had been around for nearly ten years. Cowritten by Keith Allison and Mark Lindsay, the song originally appeared as a single for Allison, a regular on the music variety show *Where the Action Is*, in February 1967. Although it didn't do anything commercially, the song was strong enough to quickly be picked up by other artists, the first being Glen Campbell, who recorded the song in early 1968 for his album *A New Place in the Sun*. In the original Allison version, the song starts with a lone Dobro, followed quickly by the band and then Allison's vocal. In Campbell's arrangement, he starts the song with only his voice, singing, "I was born in the southland," followed by a quick run on an acoustic guitar as horns swell behind it. While changing the arrangement, Campbell also changes the lyric from Allison's "northwest" to something perhaps a little more identifiable to Campbell's country audience. After this introduction change, the song hews close to the original arrangement. The song wasn't released as a single, but the album reached #1 on the Country charts, as his previous three had and his next three would.

Soon, other country artists were recording the song, including Jerry Reed (for his 1968 album *Alabama Wild Man*), forgotten artist Kenny Vernon (who released his single just a few months after Campbell), and, perhaps most influentially, Jimmy Martin, who helped the song become a bluegrass standard after his 1968 version. In 1969, Allison reclaimed the song, this time as part of Paul Revere and the Raiders, along with the song's cowriter, recording a version for their 1969 *Alias Pink Puzz*, one that was closer to the original version than the ones popping up in the country format. And they continued to pop up, as Hank Williams Jr.

released his version as a single in 1970 and Bob Luman released his in 1971. Progressive bluegrass artists had picked up on Jimmy Martin's rowdy crowd favorite, with Bluegrass Alliance (in 1970), Tony Rice (in 1974), and J. D. Crowe (in 1976) releasing recordings of their own.

In 1976, the Outlaws released their version. Rather than using the arrangement that country and bluegrass artists were turning into a standard, the Outlaws roll back to the Allison/Raiders arrangement, though Henry Paul's voice lends it a tie to the country versions. The band makes its mark on the song beginning at 1:25, when the song goes from the hard-driving rhythm to a laid-back jazz-inflected beat. Billy Jones takes the first solo, showing his jazzy side, his smooth Les Paul tone floating effortlessly amid drummer Monte Yoho's steady high hat and bassist Frank O'Keefe's walking bass line. A minute later, Jones and Hughie Thomasson arrive at their signature method of tagging in and out of the solo. Instead of simply one ending and the other beginning, the two go into a twin-guitar riff that becomes a harmony riff until both are aggressively bending the strings in unison, Jones tagging out to Thomasson, who continues bending the strings with short bursts of notes before Jones joins him for a descending figure that becomes a harmony part that then switches to the two guitarists trading a chicken-picking break. Thomasson continues afterward for a short melodic run before Jones joins him, and the band begins to ramp back up to their original tempo, with Paul returning with the final verses before the song crescendos. Here, the band has taken a song that had become a standard into a new direction, slowing it down rather than speeding it up.

38. "Just Got Paid," ZZ Top (from *Rio Grande Mud*, 1972)

The best kinds of songs are those that you can immediately relate to—songs that are about experiences common to us all. "Just Got Paid" is about one of life's most common experiences—getting that paycheck. Whether you get paid daily, weekly, or monthly, the experience is the same. Billy Gibbons and the crew put together one of the quintessential end-of-the-workweek songs.

Every workingman and workingwoman looks forward to the end of the week, the time when the paycheck goes into the pocket and the good times ramp up for another weekend of fun. "Just got paid today," Gibbons lets the world know, and now he's got a "pocket full of change." But it's

not easy money, which is evidenced by his sore back. If you don't believe him, he invites you to step into his shoes and earn it the same way. It's a family tradition, this one of hard work and the only life he's ever known. Even though he knows that love of money is the root of all evil, he's grateful to have it, not greedy to get it. Having what he's got comforts him. When the wolf passes by the door, he can rest easy that he's taken care of.

The song is one of Gibbons's most sparse, with most of the rhythm guitar consisting of his funk-filled riff repeated while his overdubbed slide guitar work provides only snippets of sound—until the solo, that is, when the rhythm guitar takes on a syncopated life of its own and the slide carries the song forward with long sustaining notes sliding into place, then taking its place alongside the Bo Diddley–like rhythm before busting loose on its own with a long gleeful squeal. After the last verse is sung, all the instruments hammer out a beat like a craftsman's hammer pausing to let each individual instrument have its say.

But let's give the bass player some credit too. As solid and groove inspiring as Gibbons's guitar work is here, it is Dusty Hill's bass that drives the song. And "drive" might be too light a word. Gibbons's guitar rhythm is so sparse that Hill's instrument is the focal point of the song. When a bass player stays on the root of a chord for the song, it can sometimes become monotonous and overly simplistic. But here, Hill takes it as a challenge. During the verse, he alternates between locomotive-like sixteenth notes, dropping to eighth notes for a few bars before ramping it back up when Gibbons is singing. Between vocals, he even drops it to quarter notes and stays there through the solo sections. All of this is done using only the root notes, but, even so, Hill is able to add incredible texture to the song.

One of the hallmarks of Southern Rock is the way that fans were able to relate to the bands as equals, fellow workingmen and -women who just happened to be on a stage in front of thousands of people at a time. The artists gave an air of accessibility that they could come off the stage and over to the house for a beer. When that believability is encapsulated in a song, it is an instant favorite. Even today, it is played live by artists like Gov't Mule and Joe Bonamassa, who take the opportunity to expand on the solo sections while retaining the original's groove and appeal.

37. "Jukin'/San Antonio Rose," Atlanta Rhythm Section (from Red Tape, 1976)

Western swing's influence on Southern Rock crops up many times during its brief chart reign. The Marshall Tucker Band's "This Ol' Cowboy" tipped its Stetson to the music of Bob Wills and the Texas Playboys, and their influence stretched into the music of the Allman Brothers Band by way of Dickey Betts. But the best tribute to the music of western swing comes from the Atlanta Rhythm Section from the 1976 album *Red Tape*.

The opening guitar, heavily distorted and playing syncopated double-stops from the Chuck Berry school, may not immediately bring to mind western swing (though Berry himself was influenced to write "Maybelline" by Wills's "Ida Red") but may bring to mind something closer to the Texas boogie of ZZ Top. It's here, right from the beginning, that the Atlanta Rhythm Section puts a twist on paying tribute to their influences.

Ronnie Hammond first tells listeners that if they like to go jukin', he knows a great little unassuming cowboy bar just outside of Austin, Texas, that is the place to go. While other Southern Rock artists talked of their love of country music, Hammond tells us he never cared for it—until, that is, he heard western swing, which mixed country with jazz into a blend all its own. "Don't you want to go jukin'," he asks, telling the listener he has "jukin' in his blood." After a second time through the chorus, pianist Dean Daughtry rolls out a barrelhouse-style piano break, leading to the syncopated guitar reprising the song's opening.

In the second verse, Robert Nix, the Atlanta Rhythm Section's drummer and the song's writer, draws a through-line from western swing pioneers Bob Wills and the Texas Playboys to ZZ Top, commenting that the scorching boogie of ZZ Top has now taken the Playboys's place in the juke joint but is carrying on the same legacy.

After the next chorus, as if to illustrate the point, guitarists J. R. Cobb and Barry Bailey join in harmony for an instrumental version of Wills's "San Antonio Rose," giving way for Daughtry to return with his boogie-woogie piano. After his rousing spot, the guitarists return in harmony before the band returns to the original riff and Hammond repeats the chorus, imploring the listener to go jukin'.

The line they draw—from the Texas Playboys to ZZ Top—isn't a perfect one, of course, but it's an accurate summation of the influences

that drove Southern Rock forward to diverse audiences and the subgenre to include such a wide range of sounds within it.

36. "Dumas Walker," Kentucky Headhunters (from *Pickin' on Nashville*, 1989)

One of the hallmarks of Southern Rock music is a regional pride not exhibited by most other forms of rock and roll. By the end of the Southern Rock era, or at least that which is covered in this book, the regionalism that was once a celebrated part of the genre was less important than creating songs that could be universally accepted—at least from the point of view of a record label. Labels are good at pushing products, chasing trends, and helping get the word out (most of the time), but they aren't always great at knowing what audiences want to hear.

When the Kentucky Headhunters made their debut in 1989, that was the atmosphere they were stepping into. Their first single, "Walk Softly on This Heart of Mine," proved to be a surprise Country Top 40 hit. The label was chomping at the bit to improve on (or at least repeat) that success. So the second single was a crucial decision, and the band decided on "Dumas Walker."

The song is a slice of life taken from the band's daily routine—actually, two slices. Dumas Walker was a real man and marble champion who owned Walker's Package and Grocery Store in Moss, Tennessee, just over the Kentucky–Tennessee state line and about thirty-five miles from where some of the members of the Headhunters grew up in Metcalfe County. The boys would head there as kids to grab a hot dog and some firecrackers with the hopes that Walker would teach them a few marble tricks. As the boys got older, and since many of the surrounding counties were dry, Walker's was the nearest spot for a drink.

When vocalist Ricky Lee Phelps enters the song, he bellows, "Well, let's all go down to Dumas Walker's," rallying his group to head down to the store. Phelps tells us he and his girl are heading to the drive-in, but they first have to make a stop at Walker's for a six-pack. The plan after the show? To return to Dumas Walker's to shoot more marbles and maybe make a little money doing it since everyone is placing bets on the winner.

The sing-along chorus featuring the rallying cry takes a little artistic license but draws on another childhood favorite of other band members.

The famous line about a "slaw burger, fries and a bottle of Ski" doesn't actually reference Walker's Package and Grocery Store. Instead, it's about a little greasy spoon nearly sixty miles north, closer to Bowling Green, Kentucky. The story goes that before they became the Kentucky Headhunters, the band stopped at the Adolphus Ennis Lunch Room and were served by the proprietor himself. He began to take their orders without writing them down when one of the group asked him if he needed a pen and pad. Ennis told them he didn't, that he had a photogenic mind. It was a humorous misuse of words that made its way into the second verse of the song. The specialty of the Lunch Room was the slawburger, simply a hamburger topped with coleslaw and served with fries. The drink of choice in the song is Ski, a soda that is a regional favorite combining lemon and orange flavors.

The song combined strong regional references that were personal to the band with a catchy sing-along chorus. It was the kind of song that drew people in with a sense of nostalgia; even if they didn't know Dumas Walker or what a slawburger was, they knew something like it from their past.

So the record label said no. It was too regional, too specific. It wouldn't work on a national scale. But the band had seen the reaction to it every night when they played it in their live set, no matter where they were, and they stood their ground. The label reluctantly relented and released the song as a single. It went on to peak at #15, ten spots higher than their debut single. Their third single, a take on the Don Gibson classic "Oh Lonesome Me," charted even higher, landing the group their only Top Ten Country hit. Their success earned them a Grammy for Best Country Performance by a Duo or Group with Vocal (1990).

As a postscript: Dumas Walker enjoyed a bit of local and regional fame after the song became a hit in March 1990, but just over a year later, on April 22, 1991, he died of a heart attack at age seventy-five. A few months later, his widow put the store up for sale since she wasn't able to go it alone.

The Adolphus Ennis Lunch Room enjoyed the success of the song, so much so that the "A. Ennis Lunch Room" sign that hung over the door was removed and replaced with one that reads: "Ky. Headhunters. Original Slawburger, fry & bottle of 'Ski.' Grammy Winning 'Dumas Walker' Slawburger."

35. "Wild-Eyed Southern Boys," .38 Special (from *Wild-Eyed Southern Boys*, 1981)

Phase two of Southern Rock was led by Molly Hatchet and .38 Special. Molly Hatchet, who often referred to themselves as "Southern Metal," decided to continue to produce a harder-edged sound than their predecessors. With *Rockin' into the Night*, .38 Special had charted a new path for their brand of Southern Rock that led to a more commercial, mainstream pop-rock sound. The song "Rockin' into the Night" had been written by people outside the band, and the success of the song and album encouraged the band to continue to utilize outside sources. But they didn't go too far afield in doing so. For their next album, they went to one of the cowriters of their recent hit, Jim Peterik, to collaborate on songs for the album.

Before they began writing with Peterik, he offered them another song he had worked up. Peterik had been in the music business since the mid-1960s and had scored a #2 hit in 1970 with the song "Vehicle," performed with his band Ides of March. Now he was writing songs and also performing with his new band, Survivor, who were working on their second album and were just over a year away from their breakthrough smash, "Eye of the Tiger." Peterik had been writing for years, and his experience of having a song recorded by a Southern Rock–associated band inspired him to write a song from that point of view. Out came "Wild-Eyed Southern Boys."

The song is a fictional account of a southern Saturday night when the men are rough and rowdy, starting fights and picking up women in the first verse. In the second verse, the object of their affection, a mysterious lady in black, has all of the outlaws lining up to fight for her. The third and final verse describes a "man of wealth and power" driving an expensive car. But none of these things will help him pick up a lady because he "ain't no wild-eyed southern boy."

Peterik originally pitched the song to Molly Hatchet, but they turned it down (they rarely recorded work from outside the band). Now he presented it to .38 Special, who again heard the hit potential. Much like they had with their first Peterik song, the band made the song the album title. Although the band had been shying away from decidedly southern fare, "Wild-Eyed Southern Boys" served as an excellent compromise, bridging their past and future. Lyrically, it fits the Southern Rock mold of a good

time, full of bravado and machismo, and musically it leaned the pop-rock direction .38 Special was now pursuing. The band also used the song to show their unity, having Don Barnes, who had sung their biggest hit so far, trade vocals with Donnie Van Zant. The two trade lines throughout the song, showing the band as a team, a group of friends out for a good time.

At the time of the album's release, many radio stations were embracing the album-oriented rock (AOR) format and were narrowing their playlists to rock records, cutting out much of the pop, rhythm and blues, and country that might have turned up on the station earlier. This also meant that instead of waiting for record labels to send singles for them to play, disc jockeys would pick whatever songs from an album they wanted to play. Disc jockeys across the country began to pick up "Wild-Eyed Southern Boys." Because the AOR format was spinning songs that were not designated as singles, *Billboard* created the Mainstream Rock chart in 1981 to recognize those songs. "Wild-Eyed Southern Boys" rose to #35 on the chart and became another .38 Special signature song.

34. "(Ghost) Riders in the Sky," Outlaws (from *Ghost Riders*, 1980)

Even with bringing in the hot producer of the moment, Bill Szymczyk, who had helped the Eagles break away from their country-rock sound, the Outlaws's third album, *Hurry Sundown*, continued their drop down the albums chart, peaking nearly twenty spots below their second album. Although the chart success may have been disappointing, they were still a very popular live act, so to capitalize on that, they released the live album *Bring It Back Alive*. It was the first album without vocalist/guitarist Henry Paul, but it rose to #29 on the albums chart. Much like post-Skynyrd bands Blackfoot and .38 Special, the band decided it needed to change direction. Paul disagreed, and they came to an agreement for him to leave the band and strike out on his own. Clive Davis, head of Arista, the band's record label, assigned to their new project a new producer he had been impressed with, so in mid-1978, while the live album climbed the charts, the Outlaws, including new guitarist Freddie Salem, entered the studio with Robert "Mutt" Lange to begin work on their new album. The final result stripped away much of what made the Outlaws unique (including some of the vocal harmonies Paul provided), adding a little too

much gloss and polish. Sales reflected the disappointment, peaking at #60 on the albums chart.

The band decided to go back to their Southern Rock roots on their next album, recruiting one-time Capricorn staff producer Johnny Sandlin, who had produced a "who's who" of Southern Rock greats, including the Allman Brothers, Wet Willie, Elvin Bishop, Cowboy, and solo albums for Gregg Allman and Dickey Betts. The addition of Salem played a larger part here, bringing the band's "guitar army" reputation to the forefront. Although Paul had been a guitar player, he was mainly a rhythm player, while Salem and his Les Paul stood shoulder to shoulder with the band's other two guitar players, Hughie Thomasson and Billy Jones. *In the Eye of the Storm*, featuring a little harder edge, rose slightly higher than their last album, peaking at #55.

A change of producer was once again at hand, and much like the band and label had done when turning to Szymczyk, they brought in Gary Lyons, who had produced critically acclaimed albums for Wet Willie and Crawler for Epic and the platinum self-titled debut of Foreigner. The pairing proved to be a good decision, and Lyons retained much of what made the Outlaws popular to begin with while also bringing their sound into a balance between Southern Rock and the emerging arena rock. The lead single from the album, "(Ghost) Riders in the Sky," showcases that balance with the band's country roots and penchant for reaching into the past for a song they could put their stamp on.

"(Ghost) Riders in the Sky" was written in 1948 by a Death Valley ranger named Stan Jones. As a teenager working on a ranch, Jones had been told the story of "ghost riders" by an older ranch hand, and years later, after becoming a hobbyist songwriter, Jones put the story to a tune. The first version recorded was by folksinger Burl Ives, who stuck closely to Jones's demo of the song, recording it with only guitar accompaniment in February 1949. In the early 1940s, Vaughn Monroe was a successful pop singer, consistently charting Top 40 songs and making small-time movies. When RCA producer Charles Grean heard the demo of the song, he knew immediately that Monroe could make it a hit and booked a Chicago studio for him to record in while Monroe was scheduled to play a concert in the region. The record business moved a lot faster then, and by March 1949, Monroe had hit the charts with the song, retitled "Riders in the Sky (A Cowboy Legend)." His versions sold 300,000 copies in the first two weeks; spawned a number of other recordings of the song,

including a lampooning of the song by Spike Jones; and eventually hit #2 on the Country charts and #1 on the Pop chart, becoming the #1 song for 1949.

Other versions of the song popped up over the years, but the Ramrods's recording, as "Ghost Riders," in 1960 turned the song into an instrumental favorite. Their version reached #30 in February 1961 and inspired a number of instrumental surf versions by the likes of Dick Dale and the Ventures, among others. On Valentine's Day morning in 1979, Johnny Cash entered "Cowboy" Jack Clements's studio to begin laying tracks for *Silver*, his twenty-fifth-anniversary album produced by Brian Ahern. One of two songs recorded at that session was "(Ghost) Riders in the Sky," which Cash released as a single in May 1979, reaching #2 on the Country chart.

The song was one of the first that Thomasson brought to Lyons. It was a song he had wanted to record for several years and, perhaps prodded by Cash's recent success with it, decided now was the time. Lyons agreed, and the band went to work arranging the song. Opening with an arpeggiated acoustic guitar, the song retains its stripped-down origins, but where Cash's version retains the loping rhythm of the original version, the Outlaws spur it on to a gallop about thirty seconds in, when the sound of wind ushers in the chunking rhythm of a clean electric guitar. As David Dix's drums and Rick Cua's bass come in like stallions, Thomasson's entrance echoes the Ramrods's twangy introduction. Two minutes later, Thomasson's guitar breaks loose in a flurry of notes, squealing like a bronco refusing to be broken before he returns to the vocals, his weathered voice fitting the song perfectly. At nearly four minutes, the tempo increases as a devilish laugh is unleashed before Salem fires off a blistering solo, followed by Jones, who builds the solo up to let Thomasson take over again just before the song fades out at just under six minutes.

The Outlaws had not charted a song in the Top 40 since 1975, until "(Ghost) Riders in the Sky" rose to #31 on the Top 100 (it hit #15 on the recently created Top Rock Tracks chart). The album reached #25, and the band retained Lyons for their next album, 1982's *Los Hombres Malo*, though the pairing failed to produce the same results.

33. "Keep Your Hands to Yourself," Georgia Satellites (from *Georgia Satellites*, 1986)

When the Georgia Satellites burst on the mainstream scene, it was a much more diverse place than today's mainstream chart. In 1986, it included the pop stylings of Lionel Richie and Lisa Lisa and Cult Jam and resurging acts like Fleetwood Mac and Steve Winwood. There were hair metal bands like Whitesnake and Bon Jovi sitting at the top of the charts alongside one-hit wonders like Billy Vera and the Beaters and vocal titans like Whitney Houston.

In the world of Southern Rock fans, the 1980s were a time of near famine. The Allman Brothers had disbanded again, and the Marshall Tucker Band had called it quits (for the time being) in 1983. Molly Hatchet was limping along, but few other than the die-hard fans seemed to notice. The only band with deep Southern Rock ties that was still making it happen was .38 Special, though by this time their music had lost much of its hard-rock edge and fit fine alongside other arena rock acts, like Journey.

With their debut album, the Satellites made their presence known to both mainstream radio listeners and Southern Rock fans with their song "Keep Your Hands to Yourself." Cutting through the electronic drums and synthesizers of much of pop music and the bombastic guitar pyrotechnics of mainstream metal that populated radio came a simple guitar rhythm that had been the basis of countless songs before it. With a droning A string and the two-finger chunka-chunka rhythm—Chuck Berry mixed with Jack Daniel's, the band liked to call it—the song made a statement.

Part of that statement was that straight-up pure rock and roll could still excite the masses. Dan Baird's twangy Telecaster chunks out the rhythm as his dive bar–honed voice rings out just before drummer Mauro Magellan slams down a rock-solid thud with the bass drum. Rick Richards's fuzzy double-stops and string bends were no sonic match for Van Halen and his legions of imitators, but they were visceral—they were raw. The interplay between Baird's Telecaster and Richards's Les Paul Jr. sums up an entire history of rock and roll. Bassist Rick Price slides in, lending a bouncy bottom end that blends with Magellan's heavy hits.

The other part of the statement was that you didn't have to take everything so seriously. Lyrically, the song is a novelty song. The singer's girl

does not want to get physical—until there is a wedding ring involved. It's not deep, and it's not complicated, but it's real life. The story is humorously relatable, and that is what drew in listeners. Had the song been released in June rather than October, this would have been one of those windows-down, stereo-cranked songs of the summer. It might have been too cold to do that by the time the song started to rise since it peaked at #2 in December 1986. If not for Bon Jovi's monstrous "Livin' on a Prayer," which spent four weeks at the top of the chart, it would have made it there, too.

Elektra Records even sprung for a video that featured the band on the back of a pickup truck playing the song on their way somewhere, which turns out to be the shotgun wedding of Baird and a pregnant female. MTV started the video in active rotation before moving it to heavy rotation as the song rose up the charts. No offense, but these guys weren't your typical video darlings. Behind those eyes, you could see years of bar band living, and the experience they had taming those kinds of crowds served them well as they started to tour with bigger bands in bigger venues, even making appearances at European music festivals.

The album made it to #5 on the *Billboard* Album chart, but their follow-up single, "Battleship Chains," could not uphold the momentum, making the Satellites forever an entry in the "One-Hit-Wonder Hall of Fame."

32. "Caught Up in You," .38 Special (from *Special Forces*, 1982)

Like *Rockin' into the Night* had before it, *Wild-Eyed Southern Boys* broadened .38 Special's fan base beyond the Southern Rock audience they had originally targeted. As they had seen the music landscape change before them, .38 Special was smart enough to roll with the punches and adapt their sound. Their collaborations with Survivor founder Jim Peterik had yielded three of their biggest hits ("Rockin' into the Night," "Wild-Eyed Southern Boys," and "Hold On Loosely"), each one bigger than the last one. Now going in to record their fifth album, they again turned to Peterik to collaborate, cowriting three songs with him for their new album *Special Forces*.

Where *Wild-Eyed Southern Boys* saw the band beginning to find their groove, *Special Forces* is where they found a balance between the more polished pop-rock songs like "You Keep Runnin' Away" and the South-

ern Rock–edged songs like "Chain Lightnin'" and "Breakin' Loose." But again they found their greatest success with Don Barnes at the mic singing one of the band's most hook-filled numbers, "Caught Up in You."

Returning to the well once more with an eighth-note introduction similar to that used on "Hold On Loosely," the song relies heavily on the incredibly singable chorus and bridge that draws in fans. The song quickly became the band's biggest hit, making it to #10 on the *Billboard* Hot 100 and #1 on the Mainstream Rock chart, driving the album to #10 on the *Billboard* 200 Album chart. The production of videos was on the rise as the band hit its stride, and "Caught Up in You" marks the first concept video the band created, which had the band playing in a pool hall as a guy tries to woo a young barfly.

.38 Special continued their success with their next album, *Tour de Force*, though their collaborations with Peterik ended due to the demands of his career as Survivor's "Eye of the Tiger" took off and the band began its own string of hits. .38 Special, through their record label's association with A&M Film, began to do singles for various sound tracks, including *Teachers* ("Teacher, Teacher") and *Revenge of the Nerds: Nerds in Paradise* ("Back to Paradise"). While they continued to record and eventually collaborate with Peterik again, they didn't have another Top Ten hit until 1988's "Second Chance," a song that featured a new vocalist (Max Carl) and that many of their fans thought took them too far into the pop realm.

31. "Grey Ghost," Henry Paul Band (from *Grey Ghost*, 1979)

The Outlaws stood at a crossroads in 1977. They had just released their third album, *Hurry Sundown*, produced by Bill Szymczyk, who had helped the Eagles become the multiplatinum act they had become. Szymczyk's magic touch didn't translate, and the album, though good and containing songs that would live on like "Hurry Sundown," was the band's lowest-selling album to that time. With "Southern Rock" waning as a marketing point by 1977, bands began to try to figure out how to gain more longevity in their careers. Hughie Thomasson, guitarist/vocalist, was lobbying to move in a more hard-rock direction. Henry Paul, vocalist/guitarist, was lobbying to stay where they were or even to lean a little heavier on the country side. In the end, Paul decided to leave the group, and the Outlaws entered the studio with Mutt Lange, just a year away

from his long association with hard rockers AC/DC and Def Leppard. Paul struck out on his own, forming the Henry Paul Band.

In October 1977, just after Paul left the Outlaws, the plane carrying Lynyrd Skynyrd crashed, killing Ronnie Van Zant and Steve Gaines. Paul looked up to Van Zant, as many in the Southern Rock community did. The Outlaws had toured with Lynyrd Skynyrd, and it was with Van Zant's help that they got their big break and were signed to Arista. Paul's new band mate, Barry Rapp, had played with Steve Gaines in his pre-Skynyrd band Crawdad. Both were devastated by the news and worked through their grief by writing a song about it.

With the song, Paul, a Civil War buff, worked to tie the Southern Rock story into a bigger historical framework. The first verse is a poetic and succinct description of that fateful October day before the chorus employs a bit of poetic license and bring the history into the song with reference to the Grey Ghost. There was, in fact, a Grey Ghost—Major John Mosby. Mosby led a unit that excelled at interrupting supply lines that worked to keep Union troops stocked with gear and food. Mosby's raiders moved with a stealth that gained him the nickname the Grey Ghost. Paul takes that reputation and ties it to something much deadlier, making the Grey Ghost the bringer of death.

In the second verse, the writers turn the mirror to themselves. "Fast like them, the music is just a disguise," they say, admitting that their fast lifestyle could see them meet the same end. This same Grey Ghost prowls the night, "an echo of the sadness and the pain," looking for his next soul to claim. As they get to the third verse, the focus is solely on the inevitability that the Grey Ghost brings, knowing that, no matter what legacy they leave, they will be leaving it behind.

Musically, they loosely based the structure of the song on Van Zant's "Free Bird" and the Outlaws's "Green Grass and High Tides," with their extended guitar solos. "Grey Ghost" gives a showcase to the band's guitarists, Jim Fish and Billy Crain. Fish had worked with Paul in the pre-Outlaws group Sienna before leaving to form Silver Chicken. Crain had been bouncing around Tennessee and the region with the band he formed with his brother Tommy, called the Flat Creek Band. When Charlie Daniels called Tommy to join the Charlie Daniels Band, the brothers ended the band, and soon Billy was joining the Henry Paul Band.

Utilizing the configuration of Stratocaster versus Les Paul, the two guitarists played as a perfect complement to each other. Fish, brandishing

the Strat, was influenced by the country picking of Don Rich (Buck Owens's Telecaster master), the Byrds's Roger McGuinn, and b-bender creator Clarence White. Crain, with the Les Paul, had been influenced by Eric Clapton, Jimi Hendrix, Lowell George, and the Allman Brothers Band's Duane Allman and Dickey Betts. Their interplay on this song gives any Southern Rock (or any other kind of rock) guitar team a run for its money. Fish has a crisp tone and fluid speed coming into the first short solo at the 1:56 mark. Crain takes over at 2:08 using his volume control knob to great effect for ten seconds, leading back into the chorus. Fish roars back at 3:17 employing double-stops that would make Chuck Berry proud, then running single-note runs from one end of the neck to the other before his multinote bends take center stage. At 4:13, the two guitars engage in a little twin-guitar riffing before Crain takes over. Where Fish came on with a barrage of notes and bends, Crain slows it down a bit, like a good wrestler working a rest hold. But it's just to lure us in, to allow us to catch our breath, before he breaks loose with some heavy string bending at about the 5:00 mark before letting fire a machine-gun blast of notes. Just before the big ending, Fish joins Crain for a flurry of twin notes, putting the final celebration cry to the song. While this recording is fantastic, video of Crain playing the song (along with Dave Fiester, who replaced Fish when he was sacked for, ironically, being too country) shows that Crain is absolutely one of the most underrated guitarists in Southern Rock.

30. "Seven Turns," Allman Brothers Band (from *Seven Turns*, 1990)

When the Allman Brothers Band re-formed in 1989 and headed for the studio, their condition with Epic was that they would be able to put together the album as they wanted to with complete control. Their two records for Arista just before the band's breakup were marked with heavy label involvement, compromise, and substandard material. Getting back together, they wanted to avoid those problems and produce the best music they could. Part of that was picking the right producer. For that, they went back to Tom Dowd, who had produced their breakthrough albums, *The Allman Brothers Band at Fillmore East* and *Eat a Peach*, in the early 1970s.

As they were recording the album, heavy on blues rock, Dowd asked Dickey Betts if he had any songs similar to "Blue Sky." Betts did and showed the band "Seven Turns," a song about where the choices in life take us, based on a Navajo story.

Betts's acoustic guitar opens the song as Warren Haynes's understated, clean slide guitar plays short melodic lines. The band falls in with them as Betts begins to sing about the choices that lie ahead. "Love is all that remains the same," he sings, "that's what it's all comin' to." As the first verse ends, Betts trades his acoustic for his Les Paul (quite literally in the video) and lays down a melodic, flowing guitar line as Haynes echoes him for a few bars. Haynes drops out as Betts continues with a sweet run before they come together for a harmony restatement of Betts's initial run. When the next verse begins, the subtext of a band reunited is as strong as any obvious interpretation, ending, "How in the world could you ever know we'd ever meet again?"

Betts is joined on vocals throughout the song by Johnny Neel and Haynes as they harmonize various lines, adding emphasis and underscoring. After repeating the chorus a couple of times, they are joined, in a call-and-response style, by Gregg Allman soulfully echoing the lines to incredible effect, adding to the subtext of the song as Betts and Allman trade the lines. Haynes steps into the spotlight, providing a slide guitar solo that lifts the song and places it squarely into the Allman Brothers Band canon. The vocals return, and Haynes fades to the back with ghostly high-pitched slide notes that harken back to Betts on "Ramblin' Man."

In many ways, the song stands as a mission statement for the band going forward, though the love between Betts and Allman wouldn't last as long as many would have hoped.

29. "Flirtin' with Disaster," Molly Hatchet (from *Flirtin' with Disaster*, 1979)

Ed King may have mused that Southern Rock died the day Molly Hatchet debuted, but he'd be in the minority. Their first album was released just over a year after the Lynyrd Skynyrd plane crash, which ended the first phase of Southern Rock, and less than a year later was certified gold (half a million copies sold) and still selling. The band toured relentlessly both on their own and providing support to acts including the Outlaws, Bob Seger and the Silver Bullet Band, and Angel. Suddenly, the band had

money and fame and all that came with it as they headed back into the studio with producer Tom Werman to record their second album. In the game of Southern Rock, Hatchet led the way with their harder-edged boogie, and it was time to see if they could follow up their debut success.

Flirtin' with Disaster, their sophomore release, delivered more of what came with their debut, showing the band to have the ability to duplicate its success. In fact, the album was released in September 1979, and by January 1980, it was already certified gold and by February platinum. While the album sold briskly, only one single, the title track, broke the *Billboard* 100, landing at #42.

Just as with the first album, a Frank Frazetta painting graced the cover. "Dark Kingdom" portrays a warrior striding into a cave, stepping over the remains of those who had attempted to defeat the great snake that lives within. Only the tip of the snake's tail is visible, but its scale is obvious. He may need backup.

"Flirtin' with Disaster" starts similarly, guitarist Dave Hlubek picking a droning open E string before sounding a short riff like a call to action as Bruce Crump's drums and Banner Thomas's bass join him. Quickly, guitarists Duane Roland and Steve Holland break in like the trumpet call to battle. Hlubek answers them, and it sounds as if an army is assembling for battle as they all come together, making way for vocalist Danny Joe Brown.

With the pressure of success comes doubt—questioning if, after all of the time working for it, it is really worth it. What's the next step after you've grasped the golden ring you've been chasing for so long? After watching bands they looked up to, like Skynyrd and Blackfoot, rise from their area to become superstars, now the members of Molly Hatchet stood on stages across the world looking out at their fans. "I've got the pedal to the floor," Brown sings, telling us that this fast life is flirtin' with disaster. But in the next line, he tells us that it isn't all it seems. He's out of hope and money, and, worst of all, they don't know how much more of the corruption they can take. Ah, the music business. And the band had little idea at the time of the long-term ramifications of the greed and corruption. Their first manager, Pat Armstrong, registered the band's name and trademark to himself and would later license the name back to Brown and band mate Bobby Ingram in later years before selling it outright to Ingram in 2000, leaving the original members of the band without their original group name.

The song played out the way the band was living—full tilt and balls to the wall. After the second verse, Hlubek comes in with a blistering solo that gives way to Roland's muscular riffing before both join together in harmony. Their blues-influenced playing shows the band drawing heavily from the influence of the British blues–based bands of the 1960s that Skynyrd drew from but mixing in a healthy dose of American rockers, like Joe Perry and Ted Nugent.

But the song was also a prophecy. The fame was going to their heads, and the man out front, Danny Joe Brown, began to feel like he had outgrown the band, that they were beneath him somehow. His powerful, guttural voice was the calling card of the band, and he became unbearable to the other band members. He was spoiling for a fight, and he got one from the other band members. When the dust settled, Brown was fired from the group. The story fed to the public later was that Brown had been diagnosed with diabetes (which was true) and had left the band to deal with his health problems—a white lie to save face for both Brown and the band but suspicious when the Danny Joe Brown Band released an album in 1981.

28. "Fooled Around and Fell in Love," Elvin Bishop (from *Struttin' My Stuff*, 1975)

Throughout his career, Elvin Bishop has blended country, blues, gospel, rhythm and blues, and rock and roll into something distinctly his own. With the album *Let It Flow*, and particularly with songs like "Travelin' Shoes" and "Stealin' Watermelons," he had found acceptance by the growing group of fans identifying with Southern Rock. Bishop returned to producer Johnny Sandlin to record the 1975 release *Juke Joint Jump*, which continued with his blend but didn't produce the attention his Capricorn debut had.

Heading back into the studio later that year, Bishop made the change to red-hot producer Bill Szymczyk, though the music remained the same essential blend that Bishop had been known for. After recording the songs for the album, Szymczyk felt there was something missing and began to ask if Bishop had anything else they could try. As Bishop searched his memory, backup vocalist Mickey Thomas spoke up.

Thomas was a young white southern tenor from Cairo, Georgia, who, in 1971, dreamed of being in music as a career. While he sat in his small

town dreaming, a West Coast, African American gospel singer with wild eyes named Gideon Daniels had made the trek to Florida in search of a singer to add to his multiethnic progressive gospel group, Gideon and Power. As he made his way through Florida auditioning singers, someone told him about a singer who would perfectly fit the bill, but he didn't live in Florida—he lived in Georgia. A few days later, Thomas's phone rang and it was Daniels, the man he had recently seen on an episode of *The Sonny and Cher Comedy Hour*. The two set up a meeting, and after hearing Thomas, Daniels invited him to join the group and move to San Francisco.

The band, which included guitarist Johnny "V" Vernazza, toured the country from their base in San Francisco, and when they weren't on the road, they were hanging around Fillmore getting to know other musicians and sitting in with other bands. After the shows, the groups of musicians would often end up at Bishop's apartment, where they jammed their way through old blues and gospel songs. Gideon and Power lasted for just a couple of years before breaking up and going their separate ways, with Thomas moving back to Georgia. Vernazza joined Bishop, who soon signed to Capricorn. Knowing that Thomas was close to Macon, Bishop called him up and asked him to join his band as a backup and, sometimes, lead vocalist.

Now in the recording studio with one of the top producers in the country, Thomas suggested a song he had heard Bishop play in those apartment jams a couple of years back. Bishop ran through the song for Szymczyk, and they decided to record it. Bishop tried a take on the vocals, but it wasn't gelling for him or the producer. Thomas had at this point in the recording sung lead on half the album's songs, so they decided to put him behind the microphone for this one. It was a good decision.

The mid-tempo song leans heavily on Bishop's love of rhythm and blues as the rhythm section begins the song, soon joined by Vernazza with a distinctive guitar line that makes the song instantly identifiable. Thomas's soulful tenor serves the song masterfully, conveying the feelings of this man who has built a reputation on loving them and leaving them. But now this one can't be left. "I fooled around and fell in love," he says, part in resignation, part in joy. The album cut of the song includes Bishop's guitar solo, which takes its cues, both melodically and emotion-

ally, from Thomas's vocals, crying out at times, shouting for joy at others.

The song was also edited and shopped to radio. By mid-1976, the song had reached #3 on the *Billboard* Hot 100, making it Bishop's highest-charting song. The album was also sent to rhythm-and-blues stations and managed to peak at #82 on the R&B Singles chart—not too high but a feat not often attributed to Southern Rock songs. The song has proven it has staying power by often popping up in movie sound tracks, including as recently as (as of this writing) the summer blockbuster *Guardians of the Galaxy*. The song also remains probably the most popular in Bishop's catalog, warranting it the nickname "my little annuity."

27. "Hold On Loosely," .38 Special (from *Wild-Eyed Southern Boys,* 1981)

The collaboration between .38 Special's vocalist/guitarist Don Barnes and guitarist Jeff Carlisi and Survivor's Jim Peterik had yielded .38 Special their first charting single with "Rockin' into the Night" and their best-selling album to that time with the album of the same name. A&R man John Kalonder, who was responsible for bringing the song to the band, suggested that the three get together to cowrite for .38 Special's fourth album. Barnes and Carlisi agreed and headed north to meet Peterik near his Chicago home. When they sat down together, Peterik showed them "Wild-Eyed Southern Boys," which was already completed and ready to go. Barnes and Carlisi hadn't come empty-handed either.

Looking to incorporate some of the new rock sounds of the time into their brand of Southern Rock, Carlisi had been toying around with a riff he knew had potential. As the 1980s dawned, the music labeled as New Wave began to merge with rock to form something a bit different, and one of its most popular practitioners was the Cars. Carlisi, along with everyone else in the country, heard their song "Just What I Needed" on the radio in 1979, and the idea of starting a song with an eighth-note rhythm rolled around his mind, but he had no direction. At the same time, Barnes was formulating an idea for a song based on something he had heard talk show host Dinah Shore tell a guest. The guest was talking about how she didn't try to tightly control her husband, and Shore replied that it was a good strategy, to hold on loosely.

As the trio sat in Peterik's kitchen, Carlisi began to play the now famous opening riff of the song. As it began to sink in, Barnes sang the melody to the song. They told Peterik it was called "Hold On Loosely," and the words began to pour from his mouth. In a short time, the three had finished the song and were ready to take it back to the band to record. His voice better suited to the song than Donnie Van Zant's, Barnes performed the lead vocal, as he had on "Rockin' into the Night." Barnes sang the song with conviction, and the band poured everything into it.

When *Wild-Eyed Southern Boys* was released, the title track began to receive widespread airplay on AOR stations across the country, but the first official single was "Hold On Loosely." "Rockin' into the Night" had begun the process of melding the band's penchant for melodic pop rock with their Southern Rock roots, and "Hold On Loosely" furthered them down the path. *Wild-Eyed Southern Boys* became a popular album for the band, and by the end of 1981, ten months after its release, the album was certified gold. "Hold On Loosely" had certainly done its part in growing the popularity of the band. In April 1981, the single peaked at #27 on the *Billboard* Hot 100, becoming their first Top 40 single, and #3 on the nascent Mainstream Rock chart.

Two more songs were cowritten with Peterik for the album. "Hittin' and Runnin'" was cowritten with Barnes and became a fan favorite, while his cowrite with Carlisi, "Fantasy Girl," became the album's second single, peaking at #30 and driving the album sales even higher. In February 1982, the album was certified platinum.

26. "That Smell," Lynyrd Skynyrd (from *Street Survivors*, 1977)

By 1977, Ronnie Van Zant had grown tired of the emphasis on Skynyrd's rough-and-rowdy image. While admitting it was earned rather than just given, he was essentially a kind man who had a wife at home and a new baby daughter. He had given up the partying to concentrate more on his songwriting and making the band bigger than ever. Not everyone in the band shared the same driving ambition, but with Van Zant as their leader, they fell in line.

Skynyrd had recorded cautionary tales before, but the tale of "That Smell" wasn't a generalized tale (like "Poison Whiskey") or played for laughs (like "Gimme Three Steps"). It was a pointed warning to one of their own—Gary Rossington. Rossington was the ladies' man of the

group, partying hard with starlets and living hard. Prince Charming, they called him. On a break from recording while heavily under many influences, Rossington wrapped his brand-new car around an oak tree, landing him in the hospital. His two oldest friends, Van Zant and guitarist Allen Collins, wrote the song directed squarely at their injured road warrior.

In true Skynyrd style, they made it not only a warning but also a guitar tour de force. Live, the band had routinely used "T for Texas" as a showcase for their three-guitar attack, but "That Smell" marks the first time they had laid down an original one on record. Prince Charming himself starts the song off as the band hits the first note with the force of his car into the tree. His unmistakable sound powers the opening with his unbelievable sustain that morphs into his trademark controlled feedback. After Van Zant recounts Rossington's dangerous driving habits, Steve Gaines makes his entrance with his inimitable finger-picked flurry of notes before giving the spotlight back to Van Zant for the chorus. Gaines returns as Van Zant and the Honkettes warn Rossington that "the smell of death surrounds you." Gaines picks up where he left off, showing why his new energy had lifted the band out of their doldrums, and as he winds down his section with a series of short bending notes, Collins soars in with his staccato attack before the three guitars combine for a forceful riff that could have made up a song of its own. Out of the power trio races Rossington with his double-stops and artificial harmonics squealing his declaration. The singers return with the chorus as Rossington weaves in and around, bending his notes and hitting his harmonics at the same time Collins races in to take over with a rapid-fire delivery as Rossington fades out. Collins lets loose a melodic string of notes before mimicking Rossington's earlier note bends, making room for Gaines's understated and syncopated Stratocaster lines. Seconds later, Gaines and Collins are locked together, doubling their lines until they fly apart, trading short bursts back and forth, and joining again in a tandem of guitar fury. The three guitars lock together once again for that power riff before slamming to a stop, with only the sound of Artimus Pyle's hitting his high hat like the tick of a second hand on a clock, a quickly beating heart, or both, as the guitars rise into a feedback that counteracts it like the sound of a patient flatlining.

Three days after the album was released, Lynyrd Skynyrd's plane went down, killing Van Zant and Gaines, among others. "That Smell" was released as a single soon after, but it's message was obscured by the

tragedy that had come before it, only the words "the smell of death's around" echoing in the ears of listeners.

25. "Ain't Wastin' Time No More," Allman Brothers Band (from *Eat a Peach*, 1972)

When forming the band that would come to be known as the Allman Brothers Band, Duane Allman said only one man could be the voice of the band that he heard in his head—and that was his little brother Gregg. But while Duane was in the South making plans and connecting with players, Gregg was in California working off a bum record deal and stockpiling songs for later. When the time came to break free, he made his way south to join his brother to form the band of their dreams.

Just two years later, fate bucked at the idea, removing Duane Allman from this world. It shook the band and all who knew them. The fleeting nature of life had suddenly made itself unavoidably noticeable. Their leader had fallen in the space of a thought, any idea of immortality wiped clean from their minds.

As Gregg sat stunned by grief, he decided to write as a way of coping with the pain. "Last Sunday morning," the song begins, "the sunshine felt like rain." Sorrow permeated his every thought to the point that even a ray of sunshine felt to him like a pelting of raindrops. But, oddly, this was an improvement from the previous week, when "they all seemed the same," when, rain or shine, the pain was overwhelming. Slowly, he was coming out of the cloud left by death, and with "the help of God and true friends," he was finding a new strength to continue. Along with that new strength came the realization that all things pass quickly and can be gone in an instant. His friends had pointed out the good things remaining in life, and his decision was made: "I ain't wastin' time no more."

Gregg's voice is raw with emotion, his usual soulfulness amplified by the personal lyrics. Although he had already written some fantastic lyrics for songs up to this point, this is his most personal. But the raw sadness in his voice is trumped by the near fatalism that seeps through, dealing with grief in ways that might hasten the end. His recommendation to "Miss Sally" to move through the grief is to "go on downtown, baby, find somebody to love." He recommends looking inside of yourself, and if you don't like what you see, then leave it behind by getting high. These are the thoughts of someone who is still deep in grief; even when he

looked, in the first verse, to be getting through the pain, it was still clouding his vision with nihilistic thoughts of the world.

It is apparent to any listener that Gregg was singing about the loss of his brother, but the point is driven home by the accompanying guitar. Duane had been making a reputation for himself as a slide guitar player. It's what prompted Eric Clapton to ask him to record with him for the now legendary Derek and the Dominos sessions. In Allman Brothers Band songs, he utilized the slide to play off of the style of Dickey Betts, allowing the two tones and techniques to complement each other. To that point, Betts had enjoyed playing slide on acoustic guitars, often when jamming with Duane. Here, he makes his recorded debut as an electric slide player, paying homage to his friend. Even though he sticks to the basics, never attempting more intricate lines associated with Duane, it fits the song, adding a haunting tribute.

24. "Heard It in a Love Song," Marshall Tucker Band (from *Carolina Dreams*, 1977)

Coming off of the success of *Searchin' for a Rainbow*, the band continued their hectic tour schedule and managed to record a new album, appropriately titled *Long Hard Ride*. The album charted much lower than its predecessor (#32 versus #15 on the Hot 100, though both peaked at #21 on the Country Albums chart). Only one single, the title track, charted, and it was not on the Country Singles chart. But the band was as popular as ever, even appearing at the inaugural ball of newly elected President Jimmy Carter. By 1977, the band was getting tired. Their pace was grueling, and while their work was still good, their new album seemed to coast a bit.

But it was time for a follow-up, so the band scheduled studio time with longtime producer Paul Hornsby and began to prepare. Recording sessions generally were loose, and the material would be brought in as half-baked or less-than-fully-formed ideas in most cases and then worked out in the studio. Occasionally, full songs were brought in by Toy, and the band would flesh them out. As they began to gather in the studio this time, Hornsby asked Toy what he had. Toy pulled out his acoustic guitar and began to sing "Heard It in a Love Song," to which Hornsby told him he had the band's first hit single.

The song leaned a little more to the pop elements of the band's influence, though it shouldn't be surprising since they were as influenced by songs of the British Invasion as much as they were those of western swing. Lyrically, the song stayed right in line with the band and, maybe more important, with their listeners' blue-collar roots, as exemplified by the first line, in which Toy measures the length of his relationships by the wear on his boots. But, for whatever reason, even though he claims to love her, he insists that he must leave. His only justification: that he heard it in a love song.

Led by Jerry Eubanks's flute and accompanied by Hornsby's piano featured throughout, the music is softer than previous Marshall Tucker Band releases, which probably helped it make an appearance on the *Billboard* Adult Contemporary chart (where it hit #25) but at the same time peak lower on the Country chart, at #51, though still their highest on the Country chart. Yet those elements don't bury Toy's distinctive guitar. His tone plays sharply against the flute, tinkling piano, and George McCorkle's acoustic guitar. And in a move they rarely made, the song features Toy and McCorkle playing harmony guitar lines following Hornsby's piano solo.

The song's sing-along chorus to this day embeds an earworm that is nearly impossible to shake once it is heard. Toy's enigmatic lyric pulls together a fictitious tale of a man leaving his woman and mixes it with the longing feelings he had when needing to head out on the road again, leaving his wife at home. It's a theme that permeates a chunk of Marshall Tucker Band material but never in an obvious context that elicits a sympathy for their world-traveling ways. Instead, when the subtext sinks in, it strikes listeners in a way that allows them to relate it to personal experience.

The song marked the peak of their commercial success and in many ways the end of an era. The following year, Capricorn would declare bankruptcy shortly after the release of the band's seventh album, *Together Forever*. After the country-leaning *Searchin' for a Rainbow* and the more pop-inflected *Carolina Dreams*, *Together Forever* made more of a play for mainstream rock. The sonics changed with producer Stewart Levine taking over for Paul Hornsby. More songs were contributed by band members as well, giving the album a different sound. The band soon moved to Warner Bros. records, who wanted them to move in a more pop-rock direction à la .38 Special, which was a bit of a misstep, as bands

like Alabama, building roughly on the template laid out with "Heard It in a Love Song," were climbing the country charts and finding big success.

23. "Statesboro Blues," Allman Brothers Band (from *The Allman Brothers Band at Fillmore East*, 1971)

Early Allman Brothers Band recordings tied themselves heavily to the blues, exhibiting its heavy influence on the band's songwriting, singing, and playing. "Statesboro Blues" is a song that was originally recorded by Blind Willie McTell in 1928. McTell's original blends his blues with a hint of ragtime and a dash of hokum, featuring a quickly sung section simplified in future versions of the song. Forty years later, bluesman Taj Mahal recorded a version of the song for his 1968 debut album.

Mahal had been performing the song since at least 1965, when he recorded it with his band Rising Son (also featuring Ry Cooder), though the album was not released until 1992. Recording his first album, Mahal revisited the song. Where the 1965 version is an up-tempo near-pop song, the 1968 recording returns the song to its blues roots, powered by the slide guitar playing of Mahal's guitarist, Jesse Ed Davis. During the time that the album was released, Duane Allman and the members of his band Hour Glass (including Gregg Allman, Paul Hornsby, and Pete Carr) were chasing the dream in Los Angeles. One night after a recording session, the group went to see Mahal perform at a local club. Duane was transfixed by Davis, particularly on "Statesboro Blues." Davis's playing on the song struck something in Duane, and after that night, he spent hours practicing slide guitar, eventually becoming a master of the craft.

A few years later, after two excellent but less than blockbuster albums, the Allman Brothers Band were set to record a few shows at Fillmore East in a "Hail Mary" to connect with an audience by showing their incredible live act on record. To start the show, Duane chose "Statesboro Blues."

The Allman Brothers Band arrangement is essentially the same as the Mahal version, but Duane brings something unexplainably different to the slide guitar playing. From the opening, crying note, he packs a lifetime of emotion and feeling into the guitar parts. For his part, Gregg brings his own style to the vocals while hewing closely to what the earlier version had mapped out. His voice is vibrant, giving the lyrics, often

about hardship and pain, an immediate quality without milking them for effect.

Due mainly to Duane's solo break in the middle of the song, the Allman Brothers Band version clocks in at nearly a minute and a half longer than the Mahal version. At first, he replicates Davis's solo but soon breaks out on his own, reaching higher on the neck with an intensity that cuts through Berry Oakley's tumbling bass and Butch Trucks's and Jaimoe's dual drum sets. Although Duane's slide playing is the featured act in the song, Dickey Betts gets to take a ride after Duane's slide solo, showing off his blues chops.

The recording, included as part of the original release of *At Fillmore East*, remains the definitive recording of the song, but between then and now, three other versions that were recorded during the shows for the album have been released (as well as a few other archival releases recorded in other shows featuring Duane). In each, Duane plays with the introduction, changing up the notes slightly but never duplicating Davis's version, as he does on the originally released version.

Over the years, the song has come to be one of the main signatures of the Duane-era band. It encapsulates the band's ability to take an old blues song, even one that has been arranged by someone else, and essentially erase all other versions from the minds of most fans. Even when played in the latter years of the band by guitarists who weren't on the original recording, the song transports listeners to this version.

22. "Tuesday's Gone," Lynyrd Skynyrd (from *Pronounced Leh-nerd Skin-nerd*, 1973)

For as hard as Skynyrd rocked, they also had a tender side that showed up occasionally. On their debut album, it took until only the second song for it to make its appearance. Musically, the song is an example of how orchestrated many of Skynyrd songs were. Maybe due to the "redneck" stereotype often played up by music journalists at the time or just a general bias against things from the South, many over the years have mistakenly remembered Skynyrd's music as simple, but with three guitars that never step on each other, there is more planning and orchestration than many consider.

For "Tuesday's Gone," add to those guitars Billy Powell's piano, producer and session man Al Kooper's mellotron and bass (credited to

Roosevelt Gook), and drums provided by Robert Nix, drummer for the Atlanta Rhythm Section. The music, particularly Gary Rossington's evocative lead playing, builds with the emotions of the song laid bare by Van Zant.

Lyrically, "Tuesday's Gone" may very well be Van Zant's songwriting masterpiece. He opens the song by talking to the train he rides, pleading with it to "roll on down the line," to take him far from his home. He then directs his voice to us, telling us that the wind he feels reminds him that he's leaving "his woman at home." "Lord," he nearly cries out through clinched teeth, "Tuesday's gone," he tells us, with that wind. His voice raises, met with other voices before Rossington takes over the pain-filled cry with his sympathetic Les Paul.

Van Zant continues—to us or to no one in particular—saying he doesn't even know where he's going, only that he wants to be left alone. Cryptically, he announces that when this ride is finished, he'll try again, and then, almost as if he snaps back to the present, he reminds us why he's on the train to begin with—to leave his woman, dragging out the words into a moan that leads into the cry of the chorus again. "Train roll on," he cries as Powell brings a beautiful piano piece to play, backed by Ed King's sliding Steve Cropper-esque fills that go by like trees seen through the railcar window Van Zant is looking out of. Suddenly, mellotron-produced strings swell like the boiling emotions inside of him, but he's at a loss for words, letting the strings play out the melody while Powell provides a lullaby of sorts until Rossington's guitar returns with a crying moan that releases the pent-up emotions.

With that, Van Zant is transported, freed. He starts the conversation over, repeating to the train to roll on, reminding us he's now "many miles" from his home, "riding his blues away." At this point, the honesty overwhelms him. It's all been a facade. A hint of anger rises in his sorrow as he nearly growls that Tuesday "had to be free" and that now it is up to him to carry on. He was never leaving his woman behind as he claimed. She had already left him. This was a man on the run from a memory. Now his line about trying again comes into focus. His sorrow is deep, as he repeats the lines about riding his blues away. "Goodbye Tuesday," he sings twice before he can't say it again and lets out a prolonged moan accompanied by Rossington's more impassioned playing. Beside himself with grief, Van Zant can let loose only one final word—"train." It is his salvation, his escape from the pain as he leaves his empty house behind, a

site he can't bear to look back on, so he only looks to the present, to the train that carries him.

The song was never a single, but it became one of Skynyrd's most beloved songs. It's been covered by acts like Metallica and Hank Williams Jr. (both of whom featured Rossington on guitar) and translated into bluegrass and hip-hop.

21. "Melissa," Allman Brothers Band (from *Eat a Peach*, 1972)

Gregg Allman is well known for his organ work, but one of his best songs was written on brother Duane's guitar that was lying around their shared hotel room in 1967. It was the early stages of working on the craft of songwriting, and Gregg was struggling to come up with something he felt good about, when he picked up the guitar, tuned to the open chord of E, and began to strum. The melody began to swirl in his mind while the words slowly formed on his lips. As he told Alan Paul, when he got to the line "But back home he'll always run to sweet . . . ," he could not come up with a name. Nothing he tried worked for him, so he sat the guitar down and chalked it up as another failed attempt. After about a week, he told Paul, he was in a grocery store and heard a woman call out for her young daughter. It struck him suddenly, and he sang that line, finishing it out with "Melissa." He immediately returned to the guitar and finished out the song.

When he played the song for Duane, he loved it. Soon after, the brothers were acting as studio musicians for the band of friend (and future Allman Brothers Band drummer Butch Trucks) 31st of February, when they got the opportunity to record a couple of songs of their own. "Melissa" was one of their first choices. Released in 1972 on the Polydor cash grab *Duane & Gregg Allman*, the song features an altered version of the well-known melody and early examples of Duane's slide guitar work.

The same year as Polydor released the early version of the song, it appeared on the Allman Brothers Band's first release since the death of Duane, *Eat a Peach*. The first three songs of the album serve as a tribute to a brother gone too soon. "Ain't Wastin' Time No More" starts the album with Gregg's life-affirming lyrics about the fragility of life. "Les Brers in A Minor," Dickey Betts's instrumental offering, follows before Gregg revisits one of his brother's favorite songs, "Melissa."

Initially, Gregg was hesitant to play it for the rest of the group, fearing the song was too "soft" for the band." But his brother's years of encouraging words about the song gave him the courage to play it for them. With Duane now gone, the guitar parts fell to Betts to work out. Rather than attempting to replicate Duane's reluctant early slide work, Betts took a copy of the song home to work on.

Just as he had originally written the song, Gregg picks up the acoustic guitar to open the song. Betts enters with a series of Roy Nichols–like reverse string bends over Berry Oakley's descending bass figure just before the rest of the band falls in. Even as he sings in a softer voice than on previous recordings, Gregg's voice stills carries a power and immediacy as he sings about the young road warrior who, no matter where his carefree journey takes him, always returns home to "sweet Melissa."

Betts's guitar winds melodically through the verses and choruses throughout the whole song, leaving the acoustic guitar and B-3 organ to fill out the space his electric rhythm guitar would normally occupy. Weaving between words and phrases without distracting from them, Betts turns in some of his best guitar work in a fitting tribute. A slight echo supplied by his double-tracked guitar gives the lines that close out the song a spectral edge.

The song provided such a bond between the brothers that Gregg sang it at Duane's funeral, turning the song about a wandering lover into a fitting eulogy—"will he lie beneath the clay or will his spirit float away?"

While the song barely entered the charts at the time it was released, it has grown over the years to be one of the best ballads in the rock catalog and is being used in movies, television, and even cell phone commercials.

20. "Highway Song," Blackfoot (from *Strikes*, 1979)

In the post–Lynyrd Skynyrd world of 1978, a new wave of Southern Rock bands worked to forge their way in the rock world. All of the main bands of that wave had a connection to the fallen Southern Rock pioneers. The Rossington Collins Band was, of course, the remnants of Skynyrd. .38 Special contained Ronnie Van Zant's younger brother, Donnie. Molly Hatchet members had grown up in the same neighborhood as Skynyrd in Jacksonville, Florida, and had been nurtured along by Van Zant, who had planned to produce their debut. Blackfoot contained two members, guitarist and lead singer Rickey Medlocke and bassist Greg T. Walker, who had

filled in for missing Skynyrd members when the band recorded their demos in Muscle Shoals before signing to a label.

Drummer Bob Burns and bass player Leon Wilkeson returned to Skynyrd, and Medlocke and Walker went back to the band they had been trying at the time to get signed, Blackfoot, basing themselves out of New Jersey. Shortly after Skynyrd debuted with a smash, Blackfoot was picked up by Island Records. Their debut, *No Reservations*, made no impact, and soon the band was off the label but quickly picked up by Epic Records, then riding on the early success of the Charlie Daniels Band. Produced, as their debut was, by two Swampers (David Hood and Jimmy Johnson, who had produced the Skynyrd demos), their second album again made no noise. But the band continued to tour and make a reputation for themselves as a live band.

It began to pay off in 1978 after a tour of Texas with the band Brownsville Station. Reports of their show reached Brownsville Station manager Al Nalli. After conferring with the band, he was interested in checking out Blackfoot himself. After catching a few shows, he purchased their contract from their manager and got them started on working up songs for a new record. As it turned out, Al Nalli had a sister, Reen, who was the right-hand woman of Atco Records president Doug Morris (she soon became vice president). The team signed the band to the label, and the band was off and running. Taking the band out of their comfort zone and into his, Nalli brought them to his studio in Ann Arbor, Michigan, where, accompanied by Henry Weck, Brownsville Station drummer as engineer, they began to go through the songs they had worked up for the album.

One of the breakout songs was "Highway Song." Unlike a lot of songs about the road life that come from artists living in their tour bus going from arena to arena, "Highway Song" was written by a band scraping from gig to gig in an old van overloaded with equipment. It's by a band who had recorded two records for national labels but who had little to show for it but the miles on the tires.

The song builds on the "Free Bird" model of starting as a ballad and ramping up, but guitarist Charlie Hargrett provides fantastic melodic lead breaks and fills as Rickey Medlocke sings about the toll the road takes on their spirit and relationships. (In an extended live cut available for viewing online, the ballad portion of the song is extended showing Hargrett's melodic chops.) At about the 2:30 mark, Hargrett and Medlocke have a nice twin lead break, showcasing the band's melodic sense before the

background vocals rise like a chorus. At about 4:30, Medlocke takes over the lead as the band speeds up. After about a minute, Hargrett begins to add echoes to Medlocke, punctuating his break before he takes over the lead for a minute. The two trade leads for the remaining minute or so of the song.

"Highway Song" shouldn't be mistaken for a "Free Bird" rip-off or derivative; rather, it is a showcase of a powerful road-tested band finally getting their big-label push. The song reached #26 on the Top 40, although the album failed to chart. *Strikes* would go on to reach gold status in 1980 and platinum status in 1986, proving to be the band's most commercially successful album.

19. "There Goes Another Love Song," Outlaws (from *Outlaws*, 1975)

The Southern Rock landscape had widened by 1975 with a range of music that covered the Allman Brothers Band's deep blues roots, ZZ Top's Texas boogie, and the Charlie Daniels Band's country leanings as well as Wet Willie, the Marshall Tucker Band, Lynyrd Skynyrd, the Amazing Rhythm Aces, the Atlanta Rhythm Section, Grinderswitch, Eric Quincy Tate, Hydra, the Ozark Mountain Daredevils, and Elvin Bishop. It was into this mix that the Outlaws released their debut album. It was the first rock band released by the Arista label, and Clive Davis, the label's head, had great expectations for the band. When their first single was released, Davis wasn't disappointed. "There Goes Another Love Song" quickly began climbing the charts, finally peaking at #34.

According to Hughie Thomasson, the song's cowriter and the vocalist, he was sitting backstage when drummer Monte Yoho ran into the room yelling, "I got it!" He then sang the chorus to Thomasson, who then built the verses around it. (At least one telling of the song's origin has the two backstage, and when a beautiful woman walks by, Yoho leans over and says to Thomasson, "There goes another love song.") It's the chorus of the song, melodic and lending itself to being a sing-along, that moved it up the charts. It also helped set the Outlaws apart in this new and growing group of rockers. The band's melodic sense had been one of the things that captured Clive Davis's attention. Davis had made a reputation of making pop stars, and the Outlaws were proving no exception.

Their vocal harmonies set them apart from other Southern Rock bands and more in line with the Eagles, who were becoming superstars themselves using tight harmonies and, initially, country roots. But while the Outlaws drew from their country roots, they didn't wear their influences on their sleeves. They were able to blend their love of British Invasion groups (particularly the Beatles and the Rolling Stones), their respect for country music, and even the influence of peers like the Allman Brothers Band and Lynyrd Skynyrd into something that was different, bearing little resemblance to the other Southern Rock bands in their category.

As is the case for most bands, the songs on their debut album had come together over a period of several years, years that the band spent traveling across the South in a van playing what gigs they could find to sustain their dream. As a result, even a song like "There Goes Another Love Song," with its upbeat tempo and sing-along lyrics, is laced with a bit of melancholy. The band was away from their friends and family, with only the guys in the band and crew to interact with on a regular basis. When people dream of being a star, they see only that time onstage, not the hours and hours of time spent around people they will more than likely never see again.

The song also hits a chord that so many people, from high school through adulthood, have dealt with. In the song, he is singing about a girl who he has feelings for but who isn't returning them. He's been hard-core friend-zoned. But the time on the road, the loneliness that creeps in during those offstage hours, has increased, intensifying his feelings: "Now I need you more than a friend." Sitting in a room surrounded by people, the singer still feels a deep loneliness, pulled out only by a love song that reminds him of this friend he wishes could be more.

It would be five more years before the Outlaws would crack the Top 40 Singles chart again, though their albums consistently charted, and they became a top concert draw through the late 1970s.

18. "Homesick," Atlanta Rhythm Section (from *Quinella*, 1981)

After the success of *A Rock and Roll Alternative*, the Atlanta Rhythm Section focused on making a name for themselves as a touring act, spending much of 1976 and 1977 on the road before returning to the studio to record *Champagne Jam*, which continued their chart fortunes, landing at #7 on the Pop Albums chart. As Southern Rock began to fall out of favor

with disc jockeys and audiences, their subsequent album, 1979's *Under-dog*, peaked at #26. Live album *Are You Ready!* hit #51 on the Pop Albums chart in 1979, but 1980's *The Boys from Doraville* failed to chart at all. With something to prove, the band returned to the studio and in 1981 released *Quinella*. Leading off the album is the rocker "Homesick," a song that brings back their Southern Rock roots while also making a bid for the arena-rock success that bands like .38 Special were enjoying.

But deeper than the Southern Rock roots that show up in the riffing guitars, the song points to the influence of guitar great Jimi Hendrix, mentioning him only once. The song is one of the most poetic the band put together.

"A native son in a foreign land" references Hendrix's time in England, where he grew in popularity, but the second verse changes perspective to that of a fan with "black posters on the wall" and "hazy dreams of Monterey." Where in the first verse Hendrix was homesick for his literal home, in the following verses the fan is homesick for a past time, a time when he first experienced the pull of the six-string.

The guitars of J. R. Cobb and Barry Bailey punch out a riff as heavy as any they had laid down in their catalog. While the beat drives them, Bailey steps forward to show that he himself may have been the one who had been homesick. Cobb falls back in with Bailey for a few harmony guitar lines that bring to mind an Allman Brothers Band influence before Bailey finishes the song out.

The song wasn't the big hit from the album—that was "Alien"—but it showed that the band could still rock when they wanted to. Ten years later, Travis Tritt, then riding high on the country charts and never one to hide his love of Southern Rock and its influence on his music, included a faithful rendition of the song as the closing track of his second album, which landed at #2 on the Country Albums chart.

17. "Gimme Three Steps," Lynyrd Skynyrd (from *Pronounced Leh-nerd Skin-nerd*, 1973)

There are songs that were released in their time that made little impact on the charts but that have survived to be huge career songs for their artists. "Gimme Three Steps" is one of those songs for Lynyrd Skynyrd. When released as a single from their debut album in 1973, the songs made no

noise. Years later, thanks to the advent of the classic rock radio format, the song can still be heard today.

The song dates back to the band's earliest attempts at songwriting, and they first demoed the song in their Muscle Shoals recording sessions in 1971, where recordings released on *Skynyrd's First: The Complete Muscle Shoals Album* show that the song was fully formed even at that early stage and never underwent any significant changes over the years.

It endures for many reasons, one of which is the catchy double-stop riffing of Gary Rossington on lead guitar. The pounding opening riff is instantly recognizable by music fans around the world. Another reason is the relatable lyrics of the song.

Van Zant tells us the story of the time he was simply dancing with a pretty girl at a local dive when a man walks in, assuming he is trying to seduce his girlfriend. While our narrator tries to talk his way out of the mess, the jealous boyfriend pulls out his .44. Luckily for Van Zant, the man decides to yell at his girl, allowing Van Zant to make a break for the door, yelling back at the man to give him a head start.

The song was inspired by true events, though those events vary, depending on whom you ask. Van Zant said it was about a time someone pulled a gun on him in a club. Rossington tells the story that it was based on a time that he, Van Zant, and Allen Collins went to a bar while underage and that while Van Zant was dancing with a girl, a jealous man pulled a knife on him. Whichever it is, the lyrics ring true, and many people could relate to them.

"Gimme Three Steps" is also a rare recorded example of Van Zant's sense of humor. His reputation as a hell-raiser makes the reaction of the character a surprise to the listener. Instead of standing his ground and fighting it out in some sort of macho alpha male fantasy, he admits his cowardice, even before the gun comes into play. Van Zant even sneaks in the line "as the water fell on the floor," leaving it open to the listener's imagination as to what that water was.

16. "Blue Sky," Allman Brothers Band (from *Eat a Peach*, 1972)

Eat a Peach, the first Allman Brothers Band album released after the death of Duane Allman, was structured as a tribute to the band's founder. The first three songs—"Ain't Wastin' Time No More," "Les Brers in A Minor," and "Melissa"—are Duane-less songs that tie back to him in

some way (covered elsewhere throughout this book). Sides 2 and 4 of the double album featured an expansive live version of the instrumental "Mountain Jam" that was taken, as were the first two songs of side 3, from unused material from the band's third album, *The Allman Brothers Band at Fillmore East*, which featured Duane. The final three songs of side 3 are studio recordings made just prior to Duane's death. Between the funky blues of "Stand Back" and "Little Martha," the acoustic collaboration between Dickey Betts and Duane, sits "Blue Sky."

Inspired by his then-girlfriend and soon-to-be wife Sandy "Bluesky" Wabegijig, Betts wrote the song first as a love song but then decided to go for more of a universal meaning. In the end, the song became more about how people look at the world when they are thankful for where they are at. The river keeps running and goes where it goes as the sun shines above it. The bluebird at peace, blue skies, sunny days, and love are all spiritual in nature when looked at with thanksgiving, regardless of life situation. It all fit where Betts was at the time: in love and in one of the best bands on the planet.

But when he took the song to the band, he felt Gregg Allman should sing it. Duane would have none of it, telling him that it needed his voice. Duane was right. Of course, Gregg's soulful voice could have carried the song, but Betts's earnest delivery of such personally meaningful lyrics carries them someplace different. It also marks Betts's first lead vocal on record.

Standing in contrast to the scorching blues numbers on the album and even the softer, more melodic "Melissa," "Blue Sky" is a slight departure from the Allman Brothers Band's norm. The soulful slide guitar of Duane or Betts's burning blues are replaced here with a much more melodic structure. As much as Duane is remembered now (and was recognized then) for his masterful slide playing, this song showcases his melodic non–slide playing. His subtle, pedal steel–like oblique bends that serve as fills nearly beneath Betts's vocals in the verse and chorus demonstrate a subtlety that adds texture to the song without overplaying.

After the first verse and chorus, Duane takes the first solo, his Les Paul tone round and fat as he moves up and down the neck of the guitar. Betts soon joins him as the two play a harmony passage that serves as the handoff of the baton, where Betts takes over, his Les Paul tone round but slightly thinner that Duane's, allowing a distinction to be made between the two guitarists. Betts makes his trips up and down the frets before

Duane returns, and they reprise their harmony part. The two guitarists are in total sync, their styles playing off each other and feeding each other at the same time. Betts has said in interviews that the two discussed the urge to be jealous of one another's playing but were able to skirt the line in favor of playing what was right for the song instead of their egos.

But a band, even a Southern Rock one, isn't just made up of two guitars, however incredible the players. In "Blue Sky"—and indeed much of the early Allman Brothers Band's catalog—the often unsung player is bass player Berry Oakley. In the way that Betts essentially plays one song-length solo in "Melissa," returning occasionally to established licks and riffs, Oakley does the same in "Blue Sky." In the introduction, he holds the bottom line with root notes while also doubling the sliding riff the guitarists are playing. During the verses and choruses, he explores an octave-based walking bass line that gives the happy-sounding song its bounce. But during the solo sections in the middle of the song, Oakley stretches out, playing what amounts to a long, bouncy solo that travels from one end of the fretboard to the other and back again. The fact that he does this without tripping over or drowning out the guitars is testament to his skill.

Although the song was never technically a hit, it quickly became a crowd favorite and a classic rock radio mainstay.

15. "La Grange," ZZ Top (from *Tres Hombres*, 1973)

There isn't a song on this list as rich with trivia as "La Grange." If you're ever asked to connect ZZ Top and Dolly Parton, here's your path. Although the song is named after La Grange, Texas, the actual subject of the song sat just a few miles from there and became known as the Chicken Ranch. "The Ranch" started in 1844 as a three-woman operation that ran out of a local motel. The operation moved around and expanded as the years rolled on, generally under the guise of being a boardinghouse for girls. In the midst of the Great Depression, they began to take chickens and other small livestock as payment, gaining the nickname the Chicken Ranch.

Just as *Tres Hombres*, ZZ Top's third album and the album containing the song, was released in July 1973, Houston news reporter Marvin Zindler was taking to the airwaves to inform the city of the illegal brothel operating right under their noses. Zindler had previously worked for the

sheriff's office as a fraud officer and had joined KTRK-TV as a reporter in January 1973. In July, he appeared on the nightly newscast to report that the station had received anonymous tips that a brothel was operating openly but that one could not operate that way without someone in authority as protection. His continued exposé forced authorities to shut the brothel down.

The story inspired two *Playboy* features, one of which was adapted into a Broadway musical titled *The Best Little Whorehouse in Texas* in 1978. In 1982, nearly ten years after the closing of the Chicken Ranch, Dolly Parton and Burt Reynolds starred in the big-screen feature adaptation of the play. The movie was a huge success, grabbing big box-office numbers and award nominations.

But Zindler was correct, the Chicken Ranch had been an open secret for many years. ZZ Top's bass player and vocalist said, "A lot of boys in Texas, when it's time to be a guy, went there and had it done. Fathers took their sons there," noting that he himself lost his virginity there at age thirteen. So there's your second piece of trivia.

Musically, it is one of ZZ Top's most instantly recognizable songs. When Billy Gibbons's opening guitar riff rings out, accompanied by Frank Beard's skittering stick work, ears perk up and toes begin to tap. The song became the band's first to break the Top 50 (the album hit #8 on the Top 100 Albums chart). The song and the album cracked open ZZ Top's commercial potential and put them on their path to stardom. As their fame and bank accounts grew, so did their target. By 1992, they were world-renowned superstars, so Bernard Benson, who held the copyright to a John Lee Hooker song called "Boogie Chillen," decided the famous riff was a little too similar and sued the trio for copyright infringement.

Counsel for the band argued that the riff was based loosely on the 1948 version of the song and that Benson, to whom John Lee Hooker had assigned his copyrights, didn't register "Boogie Chillen" with the U.S. Copyright Office until 1967, making the earlier version technically an unpublished work. Under the then-current copyright law, the 1948 version of the song would have been considered in the public domain. Eventually, after a long and costly legal battle, the court sided with ZZ Top, and the case set in motion reforms to the copyright law in 1988.

But "Boogie Chillen" can't claim sole influence on the song (which makes the copyright case a bit more interesting). Hooker first recorded

the song in 1948, and in 1955, Bo Diddley recorded "Bring It to Jerome," a maracas-laden song that uses a variation of the riff as its rhythm. Blues-man Slim Harpo released "Shake Your Hips" in 1966, again using a blend of Hooker's riff mixed with a bit of the "Bring It to Jerome" rhythm. By the time "La Grange" debuted as a single in 1974, rock listeners' ears were well adjusted to the sound. John Lee Hooker teamed up with blues rockers Canned Heat to release 1971's *Hooker 'N Heat*, which contains the song "Boogie Chillen No. 2." That version fuses his earlier versions with a little more pop from Harpo's "Hips." In 1972, the Rolling Stones released *Exile on Main Street*, including a faithfully rendered version of "Shake Your Hips."

What sets ZZ Top's version apart is the sheer attitude embodied in the song, bringing into it some of the original rawness of the Hooker version brought full force into the rock scene of the 1970s. For the recording, Gibbons put his trusty Les Paul (the famed Pearly Gates) away and pulled out a 1955 Fender Stratocaster, forgoing his love of effects and plugging straight into a 1969 Marshall Super Lead 100 amp. Instead of overdub-bing various guitars for different tones, as he would do on future releases, Gibbons depended solely on the pickup selector to change tones.

The song contains one of Gibbons's finest solos. The tube-driven distortion highlights the blues-rooted solo of the first section, leaning on a few classic blues phrases. But it doesn't lean so much as to sound deriva-tive or too copycat. Instead, Gibbons pours feeling into the double-stops and harmony lines before bringing the band into a turnaround. The turn-around serves only as a brief resting spot before Gibbons bubbles up again. The second part of the solo has become one of Gibbons's trade-mark solos and the one that drove a million young guitarists crazy trying to figure out just how he got those sounds. Before hair metal axe slingers started overusing the artificial harmonics–whammy bar combination, Gibbons was making his Strat squeal with glee. An artificial harmonic is a note you can get on a stringed instrument, like a guitar, by striking it with a pick and catching it with the flesh of a thumb or finger to create a higher pitched note than what is actually being fretted by the other hand. While the first section of the solo stays rooted heavily in the blue masters of the past, the second section shows Gibbons charting his own path forward. Instead of the standard plastic pick, Gibbons uses a filed down Mexican peso. The combination of the metal peso, the steel strings, and Gibbons's thumb is like guitar alchemy. Striking the string in different

spots produces different squeals, and Gibbons uses it here to maximum effect.

14. "Midnight Rider," Allman Brothers Band (from *Idlewild South*, 1970)

The scene opens with a tight shot across what appears to be a river, tall grass, and tree branches waving in the breeze. Suddenly a man, dressed in black pants, a black button-down shirt, and a black cowboy hat perched on his head casting a shadow over the red mask covering his face, appears sitting on the bank. He turns and points his finger at the camera and disappears as quickly as he appeared. The remaining two minutes of the video feature more of the same with the mysterious man appearing in frame and then disappearing while interspersed are shots of a silver dollar. Mystery surrounded the figure in this video announcing the appearance of the Midnight Rider in the mid-South wrestling territory. The sound track of the clip went along with the character's name, "Midnight Rider," but for this, it was the 1979 version recorded by Willie Nelson for the sound track to the movie *Electric Horseman*.

The Midnight Rider had made his first appearance in Florida Championship Wrestling to avenge his friend Dusty Rhodes, who had lost a match with the stipulation that he lose his job if he was defeated. Once that wrong was avenged, the Midnight Rider disappeared and reappeared (with a different mask) in the mid-South territory. A few years later, he would reappear in the National Wrestling Alliance territories of the South, avenging, once again, wrongs done to his friend Rhodes.

The choice of song and character name was perfect. Wrestling, particularly in the late 1970s and early 1980s, appealed to working-class viewers who used that weekly hour to escape their daily problems and root on wrestlers like Dusty Rhodes, the son of a plumber, who routinely wore hats and shirts emblazoned with the names of Southern Rock bands or country artists as he tangled with the avatars of avarice, the Four Horsemen, whose leader, the champion Ric Flair, bragged routinely about his $1,000 shoes and was shown boarding private jets and escorting beautiful ladies into the back of limousines.

"Midnight Rider" served as a perfect theme song for the character and struck the audience as the rest of the wrestling fantasy world did. Written by Gregg Allman and Kim Payne, a roadie for the Allman Brothers Band,

the song draws on the themes of being a loner, an outlaw, who must constantly be on the run. Its loping rhythm evokes the rhythm of a traveling horse as it goes from town to town. "I'm not going to let them catch me," Allman sings, identifying himself as the Midnight Rider.

Appearing on the band's second album, *Idlewild South*, the song showed a different facet of the band as Duane Allman sets aside his Les Paul to pick up his acoustic guitar, playing the distinctive riff that opens the song and serves as its driving force. Dickey Betts serves up pedal steel–inspired oblique bends to punctuate the midsection of the song and serve as its solo. It's unlike any other Allman Brothers Band solo in that it eschews the fiery playing Duane and Betts generally exhibited in favor of something that sits deeper within the framework of the song.

While this original version of the song is the definitive version, the song spawned several other recordings. It became a part of their live set and was recorded during the concerts at Fillmore that made up their third album but wasn't released until the 2003 deluxe edition of *At Fillmore East* (and again on the 2014 expanded version of the concert). It has also shown up on archival releases with shows from 1972 and 1973, the latter recordings without Duane, with Chuck Leavell's piano filling in during the solo back-and-forth between guitars.

For his 1973 solo album *Laid Back*, Gregg recorded a version of the song that slightly slows the tempo and prominently features horns throughout. The following year, two years before he recorded the Marshall Tucker Band's "Can't You See," Waylon Jennings dipped into the Southern Rock world and recorded his version of "Midnight Rider" for *Ramblin' Man*. Hank Williams Jr. likewise returned to the Southern Rock catalog a few years after Nelson's release, in 1983, to record a version for his Top Five charting album *Man of Steel*. Aside from the Outlaw Country artists who flirted with Southern Rock, the song has been recorded over the years by bluegrass artists and even pop-reggae band UB40.

The song's lyrics tap into the fantasy of living the outlaw life, and many people in all walks of life have found a way to identify with and draw personal meaning from them. The song continues to be a crowd favorite in Allman's live shows.

13. "Simple Man," Lynyrd Skynyrd (from *Pronounced Leh-nerd Skin-nerd*, 1973)

"Mama" has always been an important topic for country songs, starting early in country music and the folk ballad tradition. In southern culture, she has often taken on a legendary, near mystical quality, seen as a shining example to follow and a figure of longing when far from home. It was certainly true for the boys of Lynyrd Skynyrd. After attending the funeral for leader Ronnie Van Zant's grandmother, Van Zant started talking with his partners Gary Rossington and Allen Collins about the advice she had passed onto him, and the others shared similar stories. Out of that conversation came the song "Simple Man."

In it, "Mama" draws her young boy close to her and tells him how to be happy and satisfied in life. Her first piece of advice is for the young man to slow down and enjoy life, not rushing through it missing what is around him. She quickly follows that up by telling him that in his life there will be troubles but that they are fleeting. Next, she says, find a good woman to love and be loved by. Last but not least, when those troubles come, remember to turn to "someone up above."

"Be a simple man," she tells him, something he can "love and understand." It's not the same as being told to not get above your raising, which carries with it the connotation that the person is not only leaving behind the life he grew up with but also looking back with some slight condescension or pity on those who still remain.

The second verse picks up where the first left off as she reminds him that he has been raised with the tools, the principles, and the morals that will aid him in life, so he needs to forget the lust for money because it alone won't bring him satisfaction. The chorus is repeated, and Van Zant sings at perhaps his most soulful before answering, for the first time, her advice with "Oh yes I will."

"Simple Man" marks one of the few double lead guitar parts in Skynyrd's catalog. Although they had three guitars, they often played their own parts, with only one of them taking a solo at a time. The Allman Brothers Band, a band the Skynyrd crew greatly admired, had made a mark for themselves with the intricate harmony solos of Duane Allman and Dickey Betts. But here, Rossington and Collins double the lead break in unison, playing the same notes. It is mixed so tightly on the album that it often sounds as if there is only one guitar, but the original version,

released on *Skynyrd's First: The Complete Muscle Shoals Album* and on the live release *One More from the Road*, exhibits the distinction.

After the solo, Van Zant returns with one last piece of advice that echoes the earlier advice. She tells him he will find his place in this world if he follows the advice she's just offered and the morals instilled in him throughout his early life. The earnestness in Van Zant's voice shows how much this advice, something he says in concert that his grandmother gave him, was a deeply held belief. It was a very personal statement from the band that summed up how they would strive to lead their lives.

It was something producer Al Kooper couldn't grasp at first. Legend has it that the band played him the song and that he told them they weren't recording it. Van Zant then walked Kooper out to his car and told him they were recording it and they would call him when they were finished. Kooper, on the other hand, simply says it wasn't that he disliked the song but that he liked other songs better and didn't feel "Simple Man" was a good fit "editorially" for the album. In other words, why would you want to stick a song like that on an album filled with songs about leaving women and being a rambler? Kooper didn't understand the power of "Mama" (it wouldn't be the last time a "southern thing" befuddled him). Regardless of how it actually went down, the result was that Kooper added a subtle organ part and came to love the song.

He wasn't the only one. The song has become an anthem—a representation of the fans that perfectly aligns them with the band as they perceive it.

12. "The Devil Went Down to Georgia," Charlie Daniels Band (from *Million Mile Reflections*, 1979)

The success of *Fire on the Mountain* and its two popular singles, "The South's Gonna Do It Again" and "Long Haired Country Boy," propelled the success of the Charlie Daniels Band. The group had already been touring incessantly, but their new success required even more roadwork to maintain it. During that time, the band underwent a few personnel changes, bringing in Tommy Crain on guitar and Charlie Hayward on bass. Shortly thereafter, the band headed back into the studio with producer Paul Hornsby, who had helped them define their sound on the previous album. The result was *Nightrider*, a good album that followed

the path laid out by *Fire on the Mountain* but that failed to connect with listeners outside of their core group of fans.

Undeterred, the group continued touring and in 1975 left Kama Sutra for Epic Records, debuting with *Saddle Tramp* in 1976. It was another fine set of tunes, though it produced no hit singles. With Epic's promotion, the album reached #7 on the Country Albums chart and #35 on the Pop Albums chart. In 1977, the group released two albums: *High Lonesome* and *Midnight Wind. High Lonesome* failed to chart or produce any singles, and *Midnight Wind* barely missed the Country Albums Top 40 (hitting #42) but likewise produced no singles.

In a time when album-oriented rock was wide open, the lack of singles didn't hurt the band's standing with the label. "Southern Rock" as a marketing tag was beginning to wane, but country music fans were beginning to take notice of the more country influenced of the bands, as they had the Charlie Daniels Band over the past several albums. The country music landscape was changing, too. The Outlaw Movement had opened the door to mixing country influences with more pop ones, and artists like Barbara Mandrell, Mickey Gilley, and others were mixing in adult contemporary and low-grade rhythm and blues into their songs.

Gathering in a Nashville studio in late 1978, the band was ready to record their new album. Their three albums on Epic had done little to bolster the success they had acquired with *Fire on the Mountain,* so the decision was made to switch producers. They didn't have to look very far to find one. John Boylan, who had previously worked with Linda Ronstadt, Pure Prairie League, Commander Cody, and Boston, was now the vice president of Epic. With the goal of tweaking his sound, Daniels asked Boylan to come onboard, and the collaboration produced *Million Mile Reflections.* If the goal was to change up the sound, it was certainly accomplished. Horns, string sections, and female backup singers populated the songs, taking them in a different direction than previous albums. The overall sound of the album is a much slicker affair, something that reflected a little more of what was going on in country music while still tipping its hat to their rock influences—except for one song.

As the band wrapped up recording, Daniels looked at the band excitedly and said, "We forgot a fiddle tune!" In the next few minutes, Daniels and the band worked up "The Devil Went Down to Georgia." The song utilized Daniels's knack for storytelling and drew on his knowledge of music history. It was a story that had been around for centuries, written in

places like the short story "Rival Fiddlers," from the late 1800s, and the 1925 Stephen Vincent Benét poem "The Mountain Whippoorwill," both of which feature fiddle duels with Satan. In Daniels's retelling, it is an amalgam of fiddle tunes that finally defeats the Devil.

It was the most traditional-sounding song on the album, Daniels's fiddle out front, proud and loud. The song would have fit perfectly on an album like *Fire on the Mountain*, but it stood out on *Million Mile Reflection* like an aberration. Nevertheless, the band thought the song was good enough to garner some airplay—so much so that Daniels took two passes at the vocals: the first where he calls the Devil a son of a bitch and the second where he calls him a son of a gun. This way, more progressive radio stations could play one version and conservative stations the other. Or, as Daniels is fond of saying, he recorded a Methodist version and a Baptist version, and he's not saying which is which.

Their hunch proved correct. The song exploded and soon after its 1979 release reached #1 on the Country chart and #3 on the Top 40, propelling the album to #1 on the Country Albums chart and #5 on the Albums chart. The song was a crowd favorite in concert as Daniels and band blazed stages across the country. The group was awarded the Country Music Association (CMA) Award for Instrumental Group of the Year and Daniels the CMA Award for Instrumentalist of the Year, while the song took "Single of the Year." They also took home the Grammy for Best Country Vocal Performance by a Duo or Group for "The Devil Went Down to Georgia."

Nearly a year after the song had reached its peak, the Charlie Daniels Band made a cameo, performing the song in the John Travolta movie *Urban Cowboy*. Interest in the song was renewed. Stations received requests for the song constantly, to the point that Ed Salamon, program director of New York's WHN, said it was getting as much airplay as a new release. The song was popular enough that in some places, like in Daniels's home state of North Carolina, ads for the movie trumpeted, "See and hear Charlie Daniels and his Award Winning Country Music 'Band of the Year'!"—for a scene that clocks in at less than four minutes.

The song remains an enduring classic. In 2008, the makers of the video game *Guitar Hero* included the song as the final test to beat the game. In it, you must defeat the Devil (though he is never called that) by outplaying him on a heavy metal version of the song. Daniels was quick to denounce the game on the grounds that the "Devil" won the game more

often than not and in his eyes destroyed the message of the song. (Daniels had lost the rights to the song years before.)

Even so, it remains a centerpiece of his live shows, including his appearances at the Grand Ole Opry, where he is now a member.

11. "Dreams"/"Dreams I'll Never See," Allman Brothers Band/ Molly Hatchet (from *The Allman Brothers Band*, 1969/*Molly Hatchet*, 1978)

The Allman Brothers Band undoubtedly originated Southern Rock. But when their first album, *The Allman Brothers Band*, was released in 1969, very few noticed. Commercially, the album was close to a flop. Artistically, on the other hand, it was a statement of a band forging their own creative path. Of the album's seven tracks, five were written by Gregg Allman and worked up by the band. Gregg had been persuaded to join the band by his brother Duane while Gregg was in California working to get out of an ill-fitting record deal. While in California, he worked on his songwriting, and when he finally made it back to Georgia, those songs became the puzzle piece that had been missing in his brother's band.

One of those song was "Dreams." Built on a shuffle beat, the song begins softly with Gregg's swirling Hammond B-3 organ. The band's two drummers, Jai Johanny "Jaimoe" Johanson and Butch Trucks, set a jazz pace based on the John Coltrane version of "My Favorite Things." Berry Oakley serves up a hypnotic walking bass run as the guitars remain subtly in the background.

"Just one more morning," Gregg sings out, greeting the morning with the downbeat realization that his life remains in motion as the dreams he has harbored float somewhere there in front of him. As he rolls out of bed, his goal for the day remains the same as every other day: to "climb up on the hilltop" with the sole purpose of seeing what he can see.

Gregg's gravelly moan reveals the Sisyphean task that it has become. Once on the hilltop, he can only see those things he can never have. These dreams are elusive thoughts and goals that remain out of the reach of a man who daily looks for them. "I'm hung up," he says, "on dreams I never see."

It came from where he lived at the time. He had made it to California with his brother, and they landed the recording contract they dreamed of as teens. But as so often happens, the label wanted to remake them into

something they weren't. They succeeded in separating the starry-eyed, charismatic, good-looking lead singer away from the band and bound him to a contract he neither understood or comprehended. Now he was alone in California, withering on the label's creative vine. Stardom, creative freedom, fame, musical innovation—all dreams that were just beyond his grasp.

Once he shook loose the shackles of his previous label, he joined his brother Duane and the band he had assembled. "Dreams" was fully formed lyrically when they stepped into that New York City studio with legendary producer Tom Dowd. The band worked up the arrangement. The music laid claim to being both a blues-jazz hybrid and the burgeoning psychedelic music movement of the time.

The music is both dreamlike and entrancing as Gregg soulfully sings through his pain, breaking from that only when he proclaims that "the whole world's fallin' down" around him. Then Duane's guitar comes front and center, the organ stabs, and the drummers echo the world's fall.

As the music settles back into its calmer state, Duane's guitar comes in, echoing Gregg's tone for a bit before becoming something of its own. His jazz influences on display, Duane continues to glide through the fretboard. Halfway through, a slight bit of feedback announces his switch to his slide, which adds to the swirling vibe of the song's rhythm. Three minutes later, Gregg comes down from the hilltop, carrying with him the realization once again that these dreams will not come for him and that this painful wishing will "be the end of me."

The song in its original version stretched out for almost seven-and-a-half minutes, but live versions ran from around the 10:00 mark to just under twenty minutes, each version featuring longer versions of Duane's exquisite guitar work.

That guitar work laid the foundation for what was called Southern Rock, and the first wave of southern rockers, led by Marshall Tucker, Wet Willie, and Lynyrd Skynyrd, effectively came to an end with the 1977 plane crash that killed Skynyrd's Ronnie Van Zant and Steve Gaines. The second wave of southern rockers leaned a little more to the pop end of the spectrum, led by groups like .38 Special and even the Rossington Collins Band, made up of survivors of the Skynyrd tragedy.

One of the hardest rocking of the bands in the second wave was Molly Hatchet, who on their self-titled debut album offered up their version of

"Dreams" (titled "Dreams I'll Never See") as an homage to the band that had started the genre nearly ten years before.

But the version present on *Molly Hatchet* bears little resemblance to the "Dreams" of the Allman Brothers Band. Instead, it owes its arrangement to a little-noticed version of the song released not long after the Allman Brothers Band's own version.

In May 1970, six months after the release of *The Allman Brothers Band*, Buddy Miles of Jimi Hendrix's Band of Gypsys and the Electric Flag released his third solo album, *Them Changes*. Among the songs included on the album was his straightforward version of "Dreams." Replacing the breezy shuffle beat with a powerhouse 4/4 rock beat, Miles moves the song to another place.

Molly Hatchet grabbed ahold of the Miles version, including the instantly identifiable opening guitar part and even the opening figure of the first guitar solo, and continued to move the song on, making it their own.

Replacing the B-3 of the original and even the funk-inflected Buddy Miles opening with a hard-edged distorted guitar, Hatchet proclaims their differences with previous versions right away. Gone are Gregg Allman's soulful vocals filling the lyrics with remorse for what couldn't be attained. Instead, vocalist Danny Joe Brown's contemptuous growl spits out the words. The regretful looking forward to elusive dreams is replaced with a fatalist acknowledgment that the dreams are gone.

While Allman climbs the hill to look over a paradise just out of his reach, Brown looks over the smoldering rubble of what remains. The dreams are not dangling before him as some sort of carrot on a stick. Instead, they lay in the road trampled under the feet of those who've gone before him. The heavy stomp of the drums reinforces the weight of the lyrics and the meaning Brown drenches them with.

What sets the Molly Hatchet versions apart from either of the previous versions and has made it a fan favorite are the guitar parts. Gone is Duane's jazz-infused slide. Aside from the opening notes of Charlie Karp's guitar solo on the Miles version, with its Leslie speaker effect, Hatchet guitarists Duane Roland and Steve Holland take the guitar work on as a showcase. Their guitars take the song from its psychedelic beginnings to somewhere deeper into hard rock.

This is the only time on this list where one song performed by two different bands is highlighted and there is a reason for that. Fans can choose which they prefer the most, but the fact is that both bands owned

their version of the song. The Allman Brothers Band put down a proclamation of the type of music they were setting out to make. Molly Hatchet offered up an homage to those founders and at the same time put their own mark on the song.

10. "The South's Gonna Do It Again," Charlie Daniels Band (from *Fire on the Mountain*, 1974)

Charlie Daniels had been a studio musician playing on albums by Bob Dylan and Leonard Cohen before initially signing with Capitol. His first album owed more to the Band than his country roots. He was soon gone from Capitol and signed to Kama Sutra, home to acts like Sha Na Na, Flamin' Groovies, Gunhill Road, and NRBQ. Rather than another solo project, Daniels formed the Charlie Daniels Band and released their first album, *Te John, Grease, & Wolfman.* With one notable exception, neither it nor its subsequent follow-ups (*Honey in the Rock* and *Way Down Yonder*) made any impact.

That exception was the single from *Honey in the Rock*, "Uneasy Rider," which reached the Top Ten on the Pop chart. Follow-ups to the song failed to make a mark, and it is easy to see why. "Uneasy Rider" was a recitation atop a rambling acoustic band, a good-humored poke at rednecks featuring the triumph of a long-haired country boy. Listeners looking for something musically similar to this on Charlie Daniels Band albums were out of luck. While the band was made up of top-notch musicians (including Jimi Hendrix bassist Billy Cox) and the jams were sufficiently kicking, the music didn't stray from the Allman Brothers Band mold, complete with dual drummers and twin guitars. Daniels's fiddle was faintly heard in the background on a few songs over the three albums, but there was nothing that set the group apart.

The Southern Rock fraternity was growing, and the band was touring as a support act for Lynyrd Skynyrd and the Marshall Tucker Band, a band Daniels had come to consider brothers. The Marshall Tucker Band's debut album had been a success, and Daniels decided to approach their producer, Paul Hornsby, to produce a new album. Hornsby had played with Duane and Gregg Allman in Hour Glass and had become a staff producer at Capricorn Records. After a few failed tries at producing, Hornsby hit a home run with the Marshall Tucker Band's debut and soon became an independent producer. He agreed to come out to see a few

Charlie Daniels Band shows but came away with the opinion that, while talented, there wasn't anything that stood out about the band—until Daniels brought out the fiddle and did "Orange Blossom Special" as an encore. The crowd reaction sealed the deal for Hornsby.

The result was *Fire on the Mountain*, an album that is sonically very different than previous Charlie Daniels Band albums, featuring the fiddle prominently. With a new producer and a new sound, the band caught the proverbial lightning in a bottle. Due to touring requirements and a low budget, the band had only eleven days in the studio to complete the album. For the most part, Daniels brought in finished songs, along with a few ideas, like the instrumental "Fiddle Boogie." The band and the producer liked it well enough, but Hornsby felt it could use lyrics because he didn't think it was strong enough to stand alone as an instrumental. Each morning, he asked Daniels if he'd thought of anything for it. Daniels would wave him off and tell him not to worry. On the last day of recording, Daniels still hadn't shown Hornsby anything, so the band took a break. When Daniels came back in, he asked them to put on the track so he could show them an idea he had. In the studio, he began to sing the lines now known as "The South's Gonna Do It Again."

The song was chosen by the label as the lead single and was a hit (hitting #29 on the Top 100) that became a rallying cry for Southern Rock fans across the country. By name checking other groups given the "Southern Rock" tag, including Lynyrd Skynyrd, Dickey Betts of the Allman Brothers Band, ZZ Top, Elvin Bishop, Grinderswitch, Barefoot Jerry, and others, the Charlie Daniels Band had created a theme for the movement. To Daniels, it was simply a shout-out to friends and peers utilizing the common phrase as the song's title; it wasn't meant as a political statement, though that might have been a naive mistake on Daniels's part.

The mid-1970s had seen the rise of Nixon's Silent Majority, the forgotten people who had no one to speak for them. It was a group often characterized as angry white men that at this time in pop culture, particularly in country music, was beginning to boil. Merle Haggard had seen great success in 1969 with "Okie from Muskogee," a song that cast dispersions on hippies and the youth culture, and again in 1970 with "The Fightin' Side of Me." In 1975, country singer Jim Mundy recorded one of Haggard's songs (one that Haggard wouldn't record until 1977), "I'm a White Boy." Mundy's label, ABCDot, had been waiting for the right

political climate to release the song and decided that late 1975 was the time. Although Mundy had high hopes for the song, it failed to do more than generate some publicity and polarize some listeners.

And while Southern Rock fans latched onto "The South's Gonna Do It Again," others looked at it as a cry to return to the old ways of the South. While Daniels remained noncommittal to any translation that veered away from the song being a play on the "Southern Rock" marketing tag, he made remarks in the press that could give others fuel for the fire. For example, when asked why Southern Rock was so popular, Daniels explained it was because southern bands made music that the people could understand. But in making the comment, he cited the speeches of George Wallace, the controversial segregationist governor of Alabama, saying, "I wouldn't vote for Wallace, but I can understand every word that comes out of his mouth."

By the same token, shortly after the song was released, the national director of the Knights of the Ku Klux Klan, David Duke, began to put together radio commercials to recruit new members, choosing "The South's Gonna Do It Again" for the musical sound track. In response, Daniels said that he was proud of the South, but "I sure as hell ain't proud of the Ku Klux Klan." After the threat of a lawsuit, the Klan dropped their use of the song.

Regardless of political intent or implication, the song remains one of the finest examples of Southern Rock. From the opening fiddle line to the toe-tapping rhythm, the song is a new rebel yell, calling fans of this thing called Southern Rock together.

9. "Train, Train," Blackfoot (from *Strikes*, 1979)

It's not unusual for a Southern Rock band to pay tribute to the music that came before them, as we've seen several times throughout this book, but none did it as directly as Blackfoot. In Blackfoot's case, it was honoring not only the music but also the man who made the music—Shorty Medlocke, the maternal grandfather of Blackfoot founder Rickey Medlocke.

Medlocke was a regionally popular bluegrass and country artist who hosted his own local television music variety show in the Jacksonville, Florida, area. It was Shorty who showed young Rickey how to play a variety of instruments, featuring him on the television show at a young age. When Rickey was entering his teenage years, Shorty took him to see

two concerts, one starring Elvis Presley and the other Buddy Holly, that would change Rickey's world. When Rickey formed his own band, Shorty leased a building that he nicknamed "The Barn," where he hosted Friday and Saturday night dances featuring a set of rock and roll by Rickey's group and a set of bluegrass and country by his group, Shorty Medlock and the Fla. Plow Hands.

Soon, Rickey and the band were playing local clubs and trading members with other groups. By 1969, the group that would be known as Blackfoot formed: Rickey on guitar and vocals, Greg T. Walker on bass, Jakson Spires on drums, and Charlie Hargrett on lead guitar. After gigging around the South, the band decided to move to New York to try to land a recording contract.

Times were lean for the band, and in 1971, they were ready to throw in the towel. Rickey, Walker, and Spires returned to the South with Rickey and Walker going with Lynyrd Skynyrd to record some demos in Muscle Shoals, Alabama. In the meantime, Shorty and his group continued to entertain and that same year decided to try a little recording of their own. Joined by daughter Mickey (Rickey's mother) and billed as Shorty Medlock & Mickey with the Fla. Plow Hands, the group recorded two songs. The A-side is a steel guitar–drenched country number called "If I Could Live It Over (I'd Be a Different Guy)." The B-side is a high-octane country-blues tune written by Shorty called "Train, Train." The song kicks off with propulsive acoustic guitar before Shorty's harmonica charges in emulating the sound of an approaching train while a train whistle sounds in the background. The 45-rpm recording was strictly for regional distribution (and is extremely rare today). Although he didn't record any other songs, he continued to write and perform.

Shorty's influence first pops up in Southern Rock on Lynyrd Skynyrd's 1974 album *Second Helping*—though anonymously—where his influence on the young Ronnie Van Zant is woven in with an amalgam of influences that make up the old musician in "The Ballad of Curtis Loew." *Nuthin' Fancy* (1975) included "Made in the Shade," a laid-back blues that borders on jug band music that Ronnie introduces: "Well when I was a young-un' they used to teach me to play music like this here." In the liner notes, the song carries the dedication "This one's for Shorty Medlock."

That same year, Blackfoot released their debut album, *No Reservations*, on Island Records. The album opens with "Railroad Man," a song

written by Shorty. Going a step further, the album also closes with "Railroad Man," but instead of the band's overdriven guitars and twin riffing, it featured acoustic guitar, mandolin, harmonica, banjo, and vocals, all by Shorty. Neither the album nor their second release did anything commercially, but the band was picked up as a supporting act for a few small tours with Peter Frampton, Kiss, and Ted Nugent.

The band's breakthrough came with their Atco Records debut *Strikes* and another song written by Shorty, "Train, Train." As the song opens, it is only Shorty, solo on the harmonica, repeating his chugging train, growing faster until at about the thirty-eight-second mark the band comes in, the guitars and bass chugging in place of the harp, Spires's drums hammering them on. Suddenly, the harmonica wails though this time played by coproducer Henry Weck's Brownsville Station band mate Cub Koda, who also takes a blistering solo in the middle of the song. Guitar-wise, the studio version is a showcase for Rickey's adept slide playing. (The live version, released on 1982's *Highway Song Live*, which is slightly sped up and thunders forward even harder than the original take, replaces the harmonica solo with a little guitar back-and-forth between Rickey and Hargrett before involving the crowd in a little sing-along. It also shows that before management tried to steer them toward pop, they were a hell of a hard-rocking act.)

"Train, Train" was a hard-hitting song that has become a favorite hard-rock sing-along for fans everywhere. Shorty passed away in 1982, and in the few years between the song's release and then, he enjoyed every bit of the attention, appearing, at age sixty-seven, at shows close to home to play his now famous harmonica intro. In 1999, country superstar Dolly Parton took the song back to its acoustic roots when she recorded it on her first-ever bluegrass album, *Grass Is Blue*.

8. "Keep On Smilin'," Wet Willie (from *Keep On Smilin'*, 1974)

Even a short trip through Wet Willie's catalog will show you they are a band about excitement, joy, and enthusiasm. Vocalist Jimmy Hall's exuberance is one of the prime characteristics of the group, cheered on by the gospel-flavored vocals of the Willettes. Even when they get the blues, there is an optimistic hope embedded within them.

Wet Willie's first two albums, containing some fine examples of their rock and soul music, garnered very little notice from music consumers or

critics. In a move that imitated their heroes, they set their sights on a live album for their third release. It at least charted on the *Billboard* Top 200, but it still got little reaction. Undeterred, the band continued to grind it out on the road, winning fans with their live shows. During those years they toured heavily, opening for ZZ Top; the Allman Brothers Band; Foghat; the supergroup of Jeff Beck, Tim Bogert, and Carmine Appice; and Sly and the Family Stone. Those who couldn't make it to a show could see them on syndicated late-night live music shows such as *Don Kirshner's Rock Concert* and *Midnight Special*.

In addition to keeping a high profile, the decision was also made to move from producer Eddie Offord, who had produced their first two albums, to Tom Dowd, who had worked with soul artists Wilson Pickett, Otis Redding, Solomon Burke, and Aretha Franklin and rock artists Derek and the Dominos (the Eric Clapton project including Duane Allman) and Eric Quincy Tate.

While things were gearing up in his career, Jimmy Hall was suffering loss in his personal life with the toll of the road claiming yet another relationship. Rather than sink into a depression or wallow in the pain, he comforted himself to "keep on smilin'" and put it into a song.

Lewis Ross's drums beat out a short rat-a-tat rhythm, seconded by Ricky Hirsch's guitar, John Anthony's electric piano, and Jack Hall's bass, the two factions trading their licks back and forth, introducing Jimmy Hall's soul-felt vocals. "Well you say you got the blues," he sings sympathetically, noting the person he's talking to has holes in both shoes and is feeling alone and confused. The person is about to go insane because of his cheating woman, who blames him for her shortcomings. Hall offers this advice: "Keep on smilin' through the rain / Laughin' at the pain / Just flowin' with the changes / 'til the sun comes out again."

It's the emotional equivalent of "fake it until you make it." Yet what Hall proposes is something fundamentally deeper than the surface act of smiling. Here he digs into the joy of the band and encourages others to power their attitude with a smile. He was speaking from experience not just from the loss of his beloved but also fronting a high-octane, unique band that in every respect should have been a huge band but instead were stuck in the perpetual opening-act slot.

The second verse could easily be talking about himself, telling, in the first half, of playing small-time gigs and wondering if anyone is even hearing the music. In the second half of the verse, he talks about moving

to the country to escape it all, echoing the sentiments of the album's other single, "Country Side of Life."

Following the verse, Jimmy launches into a harmonica solo, its first notes evoking the hymn "Amazing Grace," giving a clue to where he is looking for the strength to keep on smiling. Indeed, the song that follows it on the album, "Trust in the Lord," is an out-and-out gospel song.

Coming out of the solo, his vocals turn from the sympathetic singing to a soulful shout, perhaps to himself, about hanging out in the local bar wondering "who the hell you are." "Are you a farmer? Are you a star?" he asks, the band returning to the rat-a-tat rhythm of the opening before returning to the chorus, alternating "smilin'," "laughin'," and "flowin'" as the song fades out.

With *Keep On Smilin'*, all of the one-night stands, opening slots, and self-doubt paid off. The album reached #41 on the *Billboard* Albums chart, while the single of the same name made it to #10 on the Hot 100, becoming the band's breakthrough. The song encapsulates the optimism ingrained in the band and is an infectious reminder to press on through trials and hardship.

7. "Take the Highway," Marshall Tucker Band (from *The Marshall Tucker Band*, 1973)

When the needle touched the wax on the Marshall Tucker Band's debut album, listeners were greeted by the fanfare announcing a new and different band in the soon-to-be-called Southern Rock space. Paul Riddle's heavy hit sounds simultaneously with Tommy Caldwell's bass and Toy Caldwell's guitar, while George McCorkle's sparkling electric guitar arpeggiates through them before they hit again and McCorkle is joined by flautist Jerry Eubanks. This was Southern Rock but something different at the same time. When producer Paul Hornsby swoops in with his Moog synthesizer, all bets are off. The Allman Brothers dipped heavily into the blues, sprinkling in heavy shakes of jazz, while Lynyrd Skynyrd strove to be America's Rolling Stones while leaning more on the influence of Free. The Charlie Daniels Band held on to a country influence, while Wet Willie caressed rhythm and blues. Into this soundscape, the Marshall Tucker Band brought all of this and a dash of progressive rock.

After the band makes their introduction in the song, vocalist Doug Gray appears, his soulful voice telling us that, with his love affair ended,

it's time to pack his bags and hit the highway. The road—missing loved ones and leaving them behind—is a theme that weighs heavily in the lyrics of the band throughout their career, perhaps more than any other band in Southern Rock. It's never played for sympathy or pity but is always stated as a fact of life, something that comes with the territory.

But the lyrics, while good, are secondary in this song, which introduced the band to the world. For the minute they last, they are punctuated by Toy's distinctive guitar style. When Gray's minute is up, the band shifts gears, going from the swinging rhythm to a heavy downbeat. McCorkle lays a funky syncopated guitar counter-rhythm down, moving under the Caldwell brothers' insistent riff. Floating atop this is Eubanks. His flute duplicates the pulsing riff but then breaks loose into a solo that moves the song higher into a spacey progressive-rock setting. After a minute, he rejoins the Caldwell brothers to restate the riff before brother Toy breaks loose.

Toy Caldwell had learned to play guitar from his father, and when learning adopted a thumb-picking style all his own. Although he used a solid-body Gibson Les Paul, he was able to coax a sound close to his hero BB King, who used semihollow bodies like the L-30 (the original Lucille) and ES-355 (the most famous Lucille). The combination of guitar, Fender Twin amp, and that thumb gave Toy an unmistakable sound all his own. At the 2:47 mark, he bends into the opening, letting the note hang like his hero does. He follows it with a series of syncopated phrases that break alternately into bursts of speed and squeals of bending strings. Just under a minute later, Toy joins the other for that pulsating riff before the band lands down just as they had opened the song.

Gray reenters, repeating part of the verse and the chorus before repeating "take the highway" over the band with Toy's guitar fills surrounding the words. Gray announces it's time to "pack his bags and walk away," and the music begins to build underneath him. Suddenly, Hornsby's Moog returns, giving a bit of a progressive-rock edge to the song's ending.

The song is a powerhouse that immediately let listeners know there was more to this band than just another rock act from the South being thrown into the market. While the song wasn't released as a single, it became a frequently played track on FM radio, driving the album up the charts and landing them at #29 on the Hot 100. Bands they had opened show for regionally, like the Allman Brothers and Wet Willie, who had

introduced them to Capricorn Records, were now commanding national stages and bringing the Tucker boys along with them.

The opening of the song announced their arrival, their fans gave them a stage, and the band proved the blend that only they could provide: The jazz drummer and flautist, the country-influenced bass player, two blues- and rock-inspired guitarists, and a rhythm-and-blues singer drew all of the influences that fed into the wide range of Southern Rock and put them all in one band, blended together and producing a sound unlike any other.

6. "Whipping Post," Allman Brothers Band (from *At Fillmore East*, 1971)

When Gregg Allman returned from California to join his brother's new band in Jacksonville in 1968, he came with a notebook loaded with new songs. But being back in his old stomping grounds spurred on his creativity even more when he began to write. One of the songs from that fresh batch was "Whipping Post," though initially he didn't feel strongly about the song. Even the band was a bit indifferent, hearing the song as a good blues song but nothing that outshone the songs they were already working on with the goal of recording. But bass player Berry Oakley heard something different and wanted to keep the song in consideration. So, he went home and worked through the night to craft an introduction to the song, playing with the tempo and feel of what Allman had shown them. When he showed it to the group, they immediately got it.

His introduction sounds like the ominous sound track of a group of riders entering the scene. Most impressively, Oakley's introduction completely sets up the tone of the song, giving it a gravitas that is picked up by Allman's vocals—and it's only five seconds long. At just before the five-second mark, a lone high hat enters before Duane Allman enters, duplicating Oakley's riff in a high register. A few seconds later, Dickey Betts enters, at first playing opposite of Duane, then joining to punctuate the riff. By this time, both Butch Trucks and Jaimoe have joined in with cymbal-heavy percussion that moves the song into a much jazzier territory before Gregg's Hammond B-3 enters at the twenty-second mark.

When Gregg begins to sing, the song is barely thirty seconds in, but the arrangement of the instruments, from Oakley's foreboding introduction to the rest of the band's complementary accompaniment, has set the stage for the pain that forces the first few words out through seemingly

gritted teeth. Those early notes make it sound as though those teeth are gritted in anger. "I been run down, I been lied to," he sings, wondering why he let his woman play him like a fool. His mouth opens more and his voice rises as he tells us she took all of his money, wrecked his new car, and ran off with one of his friends to a bar across town. He finally lets loose when he comes to the chorus, and we wonder if his teeth were gritted not because of anger but to fight back the tears. While Gregg is letting out his emotion, Duane is seconding it with knife-like fills. After Gregg releases some of his pain, the band drops out, allowing him silence as he falls back, saying, "Good Lord I feel like I'm dyin'."

The song's original release came on the band's self-titled 1969 debut album and clocked in at just over five minutes. When it made it into their live sets, the song stretched into a massive jam, ranging from fifteen minutes to the twenty-three-minute version released on 1971's *At Fillmore East*. Even with its incredible length, that live version has become the definitive recording of the song.

Following a spirited version of the instrumental "In Memory of Elizabeth Reed," Duane announces they'll be doing a song from the first album and is met with cries of "Whipping Post." The song had become a crowd favorite and a staple of their live show, often serving as the set closer. This live version follows the original recording in form but offers extended solos by both Duane and Betts. Behind them, Oakley explores the neck of his bass with precision, laying down a bass line that weaves between the two guitars, providing a solid foundation.

Other live versions—some featuring both Duane and Oakley, others after their untimely passing—have been released and exhibit variations of the jams the soloists provide. While they all offer an exciting take on the song, none live up to the immortal Fillmore recording.

Over the years, the song has become a rock standard recorded by rockers like Frank Zappa, Jeff Healey, and Pat Travers and crossing genres with a recording by bluegrass group Mountain Heart and appearing as a sample in "Oh My God" by Jay-Z.

5. "Green Grass and High Tides," Outlaws (from *Outlaws*, 1975)

Every artist wants to hit on a career song, one of those tracks that is forever associated with the artist, at times buoying their career. For the Outlaws, that song came even before they had a record deal. The band

had come together in the early 1970s and toured all over the South and the East Coast. They picked up a young manager, Charlie Brusco, who went to work promoting the band and landing them several dates, opening for Lynyrd Skynyrd, who were heating up at that time. Skynyrd's leader Ronnie Van Zant was impressed by what he saw out on the stage each night and called Skynyrd manager Alan Walden. He told Walden he needed to come out and see this new band and pick them up. Walden was busy with the booming career of Skynyrd and was hesitant to pick up an unproven new client. And then Van Zant said to him, "They've got themselves a 'Bird,'" referencing Skynyrd's "Free Bird," a song that brought audiences cheering to their feet and showcased the prowess of the band. With that, Walden reconsidered and made the trip to see the band. Once he did, he wasted no time striking a partnership with Brusco. Brusco hoped it would get them more dates with Skynyrd; Walden hoped to make them superstars.

The song Van Zant and Walden heard was, of course, "Green Grass and High Tides," a poetic epic resting on a bed of frenzied guitars. In its original form, the song rested between fifteen and sixteen minutes long. Once the group was signed to Arista and entered the studio with producer Paul Rothchild, the song was trimmed to a more manageable length of just under ten minutes. FM radio disc jockeys began to pick up the song and spin it regularly. Trade magazine *Radio and Records* named it the twelfth most played song on FM in the 1970s. In concert, the song took on a life of its own, often stretching to twenty-five minutes, making it a third of their set.

Of course, the song was met with those who believed it was an ode to marijuana, but the band has always flatly denied those accusations. Instead, the often-cryptic lyrics that speak of "castles of stone" and kings and queens reference other rock stars. In interviews, Hughie Thomasson recalls in vivid detail how he came to write the song, standing on a Florida beach and the wind blowing his long hair, he imagined a concert in the night sky, put on for him by superstars who had left this world— Jimi Hendrix, Janis Joplin, and Jim Morrison.

But the mystery of the song goes beyond its poetic language to the question of the song's authorship. The song is credited to and claimed by Thomasson as his, but rumors have persisted for years that the lyrics for the song were actually written by a friend of the band, James Peter Britton. Britton had been a friend of and crew member to the band since its

very early days. He was also a dreamer and a poet who idealized the Rolling Stones, and after the death of their guitarist Brian Jones in 1969, Britton wrote this eulogy to one of his favorite musicians, even borrowing the name of their 1966 greatest-hits album for the song's title and chorus. But for reasons unknown, Britton never asserted ownership of the lyrics, choosing instead to allow them to flourish as his friend's signature song.

Regardless of authorship, the song stands as an incredible tour de force that helped define the hard-rocking edge of Southern Rock. The song is sung by Thomasson, one of the group's three vocalists but the vocalist most associated with the band, as he sang two of their most well-known songs. Both Thomasson and second guitarist Billy Jones stretch out within the song, showing the power and enthusiasm that connected with Ronnie Van Zant. As has popped up several times throughout this book, one of the keys to the power of the guitars in this song lies in the fact that Thomasson chose a Fender Stratocaster, while his guitar-playing partner picked up a Gibson Les Paul.

The differences are immediately distinguishable as Thomasson sports the bright tone heard at the 2:24 mark with a flurry of country-inspired licks, using multinote figures leading to Jones's entry at 3:23. His tone is more rounded and deep than Thomasson's as he contrasts his bluesy licks with Thomasson's country feel. This section between verses sets up the theme of the rest of the song, which increases in tempo after the last verse. Setting it apart from other guitar fests is the way the band is incorporated into the song. For example, at 6:54, Thomasson goes into a Wes Montgomery–inspired octave phrase that is mimicked by Henry Paul on rhythm guitar before Thomasson unleashes a flurry of triplet notes, but instead of doing so in a solo context, he begins them very quietly and raises in volume. The band does the same behind him, dropping their volume and rising along with him. Coming out of this, all three guitars join before Jones emerges on the other side with his solo turn.

Toward the end of the song, the two guitars of Jones and Thomasson are occasionally joined by Paul, who comes in to harmonize a part here or there while the guitarist not being doubled lays down the rhythm part. As the song enters its final minute, Jones and Thomasson lock in to a series of harmony lines that blaze faster and faster, leading to the big ending.

Decades past its release, the song is still held up as a prime example of the guitar supremacy of Southern Rock. *Vintage Guitar* ranked it #33 on

its "Top 50 Guitar Songs of the '70s" list, and the song remains a crowd favorite of the reconstituted Outlaws led by Henry Paul.

4. "Sweet Home Alabama," Lynyrd Skynyrd (from *Second Helping*, 1974)

Ed King originally joined Lynyrd Skynyrd as bass player at the invitation of Ronnie Van Zant. Skynyrd had opened a series of dates for an incarnation of King's first band, Strawberry Alarm Clock, and the two struck up a friendship. When the band fell apart at the end of that tour, King called Van Zant and soon relocated to the South from his native California. Skynyrd had recently lost their bass player, Leon Wilkeson, and were getting ready to head into the studio to record their debut album, so King moved from guitar to bass. After the first album was released, Wilkeson came back into the fold, and King moved back to guitar, staying with the band to help re-create in concert the layered guitars of the album. In their first rehearsal featuring King on guitar and Wilkeson back on bass, the band wrote two songs, one of which was "Sweet Home Alabama."

The opening four notes are arguably the most recognizable opening four notes in rock music. King's tone, the alchemy of the seashell on the steel strings, fires a rush through any crowd that hears them ring out from the stage or radio speaker.

Lyrically, the song is a prime example of Ronnie Van Zant's stream-of-consciousness style of writing, and they cover a lot of territory—more territory that can be given space here, in fact, so we'll stick to the surface for now. In the first verse, the narrator is traveling back home to Alabama, his missed home. It's an innocent and brief travelogue in the vein of something like Johnny Cash's "Hey Porter," where a young southern man is so excited to be returning home that he continually requests updates from the train's porter.

The second verse was the first to catch the attention of rock music fans when the song was released in 1974. In this line, Van Zant calls out Neil Young for his song "Southern Man," which dealt with racism in the South (though Young said it was more of a response to his 1972 song "Alabama"). By the time "Sweet Home Alabama" was released, the Young song was four years old, but Young was a legend in the rock world. Interestingly, one of the background singers Kooper brought in to sing on the track was Merry Clayton, who had recorded her own version of

"Southern Man" in 1972 and who initially refused the "Sweet Home Alabama" session due to the band's southern ties.

Perhaps the verse that has resonated with the longest-lasting controversy is the third. There isn't enough space here to delve into it as deeply as others have, and it might not matter if we did. Even the band members seem to have different takes on the song over the years, with most centered on line being the first of the verse: "In Birmingham they love the governor." This is followed by the most analyzed "boo boo boo" in the history of music. Did they mean to boo the governor, George Wallace, a noted segregationist? Or were they booing the ones trying to take him out of office? Or was Van Zant simply leaving it open to interpretation so listeners could lean whichever direction they wanted to take it? Now that Van Zant is gone, we will never know the exact meaning behind the verse.

Coming out of the two verses of controversy, Van Zant pays tribute to the legendary staff band of Muscle Shoals Sound Studio (and previously FAME studios), nicknamed the Swampers. It was members of that band, notably Jimmy Johnson and Barry Beckett, who worked with the band to record many of the early demos that became the foundation of their debut album. Their experience creating the Muscle Shoals sound as members of the session bands for artists like Aretha Franklin, Wilson Pickett, and Leon Russell helped Skynyrd become a tighter unit, teaching them how to craft the parts for their songs.

As memorable as the lyrics are Ed King's bright and taut guitar lines, from the opening notes to the unforgettable solo that came to him note for note in a dream. When he made it to the studio and ran through it, Kooper told him to start over because the solo was in the wrong key. King disagreed, and the band backed him up, saying that if it came to him in a dream, they needed to leave it that way—a superstitious "southern thing" that Kooper didn't understand, but he agreed to disagree, and the solo stayed.

With little fanfare, the single was released to radio, and to everyone's surprise, it caught fire, becoming the band's first charting single and staying on the chart for eleven weeks and peaking at #8. The success of the song took the album to #12 and pulled their debut album along with it to #27. It was a career-making song for the band and has endured over the years, being used in commercials and movies.

Skynyrd devotee Kid Rock used a snippet of the song, mashed up with Warren Zevon's "Werewolves of London," in his 2008 hit "All Summer Long." Because Kid Rock's catalog was not available on iTunes, listeners looking to buy the song instead turned to "Sweet Home Alabama," making it a popular song during that summer.

3. "Ramblin' Man," Allman Brothers Band (from *Brothers and Sisters*, 1973)

After two albums of great material that garnered little notice from the general public, the Allman Brothers Band broke through with their double live album that showed them in their element. They became an in-demand touring act, but the tragic death of founder Duane Allman presented a double-edged sword. On the one side, the band suffered a devastating personal loss, but on the other side, as it often unfortunately does, death brought more coverage of the band by more mainstream sources and prompted a new audience of listeners to take notice. The bulk of their fourth album, their first without Duane, featured only three songs that didn't include Duane, the rest being recorded at earlier sessions. With breakout FM hits like "Melissa" and "Blue Sky," the album continued their successes. But the group was still suffering from Duane's death, with the two members perhaps the closest to him, brother Gregg and Berry Oakley, completely devastated.

Through his grief, Dickey Betts knew the band needed to continue on, moving forward and capitalizing on the momentum that was building. It was time for him to step forward and lead the band through this difficult time. The band had recorded his songs in the past, most notably the instrumental "In Memory of Elizabeth Reed" and his first vocal performance with the group, "Blue Sky." As has been discussed earlier in this book, Betts was initially reluctant to show the band "Blue Sky" to the band, deeming it perhaps "too soft." Now he had another song to present to the band that he felt strongly about, though some of those same feelings were present.

Inspired in part by the Hank Williams song "Ramblin' Man," Betts set out to tell a story of a character who was born on the road and would continue to live his life that way. In tone and content, he felt it was a country song, a genre he would explore more thoroughly on his first solo release, *Highway Call*, but he took it to the band, who also felt it might be

more country than they normally recorded. After some time, the band decided to record it for the album.

From the song's opening notes, it is evident that it was something different from what the Allman Brothers Band normally presented. While rooted in blues, its roots, as noted, were deeper into country, with a happy bounce to them. The introduction also includes something more calculated, designed to subliminally affect listeners who had become familiar with the band's powerhouse twin guitars. The song opens with Betts's guitar playing the descending figure, but before a second guitar is introduced for the ascending section, Chuck Leavell's piano duplicates the figure Betts has just played. Leavell was added to the band just prior to the recording to allow Gregg Allman to concentrate on vocals and organ and also to fill in some of the space left by Duane's absence. The almost subliminal placement of the piano in the mix of the song sets the expectation that it is there to fill a void.

But there is a second guitarist present in the form of longtime friend of the band Les Dudek, whom Betts had been working with to put together the song's harmony guitar parts, which Betts intended to record himself through overdubs. Betts provides the rhythm guitar track and the lead playing, turning in an upbeat and infinitely memorable solo, but when it came time to do those harmony parts, Betts was just too used to cutting them live with Duane and invited Dudek into the studio to record them with him. Over the outro of the song, Betts did record an overdubbed slide part that comes in like a specter over the harmony guitar lines.

Producer Johnny Sandlin told Allman Brothers Band chronicler Alan Paul that he thought it was the wrong decision to release the song as a single, noting that the only other thing in their catalog that sounded like it was "Blue Sky." What "Blue Sky" foreshadowed, "Ramblin' Man" brought to fruition. Betts's songwriting took a larger role in the band (he penned four of the six original songs on *Brothers and Sisters* and three of five originals on the follow-up *Win, Lose or Draw*). Whether it was representative of the Allman Brothers Band sound or not, listeners took to the song, taking it to #2 on the *Billboard* chart and making it the first Top Five hit by the newly labeled Southern Rock band. It, along with other pop culture and political happenings, opened the door for other Southern Rock bands to step through and claim spots at the top of the charts and as opening acts—and soon headliners—in arenas across the country. It became a benchmark, evidenced by Ronnie Van Zant's remark after the

writing of "Sweet Home Alabama": "That's our 'Ramblin' Man'," meaning the song that would take their music, as "Ramblin' Man" did for the Allman Brothers Band, to the mainstream, casual listener.

A *Billboard* article on the band in 1973 pointed out that it had been a slow sales year for albums until the release of *Brothers and Sisters* and the immense popularity of "Ramblin' Man," moving people to get out and purchase the album. The album and single had moved the band from a band with fans in rock circles to one with fans in many circles, making them a household name.

2. "Can't You See," Marshall Tucker Band (from *The Marshall Tucker Band*, 1973)

The Marshall Tucker Band's debut leads off with a powerful one-two punch. Opening with the epic statement of "Take the Highway," the band then downshifts a little, introducing "Can't You See," a song that would become their signature. The loose sound of George McCorkle's acoustic guitar, now instantly recognizable, opens the song, leading to the trademark flute work of Jerry Eubanks. The band joins in and includes the Allman Brothers Band's Jai "Jaimoe" Johanson, who happened to be in the studio. Picking up an acoustic guitar and flipping it over to use as congas (thus the credit for "guitcongas"), his laid-back rhythm complements Paul Riddle's easy beat.

Toy Caldwell, guitarist and the song's writer, had written the song before the formation of the Marshall Tucker Band with his old band Toy Factory, which included brother Tommy and Eubanks. As he did on occasion throughout the history of the band, he takes the lead vocal slot here. The melody is infinitely catchy, inviting audiences to sing along, as they did by the thousands across the country. Audiences connected immediately with the universal theme of loving someone who maybe doesn't return those feelings as intensely yet doesn't (or pretends not to) realize what effect it is having on the other person. The only way for the singer to escape this pain is to leave town, hop a train, and never look back. Instead of making his case to the woman who has this control over him, he's telling someone else. "Can't you see what that woman's been doing to me?" he asks. Each time he asks the question, the passion in his voice increases. What starts out as a rather mundane question ends with a full-throated asking.

Likewise, Toy's guitar mimics that increase of passion. When it first enters, at the tail of Eubanks's flute introduction, his string bends evoke the pain he is feeling. When he returns at near the 2:30 mark for a short break, his vibrato is wide, bringing to mind the quiver of his lip at the thought of this love ending. At 3:43, he returns full-force, those string bends coupling with the wide vibrato and telling the internal story he can't express in words. When he ends, the tempo slows, and the band drops out, save McCorkle's acoustic guitar and Toy's vocal followed by Toy's sharp guitar lines. Slowly, the band reenters, led by producer Paul Hornsby's organ. The pace again picks up, with Toy's singing gaining more emotion and his guitar mimicking it until the song ends.

While "Heard It in a Love Song" may have been their highest- and most widely charting single, "Can't You See" remains their most important. Its commercial history tells its own interesting story and shows the link of Southern Rock and the Outlaw Movement in country music.

After releasing the song in 1973, it barely broke into the charts, bubbling under at #108 on the *Billboard* Hot 100, though it received adds on FM radio stations that didn't contribute to chart positions. Meanwhile, the Outlaw Movement was afoot, led by Willie Nelson and Waylon Jennings, who were taking over the country singles charts with songs that mixed a rock sensibility with their country music. Hank Williams Jr., who was still working on breaking out of his famous father's shadow, was watching both groups of musicians, had crossed paths with the band on the road, and was contemplating a change. With that in mind, he decided to record "Can't You See," but the people managing his career wouldn't let him, saying the song wasn't "country enough." Then Hank Jr. fell down Ajax Mountain in Montana; he survived the near-fatal fall and decided to take his career's direction in his own hands.

The result was 1975's *Hank Williams, Jr. & Friends*, friends that included Toy Caldwell, who guested on steel guitar. On Williams's version of the song, guitarist Pete Carr hews close to Toy's original parts while Williams cranks up the emotion with his vocals. The song did nothing commercially, but it served as a bridge between Southern Rock and Outlaw Country, drawing into question what was or wasn't country enough anymore. The album was scheduled to be released in December 1975, and because Toy played steel on that version of "Can't You See," they knew it was coming. It had been over two years since the original Marshall Tucker Band version had been released, so Capricorn dipped

into the vault of live tracks that had been recorded for *Where We All Belong* and included a live version of "Can't You See" on the band's September 1975 release *Searchin' for a Rainbow*.

In the spring of 1976, Toy Caldwell answered the phone to be greeted by Waylon Jennings, the superstar face of the Outlaw Movement. Jennings wanted to know if Toy would mind if he recorded the song. It was a courtesy to get such a call, and Toy wasn't going to turn down the opportunity. In April, Jennings recorded the song, releasing it in June on his album *Are You Ready for the Country?*, coming the year after he had topped the Country Albums chart with *Dreaming My Dreams* and the platinum-selling compilation album *Wanted: The Outlaws!* The album's title thumbed its nose at the "not country enough" line of thinking, including this new Southern Rock anthem alongside the title track (written and originally recorded by Neil Young) and Jimmy Webb's "MacArthur Park," a song that had been recorded by a slew of pop groups (though Jennings won a Grammy for Best Country Performance by a Duo or Group for his 1969 collaboration with the Kimberlys on the song), and this new Southern Rock anthem. Jennings's recording of the song went to #4 on the Country Singles chart.

Subsequent recordings of the song show that the bridge set up by Williams was dead-on. Country artist Gary Stewart recorded the song in 1978, and a decade later, country superstar group and heir apparent to much of the Southern Rock–country crossover influence, Alabama, included a version on their 1988 live album. A decade after that, honorary Marshall Tucker Band member Charlie Daniels recorded the song. That same year, New York hip-hop group Fun Lovin' Criminals released *100% Colombian*, including the song "Big Night Out," a song built on a heavy beat and rotating on a riff from Tom Petty's "American Girl." Midway through the song, the music drops out, and they begin to sing "Can't You See," though the lyrics are completely different: They repeat the title over and over, backed by a choir and piano with a guitar shredding behind them using the song's anthemic aspects to finish the song. Recordings by heavy metal group Poison, country singer Anita Cochran, jazz singer Ilona Knopfler, and Kentucky-based hard-rock group Black Stone Cherry have continued to push the song into the future.

1. "Free Bird," Lynyrd Skynyrd (from *One More from the Road*, 1976)

Face it—it's nigh impossible to do a list of the 100 Best Songs of Southern Rock without it being topped by "Free Bird." More than any other song in the genre, it has transcended beyond its "Southern Rock" tag to be counted as one of the greatest songs in rock music, period. It has taken on greater cultural significance as it ages, moving from a tour de force encore for one of the genre's most successful bands to a battle cry of sorts at concerts everywhere, often prompted by a sense of snark but at other times from a sincere heartfelt place.

While Lynyrd Skynyrd certainly didn't invent the ballad to jam conceit, they certainly went a long way in popularizing it. While the first part of the song prompts lighters to be hoisted into the air, the latter half of the song demands both hands be free for maximum air guitar efficiency. According to legend, the song, with music written by guitarist Allen Collins and lyrics, as always, by Ronnie Van Zant, was simply a ballad that elicited little response from audiences. Van Zant, looking to have a reason to rest his voice during the long nights of playing clubs, suggested the band put a jam on the end. Once added, the crowds not only began to perk up but also began to request the song.

There is also no other song in the genre that listeners can hear develop over the years. Released in various forms over the years (in thirteen versions that span the time covered in this book), fans can hear the changes in the song as it was being molded and then the subtle shifts afterward.

After bouncing around regional clubs with occasional excursions north, Skynyrd came to the attention of a small local label called Shade Tree Records. In 1968, the band released a single on the label that received little to no attention. The songs, "Need All My Friends" (A-side) and "Michelle" (B-side), show little of the fire the band would become known for and faded quickly. That fire, though, was evident in "Free Bird," and the label owners knew it as soon as they heard the band play it live. The club happened to be across from the recording studio, so the band headed across the street after their set to put it on tape. This was the first recorded version of "Free Bird," recorded in early 1970 but not available to fans commercially until the 2000 release of the rarities collection *Collectybles*.

Clocking in at 7:29, the song is shorter than its major label debut and nearly half the length of the definitive live version, but all of the elements that make the song a classic are there. Allen Collins's arpeggiated introduction churns with a little more force than it will later, using a tone that is thicker and duller than the brighter tone of the band's debut album. Gary Rossington's slide guitar is drenched in reverb, making it sound nearly otherworldly. Bob Burns on drums and Larry Junstrom on bass hold down the rhythm with little frills. Van Zant's voice is likewise covered in reverb, and as he comes to the final chorus, the fact it was recorded after a long club set is evident. But what strained and tested Van Zant's vocals was a warm-up for Collins, who unleashes a flurry of notes and string bends in an abbreviated version of the solo that helped put his name in the pantheon of guitar gods. Rather than fading as it does on the debut album, the song ends with a "Beck's Bolero"-esque run through the chords as Collins plays an intense mid-register vamp over top.

With no success to be found on Shade Tree and their sights set on bigger things, the band asked to be released from their contract. Soon after, they came to the attention of manager Alan Walden, who sent them to Alabama to record at the famed Muscle Shoals Sound Studio. Instead of taking it to Muscle Shoals, the band was sent to a smaller studio run by a partner of the recording group named Quin Ivy. This version, recorded in October 1970 (but not released until the 1991 boxed set) with the same musicians as the Shade Tree recording, retains all of the musical elements of the earlier take, though Burns throws in a couple more drum fills as the song progresses. Van Zant is in strong voice for this recording, and he is mixed clearly in front of the music, delivering a poignant performance. The major difference with this version is that it comes in at 4:07, cutting off just before the guitar solo, leaving the ramping up as it fades out.

While the songs recorded at Quinvy Studios were good, the band knew they could do better, and after hearing their tapes, Jimmy Johnson of Muscle Shoals Sound Studio decided he wanted to work with them. So in early 1971, the band returned to the studio, though the configuration of musicians had morphed in the few short months between sessions. When it came time to revisit "Free Bird" at the end of June and the beginning of July of that year, gone were Junstrom and Burns. On the drummers stool was an old friend of the band, Rickey Medlocke. But the most significant thing in the evolution of the song was the addition of Billy Powell on piano. Rather than opening with Collins's arpeggiated guitar chords, lis-

teners hear Powell's classical-inspired piano, which fades back to allow Collins to take his traditional place. Medlocke's drum pattern is a bit more busy than Burns's and seems to push the song a bit more than previous versions. To this version, Medlocke also contributes a falsetto backing vocal that is mixed closely with Van Zant's. For those used to the album versions heard through the years, the ghostly vocal is a little jarring at first but adds an interesting element to the song. When it comes time for the solo, Medlocke's slight pushing of the tempo is nothing compared to the savage energy unleashed by Collins as he tears into his Gibson Explorer. His solo pushes the tempo and seems to be near exploding from its musical confines. This version also introduces the second guitar into the solo but in a less structured way than later in its evolution. This version of the song would not be released until the 1998 release of *Skynyrd's First: The Complete Muscle Shoals Album*, a fantastic twentieth-anniversary expansion of *Skynyrd's First . . . and Last*.

Those recordings and the work of Al Kooper secured the band a record deal with MCA, and just a couple of years after recording them, the band was back in the studio, rerecording five songs from those Muscle Shoals sessions along with three new tunes. "Free Bird" from the band's debut album is perhaps the most iconic version of the song and exhibits the culmination of the time on the road coupled with Kooper's production. Instead of the sound of Powell's piano or Collins's guitar notes opening the song, it is Kooper on organ who greets listeners. He is soon joined by both as they create an atmosphere that perfectly suits the lyrics. Given the additional studio time that big-studio dollars buy, the band put great effort into orchestrating more intricate parts, including a subtly mixed but important acoustic guitar part that helps ground the band among the organ, piano, and newly added string section. With these new atmospheric elements, the reverb is lifted from Rossington's guitar, and his slide part is front and center in the mix. In this new recording, returning drummer Burns's no-frills approach fits perfectly, playing expertly with new band member Ed King, who plays bass on the first album before moving to guitar and returning the bass duties to Leon Wilkeson.

The orchestrating of parts for the song did not stop at the structure and rhythm section. When it comes to the legendary guitar solo portion, the second guitar is given distinct sections to play off of Collins's extended licks. The newly constructed solo showcases the growth of Collins as a guitarist from the first recorded version just a few years earlier. His

playing is energetic but not as frenetic as previous versions. The guitarists of Skynyrd were known for having their parts mapped out by the time they reached the studio, and Collins's progression in that area is evident here. While this studio take fades out to end at 9:07, a version later released on the 1989 greatest hits compilation *Skynyrd's Innyrds: Greatest Hits* features the unfaded version, which includes the "Bolero"-style ending with the addition of Powell's piano and a big finale.

Two live versions featuring this classic lineup of the band have been commercially released, one recorded in 1973 at radio station WMC-FM, released on *Collectybles*, and one recorded in 1974 in Hamburg, Germany, released on the 2015 *Sweet Home Alabama Live at Rockaplast*. Both of these versions contain the only versions of the original three-guitar lineup that included King on guitar. Two more live versions followed chronologically, both released in the 2009 *Authorized Bootleg* series, and feature the short-lived two-guitar version of the band left with the departure of King. The first was recorded in November 1975 at a show in Cardiff, Wales, and the second was recorded at Winterland in San Francisco.

The San Francisco show was recorded just before the arrival of Steve Gaines, the guitar spark plug that makes his recording debut on the live album *One More from the Road*. It is this show that contains the definitive version of "Free Bird." Saving the song for last, Van Zant tantalizes the audience by saying, "We've got time for one more," asking, "What song is it you want to hear?" to be answered by a thunderous reply from the audience, "Free Bird!" With that, the band launches into the song, giving a blistering performance and leaving the crowd on their feet cheering for more. An alternate take of the song was released on the 2001 twenty-fifth-anniversary deluxe edition of the album, which included two shows recorded for the album.

Through the years, it has been said that the song was written as a eulogy of sorts to Southern Rock founder Duane Allman, but the song existed several years prior to his untimely death. The story evolved from the fact that Van Zant often dedicated the song to Allman (and later Berry Oakley). In 1987, when the Lynyrd Skynyrd tribute band assembled with Rossington and King, joined by Randall Hall on guitar, they ended their shows with an instrumental version of the song dedicated to the memory of Van Zant and Steve and Cassie Gaines. The only vocals heard on the recording released on the 1988 album *Southern by the Grace of God—*

Lynyrd Skynyrd Tribute Tour 1987 were those of the crowd, who lifted the song up to the fallen in tribute. The band would continue the instrumental rendition for several years before Johnny Van Zant stepped up to the microphone to sing the song.

The song has made its way into the culture's collective consciousness, making appearances in many movies, perhaps most notably in Cameron Crowe's *Elizabethtown,* and video games. It continues to stand as the greatest Southern Rock song of all time. Now, what song is it you want to hear?

...AND 100 MORE

101. "Workin' for MCA," Lynyrd Skynyrd (from *Second Helping,* 1974)
102. "Jessica," Allman Brothers Band (from *Brothers and Sisters,* 1973)
103. "Ramblin'," Marshall Tucker Band (from *Where We All Belong,* 1974)
104. "No More Boogie," Molly Hatchet (from *Flirtin' with Disaster,* 1979)
105. "Rock and Roll Band," Wet Willie (from *Wet Willie,* 1971)
106. "Fantasy Girl," .38 Special (from *Wild-Eyed Southern Boys,* 1980)
107. "Legend of Wooley Swamp," Charlie Daniels Band (from *Full Moon,* 1980)
108. "Little Martha," Allman Brothers Band (from *Eat a Peach,* 1972)
109. "Sheila," Georgia Satellites (from *Open All Night,* 1988)
110. "You're No Good," Potliquor (from *Levee Blues,* 1971)
111. "Comin' Home," Lynyrd Skynyrd (from *Skynyrd's First . . . and Last,* 1978)
112. "Grits Ain't Groceries," Wet Willie (from *Wet Willie II,* 1972)
113. "In Memory of Elizabeth Reed," Allman Brothers Band (from *Idlewild South,* 1970)
114. "Blue Jean Blues," ZZ Top (from *Fandango!,* 1975)
115. "Mountain Jam," Allman Brothers Band (from *Eat a Peach,* 1972)

116. "Was I Right or Wrong," Lynyrd Skynyrd (from *Skynyrd's First . . . and Last*, 1978)

117. "Outlaw Women," Hank Williams Jr. (from *Whiskey Bent and Hell Bound*, 1979)

118. "Before the Bullets Fly," Gregg Allman Band (from *Just Before the Bullets Fly*, 1988)

119. "Funky Junky," Charlie Daniels (from *Honey in the Rock*, 1973)

120. "Imaginary Lover," Atlanta Rhythm Section (from *Champagne Jam*, 1978)

121. "Red Hot Chicken," Wet Willie (from *Wet Willie II*, 1972)

122. "Moonshine Runner," Doc Holliday (from *Doc Holliday*, 1981)

123. "Cumberland Mountain #9," Charlie Daniels Band (from *Saddle Tramp*, 1976)

124. "The Ballad of Curtis Loew," Lynyrd Skynyrd (from *Second Helping*, 1974)

125. "Tush," ZZ Top (from *Fandango!*, 1975)

126. "Stealin' Watermelons," Elvin Bishop (from *Let It Flow*, 1974)

127. "Hot and Nasty," Black Oak Arkansas (from *Black Oak Arkansas*, 1971)

128. "Nicole," Point Blank (from *American Excess*, 1981)

129. "Higher Ground," Grinderswitch (from *Pullin' Together*, 1977)

130. "Hillbilly Band," Marshall Tucker Band (from *The Marshall Tucker Band*, 1973)

131. "Beatin' the Odds," Molly Hatchet (from *Beatin' the Odds*, 1980)

132. "Back Where You Belong," .38 Special (from *Tour de Force*, 1984)

133. "I'm Bad, I'm Nationwide," ZZ Top (from *Degüello*, 1979)

134. "Blue Ridge Mountain Sky," Marshall Tucker Band (from *A New Life*, 1974)

135. "Struttin' My Stuff," Elvin Bishop (from *Struttin' My Stuff*, 1975)

136. "Life's Railway to Heaven," Amazing Rhythm Aces (from *Stacked Deck*, 1975)

137. "Run Gypsy Run," Dickey Betts & Great Southern (from *Dickey Betts & Great Southern*, 1977)

138. "Foolin'," Henry Paul Band (from *Grey Ghost*, 1979)

139. "Funky Refried Chicken," Dixie Dregs (from *Free Fall*, 1977)

140. "Breaker Breaker," Outlaws (from *Lady in Waiting*, 1976)

141. "Saturday Night Special," Lynyrd Skynyrd (from *Nuthin' Fancy*, 1975)

142. "Oh Lonesome Me," Kentucky Headhunters (from *Pickin' on Nashville*, 1989)

143. "Stone Cold Believer," .38 Special (from *Rockin' into the Night*, 1979)

144. "A Fool for Your Stockings," ZZ Top (from *Degüello*, 1979)

145. "Cheer," Potliquor (from *Levee Blues*, 1971)

146. "Fly Eagle Fly," Marshall Tucker Band (from *A New Life*, 1974)

147. "Song for You," Outlaws (from *The Outlaws*, 1975)

148. "Cannot Find My Way Home," Blackhorse (from *Blackhorse*, 1979)

149. "Bougainvillea," Dickey Betts & Great Southern (from *Dickey Betts & Great Southern*, 1977)

150. "Third Rate Romance," Amazing Rhythm Aces (from *Stacked Deck*, 1975)

151. "Doin' (It Again)," Doc Holliday (from *Doc Holliday Rides Again*, 1981)

152. "Hard Luck Jimmy," Blue Jug (from *Blue Jug*, 1975)

153. "Whiskey Man," Molly Hatchet (from *Flirtin' with Disaster*, 1979)

154. "Slick Titty Boom," Elvin Bishop (from *Struttin' My Stuff*, 1975)

155. "Keep the Faith," Black Oak Arkansas (from *Keep the Faith*, 1972)

156. "Mose Knows," Mose Jones (from *Mose Knows*, 1973)

157. "I'm Proud to be a Redneck," Barefoot Jerry (from *Southern Delight*, 1971)

158. "Uncle Lijiah," Black Oak Arkansas (from *Black Oak Arkansas*, 1971)

159. "Louisiana Rock & Roll," Potliquor (from *Louisiana Rock & Roll*, 1972)

160. "Rattlesnake Rock 'n' Roller," Blackfoot (from *Marauder*, 1981)

161. "Opportunity," Rossington Collins Band (from *Anytime, Anyplace, Anywhere*, 1980)

162. "Kiss the Blues Goodbye," Grinderswitch (from *Honest to Goodness*, 1974)

163. "Country Fool," Sea Level (from *Sea Level*, 1977)

164. "You Got That Right," Lynyrd Skynyrd (from *Street Survivors*, 1977)

165. "Railroad Man," Blackfoot (from *No Reservations*, 1975)

166. "Shotgun Rider," Blue Jug (from *Blue Jug*, 1978)

167. "Nights of Mystery," Georgia Satellites (from *Georgia Satellites*, 1986)

168. "Redneck Rock and Roll Band," Doc Holliday (from *Danger Zone*, 1986)

169. "Free Man," Point Blank (from *Point Blank*, 1976)

170. "Your Kind of Kindness," Bonnie Bramlett (from *It's Time*, 1975)

171. "Come On to Town Ned," Blue Jug (from *Blue Jug*, 1975)

172. "Homebound," Grinderswitch (from *Honest to Goodness*, 1974)

173. "Lord Have Mercy on My Soul," Black Oak Arkansas (from *Black Oak Arkansas*, 1971)

174. "King Grand," Sea Level (from *On the Edge*, 1978)

175. "Country House Shuffle," Dixie Dregs (from *Night of the Living Dregs*, 1979)

176. "Swamp Music," Lynyrd Skynyrd (from *Second Helping*, 1974)

177. "Ain't No Time Like the Present," Mose Jones (from *Blackbird*, 1978)

178. "Arrested for Driving While Blind," ZZ Top (from *Tejas*, 1976)

179. "Don't Look Down," Point Blank (from *On a Roll*, 1982)

180. "Revival," Allman Brothers Band (from *Idlewild South*, 1970)

181. "Too Stuffed to Jump," Amazing Rhythm Aces (from *Too Stuffed to Jump*, 1976)

182. "High 'N' Dry," Black Oak Arkansas (from *High on the Hog*, 1973)

183. "Poison Whiskey," Lynyrd Skynyrd (from *Pronounced Leh-nerd Skin-nerd*, 1973)

184. "Duane's Tune," Dickey Betts Band (from *Pattern Disruptive*, 1988)

185. "Another Chance," Georgia Satellites (from *In the Land of Salvation and Sin*, 1989)

186. "Castle Rock," Barefoot Jerry (from *Barefoot Jerry*, 1972)

187. "You Ain't Foolin' Me," Marshall Tucker Band (from *A New Life*, 1974)

188. "Ice Cakes," Dixie Dregs (from *What If*, 1978)

189. "Snuff Queen," Barefoot Jerry (from *Barefoot Jerry*, 1972)
190. "It's Not My Cross to Bear," Allman Brothers Band (from *The Allman Brothers Band*, 1969)
191. "Amazing Grace (Used to Be Her Favorite Song)," Amazing Rhythm Aces (from *Stacked Deck*, 1975)
192. "Stars and Scars," Point Blank (from *Second Season*, 1979)
193. "Just Trouble," Allen Collins Band (from *Here, There & Back*, 1983)
194. "Chain Lightnin'," .38 Special (from *Special Forces*, 1982)
195. "Does Your Mama Know about Me," Mose Jones (from *Mose Knows*, 1974)
196. "Gimme, Gimme, Gimme," Blackfoot (from *Tomcattin'*, 1980)
197. "Watermelon Time in Georgia," Grinderswitch (from *Redwing*, 1977)
198. "Brothers of the Road," Hank Williams Jr. (from *Hank Williams, Jr. & Friends*, 1975)
199. "Dixie Fried," Beaverteeth (from *Beaverteeth*, 1977)
200. "Party in the Parking Lot," Johnny Van Zant (from *Brickyard Road*, 1990)

BIBLIOGRAPHY

Bomar, Scott B. *Southbound: An Illustrated History of Southern Rock*. Milwaukee, WI: Back-Beat Books, 2014.

Brant, Marley. *Freebirds: The Lynyrd Skynyrd Story*. New York: Billboard Books, 2002.

Carlisi, Jeff, and Dan Lipson. *Jam! Amp Your Team, Rock Your Business*. San Francisco: Jossey-Bass, 2009.

Freeman, Scott. *Midnight Riders: The Story of the Allman Brothers Band*. New York: Little, Brown, 1995.

Paul, Alan. *One Way Out: The Inside History of the Allman Brothers Band*. New York: St. Martin's Press, 2014.

Popoff, Martin. *Southern Rock Review*. Ontario: Collector's Guide Publishing, 2001.

Smith, Michael Buffalo. *Carolina Dreams: The Musical Legacy of Upstate South Carolina*. Beverly Hills, CA: Marshall Tucker Publishing, 1997.

———. *Outlaws, Rebels & Renegades: Interviews with the Legends of Southern Rock and Outlaw Country*. GRITZ Publishing, 2006.

———. *Outlaws, Rebels & Renegades II: More Interviews with Southern Rock Icons*. GRITZ Publishing, 2013.

———. *Rebel Yell: An Oral History of Southern Rock*. Macon, GA: Mercer University Press, 2014.

Ward, Michael K. *Ghost Riders in the Sky: The Life of Stan Jones, the Singing Ranger*. Tucson, AZ: Rio Nuevo Publishers, 2014.

INDEX

ABOUT THE AUTHOR

C. Eric Banister is an internationally published freelance music journalist who lives in Scottsburg, Indiana, with his wife and children. He also runs the website Music Tomes (www.musictomes.com), where he interviews other authors of music and music-related books.